OFF THE BEATEN PATH® SERIES

TENTH EDITION

Off the Beaten Path®
Kentucky

A Guide to Unique Places

ZOÉ AYN STRECKER
Revised and Updated by
Jackie Sheckler Finch

gpp®

Guilford, Connecticut

All the information in this guidebook is subject to change. We recommend that you call ahead to obtain current information before traveling.

An imprint of Rowman & Littlefield

Distributed by NATIONAL BOOK NETWORK

Copyright © 2015 by Rowman & Littlefield
Text design: Linda R. Loiewski
Maps: Equator Graphics © Rowman & Littlefield

British Library Cataloguing in Publication Information Available

ISSN 1535-8038
ISBN 978-0-7627-9673-1 (paperback)
ISBN 978-1-4930-1709-6 (e-book)

♾™ The paper used in this publication meets the minimum requirements of American National Standard for Information Sciences—Permanence of Paper for Printed Library Materials, ANSI/NISO Z39.48-1992.

To those Kentuckians who, with lots of love and humor, continue to guide me off the beaten path in all realms of life. Gratitude to my Globe Pequot editors Tracee Williams and Julie Marsh for allowing me to share my affection for Kentucky in this guidebook.

To my kin and friends who help me discover the beauty of Kentucky. Thanks to my parents, Jack and Margaret Poynter, for instilling in me the desire to travel and showing me the heart of the Bluegrass State. Some of my happiest childhood memories are of visiting with my grandparents, aunts and uncles, and cousins in the Danville area. My sister Elaine and I always looked forward to staying with Aunt Doris and Uncle Walker Poynter in Danville and having fun with our cousins.

Thanks to my daughter, Kelly Rose, for helping carry the load and to my grandchildren: Sean, Emma, and Dylan Rose; Stefanie, Will, Trey, and Arianna Scott; and Logan and Grayson Peters. A special remembrance to my husband, Bill Finch, whose spirit goes with me every step of the way through life's amazing journey.

—Jackie Sheckler Finch

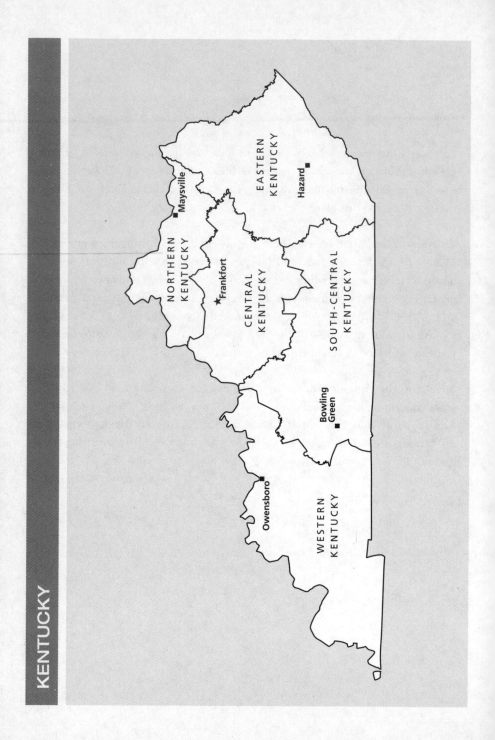

KENTUCKY

EASTERN KENTUCKY

Hazard

Maysville

NORTHERN KENTUCKY

CENTRAL KENTUCKY

★Frankfort

SOUTH-CENTRAL KENTUCKY

Bowling Green

Owensboro

WESTERN KENTUCKY

Contents

Introduction vii

Central Kentucky. 1

    Bluegrass on the Rocks 3

    In the Beginning 22

    Tradition Meets Invention 40

    City Lights 50

    Abbeys and Art 65

Eastern Kentucky 80

    Through the Gap 83

    Big Sandy Country 98

    The Gorgeous Gorge 107

    Iron Country 114

Northern Kentucky 127

    Heart of the North 127

    Sanity Land 133

    Odd Bones 136

    Metro Area 141

    Buffalo Trace Area 147

South-Central Kentucky 156

    From Caves to Culture 156

    Living-History Country 169

    Lakes and Knobs Region 176

Western Kentucky 194

    Jackson Purchase 196

    Pennyroyal Region 212

    Yellow Banks, Green River 227

Index 238

About the Author 250

About the Editor 250

Introduction

In an age when *Vive la difference!* is our cultural rallying cry, Kentucky should be a traveler's sheer delight. This 40,000-square-mile stretch of land is home to a greater variety of distinct cultures than any other rural state in the United States. Our landscapes vary wildly, our accents fluctuate county to county, and we're downright contradictory, always have been. This contradictory nature is a quality that is both enjoyable and educational for locals as well as inquisitive outsiders. Despite being a longtime victim of simplified stereotypes, the Commonwealth of Kentucky doesn't include a single "typical Kentuckian." Where the edges of Kentucky's cultures overlap, delightful contrasts abound. Where else can you find hitching posts for horse and buggy rigs in a fast-food parking lot? Where else do you hear English spoken with a heavy German lilt and a thick Southern twang? Or an Elizabethan dialect with a drawl?

Maybe the contradictions started with Daniel Boone (what didn't?), who was torn between settling the land he loved passionately and, not trusting his fellow pioneers, merging with the Native people who loved and adopted him. Maybe Kentucky's contradictory nature proved itself in bearing both Civil War presidents into the world within a year and fewer than 100 miles apart. The same waters that produce the world's smoothest bourbon and worst bootleg also sustained the life of Carrie Nation and continue to fill the teetotalers' baptismal fonts. Stereotypes of illiteracy are at loggerheads with a remarkable history of erudition and fine literary accomplishments, and the lack of national recognition for Kentucky's contributions to the high arts is suspect upon examination of the state's almost unequaled tradition of music, dance, and fine craft.

Then there's our geography, as erratic as Colorado's, yet older and more diverse in terms of flora and fauna. Vast, big-sky country dominates the western regions, where acre after fertile acre fans out, making a flat, Midwestern horizon, ending in swampland and rich arable bottomland by the banks of the great Mississippi and Ohio Rivers. Central and northern Kentucky ride on a high, fertile plateau, where game has always grazed and where livestock continue to make the region wealthy and world famous for equine and bovine bloodlines. Eastern Kentucky's lush mountains are well rounded with age, well supplied with precious seams of coal and iron ore,

KENTUCKY TRAVEL AT A GLANCE

KENTUCKY TOURISM

Kentucky Department of Tourism
Capital Plaza Tower 22nd Floor
500 Mero Street
Frankfort 40601
(800) 225-8747
kentuckytourism.com

REGIONAL AND LOCAL TOURISM OFFICES

Ashland Area Convention and Visitors Bureau
1509 Winchester Avenue
Ashland 41101
(800) 377-6249 or (606) 329-1007
visitashlandky.com

Bardstown-Nelson County Tourist and Convention Commission
One Court Square
Bardstown 40004
(800) 638-4877 or (502) 348-4877
visitbardstown.com

Berea Welcome Center
3 Artist Circle
Berea 40403
(800) 598-5263 or (859) 986-2540
berea.com

Bowling Green Area Convention and Visitors Bureau
352 Three Springs Road
Bowling Green 42104
(800) 326-7465 or (270) 782-0800
visitbgky.com

Carroll County Tourism and Convention Commission
515 Highland Avenue
P.O. Box 293
Carrollton 41008
(800) 325-4296 or (502) 732-7036
carrolltontourism.com

Cave City Tourism and Welcome Center
502 Mammoth Cave Street
Box 518
Cave City 42127
(270) 773-8833
cavecity.com

Corbin Tourism and Convention Commission
1610 Cumberland Falls Hwy, Suite 7
Corbin 40701
(606) 528-8860
corbinkytourism.com

Danville–Boyle County Convention & Visitors Bureau
105 East Walnut Street
Danville 40422
(895) 236-7794
danvillekentucky.com

Elizabethtown Tourism & Convention Bureau
1030 North Mulberry Street
Elizabethtown 42701
(800) 437-0092 or (270) 765-2175
touretown.com

Frankfort/Franklin County Tourist & Convention Commission
100 Capital Avenue
Frankfort 40601
(800) 960-7200 or (502) 875-8687
visitfrankfort.com

Georgetown/Scott County Tourism Association
399 Outlet Center Drive
P.O. Box 825
Georgetown 40324
(888) 863-8600 or (502) 863-2547
georgetownky.com

Harlan Tourist and Convention Center
201 South Main Street
P.O. Box 489
Harlan 40831
(606) 573-4495
harlantourism.com

Harrodsburg/Mercer County Tourist Commission
488 Price Avenue
P.O. Box 283
Harrodsburg 40330
(800) 355-9192 or (859) 734-2364
harrodsburgky.com

Henderson County Tourist Commission
101 North Water Street Suite B
Henderson 42420
(800) 648-3128 or (270) 826-3128
hendersonky.org

Hopkinsville–Christian County Convention and Visitors Bureau
2800 Fort Campbell Boulevard
P.O. Box 1382
Hopkinsville 42240
(800) 842-9959 or (270) 885-9096
visithopkinsville.com

Lexington Convention and Visitors Bureau
401 West Main Street Suite 104
Lexington 40507
(800) 845-3959 or (859) 233-7299
visitlex.com

Louisville Convention & Visitors Bureau
One Riverfront Plaza Suite 2300
401 West Main Street
Louisville 40202
(888) 568-4784 or (502) 584-2121
gotolouisville.com

Maysville-Mason County Convention & Visitors Bureau
2 East Third Street
Maysville 41056
(606) 564-6986
cityofmaysville.com

Morehead Tourism Commission
111 East First Street
Morehead 40351
(800) 654-1944 or (606) 780-4342
moreheadtourism.com

Murray Convention & Visitors Bureau
201 South Fourth Street
Murray 42071
(800) 651-1603 or (270) 759-2199
tourmurray.com

Northern Kentucky Visitor Center
50 East River Center Blvd.
Covington 41011
(877) 659-8474 or (859) 655-4172
nkycvb.com

KENTUCKY TRAVEL AT A GLANCE

Owensboro–Daviess County Convention & Visitors Bureau
215 East Second Street
Owensboro 42303
(800) 489-1131 or (270) 926-1100
visitowensboro.com

Paducah Convention & Visitors Bureau
128 Broadway Box 90
Paducah 42001
(800) 723-8224 or (270) 443-8784
paducah.travel

Paris–Bourbon County Chamber of Commerce
720 High Street Suite 114
Paris 40361
(859) 987-3205
parisbourbonchamber.com

Richmond Tourism
345 Lancaster Avenue
Richmond 40475
(800) 866-3705 or (859) 626-8474
richmondkytourism.com

Somerset–Pulaski County Convention and Visitors Bureau
522 Ogden Street
P.O. Box 622
Somerset 42501
(800) 642-6287 or (606) 679-6394
lakecumberlandtourism.com

Winchester/Clark County Tourism Commission
2 South Maple Street
Winchester 40391
(800) 298-9105 or (859) 744-0556
tourwinchester.com

Woodford County Chamber of Commerce
141 North Main Street Box 442
Versailles 40383
(859) 873-5122
woodfordcountyinfo.com

and laced with clear, beautiful streams. The south-central region has a touch of it all, including some of the world's most spectacular caverns.

In this book I'm just giving you leads to places that you may not have otherwise found. Your job is to immerse yourself and explore everything with fresh eyes and an open heart. The people here are so friendly, you'll get tired of smiling.

The pleasure of traveling in Kentucky begins with studying the map. Read the names of our towns and you'll begin to believe that Kentucky soil grows poets (and humorists) even better than tobacco:

Bear Wallow	Cat Creek	Dogwalk	Maddog
Horse Fly Holler	Dog Town	Dog Trot	The Bark Yard

Monkey's
  Eyebrow
Possum Trot
Terrapin
Otterpond
Buzzard Roost
Pigeon Roost
Beaver Bottom
Beaver Lick
Rabbit Hash
Chicken Bristle
Chicken City
Ticktown
Scuffletown
Coiltown
Gold City
Future City
Sublimity City
Preacherville
Fearsville
Shuckville
  (population 7)
Spottsville
Jugville
Blandsville
Pleasureville
Touristville
Wisdom
Beauty
Joy
Temperance
Poverty
Chance
Energy
Victory
Democrat

Republican
The Mouth
Mouth Card
Dimple
Nuckles
Shoulderblade
Big Bone
Back Bone
Wish Bone
Marrowbone
Cheap
Habit
Whynot
Pinchem Slyly
Mossy Bottom
Needmore
Sugartit
Hot Spot
Climax
Limp
Subtle
Geneva
Moscow
Bagdad
Warsaw
Paris
London
Athens
Versailles
Ninevah
Sinai
Buena Vista
Key West
Texas
Pittsburg
Omaha

Yosemite
Two Mile Town
Four Mile
Ten Mile
Halfway
Twenty-six
Seventy-six
Eighty-eight
Bachelor's Rest
Belcher
Brodhead
Oddville
Waddy
Wax
Dot
Empire
Embryo
Factory
Tidal Wave
Troublesome
  Creek
Vortex
Princess
Savage
Clutts
Decoy
Thousand Sticks
Gravel Switch
Quicksand
Halo
Moon
Static
Nonesuch
No Creek
Slickaway
Slap Out

Sideview
Nonchalanta
Fleming-Neon
Hi Hat
Go Forth
Alpha
Zula
Zoe
Zag
Zebulon
Zilpo
Yamacraw
Yeaddis
Yerkes
Uz (YOOzee)
Wooton
Tyewhoppety
Kinniconic
Willailla
Whoopflarea
Symsonia
Smilax
Escondida
Cutshin
Cubage
Dongola
Nada (NAdee)
Nebo
Slemp
Se Ree
Gee
Gad
Glo
Guy
Ono
Uno

Ino	Ula	Devil's Fork	Kingdome Come
Elba	Ep	Paradise	Hell Fer Certain
Ulva	Eden	Hell'n Back	

Kentucky Travel at a Glance

IN AN EMERGENCY

All regions of the state use the 911 emergency number. If you're involved in an accident, call (800) 222-5555, the emergency dispatcher's number for the Kentucky State Police.

CURRENT ROAD CONDITIONS

For prerecorded road reports call 511 when in-state, (866) 737-3767 from out of state.

A Few Facts about the Commonwealth

- **Capital:** Frankfort

- **Largest city:** Louisville, population approximately 1 million (metro area)

- **State bird:** Kentucky cardinal

- **State flower:** goldenrod

- **State fish:** Kentucky bass

- **State horse:** thoroughbred

- **State song:** "My Old Kentucky Home" by Stephen Collins Foster; written 1853

- **State bluegrass song:** "Blue Moon of Kentucky" by Bill Monroe; copyright 1947

- **Land area:** 39,732 square miles; rank, 37

- **Highest elevation:** 4,145 feet at Black Mountain

- **Lowest elevation:** 257 feet, near the Mississippi River in Fulton County

A Few of the Many Famous Kentuckians

- Bobbie Ann Mason, writer

- Cassius Marcellus Clay, abolitionist, ambassador to Russia

- Crystal Gayle, country singer

- Dwight Yoakam, country singer

- Gus Van Sant, award-winning movie director

- Harry Dean Stanton, actor

- Henry L. Faulkner, artist and poet

- James Bowie, Texas Ranger who designed the Bowie knife

- Jean Ritchie, folk singer/songwriter

- Johnny Depp, actor

- Kit Carson, agent for Native Americans

- Lee Majors, actor

- Loretta Lynn, country singer

- Muhammad Ali, boxer

- Ralph Eugene Meatyard, photographer

- Tom T. Hall, country singer

- Tom Cruise, actor

- Wendell Berry, writer

Central Kentucky

Like nowhere else in the world, central Kentucky seems to have been created for horses. For this we can thank the rocks. Water percolates through the limestone strata and brings phosphates into the soil that, in turn, enrich plants like bluegrass (actually green with a subtle blue tint), which give our thoroughbreds strong, lightweight bones—perfect for racing. The same water is the magic ingredient in this region's world famous bourbon whiskey.

Central Kentucky is also a kind of Mesopotamia of the South, a cradle of civilization west of the Allegheny Mountains. Modern buildings and businesses revolve around the region's direct links to the past. Antiques malls and bed-and-breakfasts in restored homes are ubiquitous in central Kentucky, and many of the humorous sites, like old country stores, are funny precisely because of their anachronisms. But there's nothing homogeneous about an area that can comfortably be home to everyone from Trappist monks to soul food chefs, jockeys, millionaires, Amish farmers, sculptors, and yoga teachers. And there's no chance you'll be bored exploring it all.

Bluegrass on the Rocks

Wherever there is bluegrass, there are horse farms. To get a good long look at some of the world's best-known horse farms, start in *Lexington.* Take a drive on Harrodsburg Road, Old Frankfort Pike, Iron Works Pike, Paris Pike, Danville Road, or Versailles Road. Many of these and the smaller lanes that weave through them make wonderful bicycling routes. The miles of wooden-plank fences are dizzying; these days most are sprayed with a black, creosote-based paint instead of the traditional white. Dotting the countryside are ostentatious mansions and lavish horse barns where hand-made wainscoting and brass chandeliers are not unheard of.

AUTHOR'S FAVORITE PLACES IN
CENTRAL KENTUCKY

Abbey of Gethsemani
New Haven
(502) 549-3117
monks.org

Actors Theatre
Louisville
(502) 584-1265 or (800) 428-5849
actorstheatre.org

American Printing House for the Blind
Louisville
(800) 223-1839
aph.org

Bernheim Forest Arboretum
Bardstown
(502) 543-2451
bernheim.org

Harry C. Miller Lock Collection
Nicholasville
(859) 885-6041
lockmasters.com

Kentucky History Center
Frankfort
(502) 564-3016
history.ky.gov

Muhammad Ali Center
Louisville
(502) 584-9254
alicenter.org

Shaker Village of Pleasant Hill
Harrodsburg
(800) 734-5611
shakervillageky.org

21C Museum Hotel
Louisville
(502) 217-6300
21chotel.com

Weisenberger Mill
Midway
(859) 254-5282
weisenberger.com

Lexington is surrounded by hundreds of horse farms. The most famous are the thoroughbred farms, where the top racehorses in the world are bred, born, trained, and retired. Amid those gangly-legged foals you see romping in the fields in the spring may be a future Kentucky Derby—or Epsom or French Derby—winner.

trueblue

Lexington was such a cultural center in the early 1800s that it was known as the "Athens of the West."

Thoroughbreds are just one of many types of horse breeds raised on farms in and around Lexington. Standardbreds, American saddlebreds, draft horses, miniatures—all kinds of equines call Lexington home. Visitor policies on farms vary widely. There are several local tour companies. One is *Historic and Horse Farm Tours Inc.* (859-268-2906; horsefarmtours .com), which offers tours from April 1 through the end of October. The oldest tour company, *Blue Grass Tours* (859-252-5744; bluegrasstours.com), offers horse farm tours. An excellent option for independent types is the tour of the stallion division of *Three Chimneys* (859-873-7053), located on Old Frankfort Pike between Lexington and Midway. Here you'll see racing champions. Tours are offered strictly by appointment. Call (859) 873-7053 for reservations and directions to the farm. Also check threechimneys.com or write to P.O. Box 114, Midway 40307.

The best way to find out which farms are currently open is to call or stop by the *Lexington Convention and Visitors Bureau* (859-233-7299 or 800-845-3959; visitlex.com), which keeps updated information. The bureau is in downtown Lexington at 401 West Main Street. There's no admission charge to tour individual farms, but keep in mind that it's traditional to tip the groom who shows you around, at least $5 to $10.

trueblue

More than 1,000 people attended the funeral of Man o' War, the thoroughbred racehorse superstar, in 1947. He was the first horse to lie in state. The stallion's body was embalmed and buried in an oak casket lined with black and yellow racing silks. In 1977 his grave and monument were moved to the Kentucky Horse Park.

While you're at the visitor center, pick up a free copy of the *Lexington Walk and Bluegrass Country Driving Tour* guide, which directs your attention to specific histories while you absorb horse-farm aesthetics. The visitor center also offers special guides on more than a dozen topics of special interest, from antiques stores to area museums.

The *Kentucky Horse Park* (859-233-4303 or 800-678-8813; kyhorsepark .com), located a few miles north of downtown on Iron Works Pike, is not off the beaten path in any sense, but it is a great place to see all kinds of real horses, from thoroughbreds to rare breeds. There are some lesser-known aspects of this 1,032-acre park. Everybody stops at the Man o' War statue and grave, but take time also to visit the grave of Isaac Murphy. Here's a reminder of the important and largely unheralded role African Americans played in the early days of thoroughbred racing. Fourteen of the 15 riders in the first Kentucky Derby were black. Murphy, born in Lexington in 1861, remains the all-time most winning jockey, achieving victory in 44 percent of his races.

The Kentucky Horse Park is an educational center as well as a tourist attraction. So in addition to watching the films and looking at the antique carriages and other exhibits in the museum, be sure to walk through the Big Barn. You might find future horse trainers or veterinarians hard at work or meet some members of the Mustang Troop, Lexington inner-city youngsters

Jot 'Em Down

Stop by the *Jot 'Em Down Store* at the intersection of Iron Works Pike and Russell Cave Road (859-523-0103). Once called Terrell's Grocery, this little store has long been a favorite hangout for horse-farm employees. Founder Robert Terrell remembered the late 1930s, when his father and uncle listened for 15 minutes every night to a radio show called Lum and Abner, a comedic series about two store owners much like themselves. Lum was tall and savvy, while Abner was short, dim-witted, and funny. The fictional characters ran a grocery called the Jot 'Em Down Store in Pine Ridge, Arkansas. The Terrells' customers got into the habit of calling them Lum and Abner and began adopting character names from the show, like Mousie and Grandpappy Spears. Once when the real Lum and Abner were in Lexington buying horses, they heard about the tradition at Terrell's Grocery, so they dropped in for a visit, bringing with them a sign that read Jot 'Em Down Store. The rest is history. Come by for sandwiches and beers and you will meet Robert Terrell II ("Robey"), who has run the store since his father's death in 1998.

who come to the park to care for once-wild western mustangs. The Mustang Troop rode in the 1997 Presidential Inaugural Parade.

Horses have been a favorite subject of artists, and the William G. Kenton Gallery, part of the park's *International Museum of the Horse,* is host to fascinating exhibits from around the globe. Something interesting is always on display, so don't skip over the gallery. The Kentucky Horse Park is open from 9 a.m. to 5 p.m. daily from mid-March through October and from 9 a.m. to 5 p.m. Wednesday through Sunday, November through March. There are many special shows and events throughout the year (kyhorsepark.com).

trueblue

In 1789 there were more horses than people in Lexington.

To experience other important aspects of Kentucky's equine industry, go to the races or one of the big sales. In late April through May and in late September and early October, standardbred horses race at the *Red Mile Harness Track* (859-255-0752), the second oldest harness-racing track in the U.S., located off South Broadway, just a few blocks from the downtown business district. Great trotters and pacers have been racing this track and provoking bets since 1875. Tattersalls Sales holds a variety of standardbred auctions at the track throughout the year (theredmile.com).

About 43 percent of all the thoroughbred horses sold in North America are sold at public horse sales in Kentucky. And the most prestigious horse sale in the world is the July Selected Yearling Sale at *Keeneland Race Course* (4201 Versailles Road; 859-254-3412 or 800-456-3412) in Lexington. This sale dates to 1943, and the horses sold must meet high bloodline and conformation standards. The bidders are an impressive group, too. From sheiks and film stars to international business moguls and Texas cowboys, you just never know who you'll see at the Keeneland sales pavilion. But you can bet that they will have one thing in common: the means and the desire to spend big bucks on horses. You don't have to be a millionaire just to watch the sales from the pavilion lobby or to walk through the barns while the horses are being shown to potential buyers. It's a fascinating and surreal experience. Additional sales are held at Keeneland in January, September, and November.

Race meets at Keeneland are brief (just three weeks in April and three weeks in October), but they usually attract the top echelon of the thoroughbred world. The spring meet includes the Blue Grass Stakes, an important preparatory race to the Kentucky Derby. The atmosphere is relaxed and genteel (until 1997, the track didn't even have a public address system), and this is one of the few tracks in North America where the public is allowed access to the barn areas. Keeneland is worth a visit at any time of year. The old stone buildings and grounds are lovely, and at the track's training center, you can catch early morning workouts year-round. Plan to have breakfast at the track kitchen. For more information check keeneland.com.

Lexington boasts plenty of beautiful mansions, many dating to the early 1800s. One of the historic houses open for tour is *The Hunt-Morgan House* (201 North Mill Street; 859-233-3290). This lovely Federal-style brick house was built in 1814 by John Wesley Hunt, an early Lexington entrepreneur believed to be Kentucky's first millionaire. Later residents included Thomas Hunt Morgan, who won a Nobel Prize for medicine in 1933. Civil War buffs will be interested in the collection of uniforms, weapons, pictures, and other items relating to its most flamboyant occupant, Confederate general John Hunt Morgan. The escapades of Morgan and his "Morgan's Raiders" are recounted to this day in many a Kentucky community. Tour guides tell visitors that Morgan is reputed to have ridden his horse into the front hall of the house, kissed his mother, and galloped out the back door, with Union troops in hot

trueblue

Kentucky has more than 1,500 miles of marked hiking trails.

pursuit. Morgan must have had a thing about riding his horse in the house, because there's a similar story attached to a house Morgan and his troops occupied in Lebanon, Kentucky.

Tours of the house are offered hourly Wednesday through Friday from 1 to 5 p.m., Saturday from 10 a.m. to 4 p.m., and Sunday from 1 to 5 p.m. (nps.gov/history/nR/travel/lexington/hun.htm). If you like old houses, you'll enjoy strolling in the surrounding Gratz Park neighborhood, Lexington's most posh address in the early 1800s. For more information on historic buildings call The Bluegrass Trust at (859) 253-0362.

Consider a man who was a jewelry designer known to drape diamond necklaces around the stubby red neck of his dachshund, Ernie, then send the dog out to model them for potential clients who were sunbathing by the swimming pool at the Bel Air Hotel. Try to imagine what kind of museum such a man would build. When you give up, take a drive west from downtown on the Old Frankfort Pike to the **Headley-Whitney Museum** (859-255-6653; headley-whitney.org). Originally, the late George W. Headley III established the space at his home to privately display his jewel collection, but in 1968 he and his wife opened the place to the public. Headley died in 1985, but the legacy of his museum continued. In the dramatic setting of the Jewel Room, visitors could once marvel at Headley's unusual jeweled boxes and bibelots, ranging from a ruby-encrusted abalone horse head to a scene of the moon landing in semiprecious stones. Unfortunately, in a sensational 1994 heist, burglars made off with many of the pieces. Since the robbery, the museum has increased its focus on fine decorative arts and features changing exhibits of clothing, textiles, and furniture. There are still many Headley creations on display, loaned by private owners, and if you need further evidence of his eccentricity, you need only step into the Shell Grotto—an entire room encrusted with thousands of seashells. The museum is open from 10 a.m. to 5 p.m. Tuesday through Friday, and from noon to 5 p.m. Saturday and Sunday. It's closed in January. Recently established as a Smithsonian Affiliate, the museum also hosts temporary exhibits that change every three months; these exhibits focus on the categories of decorative arts and historic fine art. The grounds are elegant for picnicking. Old Frankfort Pike is a great place for biking; part of it is an official National Scenic Byway.

true*blue*

Transylvania University in Lexington was the first university west of the Alleghenies.

For more art, the Lexington Art League has its offices and a small gallery in a strange, castellated 1852 Gothic villa in downtown Lexington, one of five designed by the architect A. J. Davis. The exhibitions at the **Loudoun House** provide a taste of the work of some visual artists in the area. A national juried exhibition every January called (and featuring) *The Nude* is the most popular event. Two alternate galleries run by the Art League are The Project Space, a space within the Loudoun House used for installation art projects, and the Metro-Lex Gallery off-site at 301 East Main Street in the atrium of the National City Bank Building. From downtown go north on North Broadway and turn right (east) on Loudon Avenue, then bear left when you reach a V in the road. Turn right onto Castlewood Drive. Hours are Tuesday through Sunday 1 to 4 p.m. (859-254-7024; lexingtonartleague.org).

Two artists who can almost always be found at work in the studio are Erika Strecker and Tony Higdon, a married couple of blacksmiths/sculptors. The public is welcome to stop by their gallery and studio, *Higdon-Strecker Studio,* on the edge of downtown Lexington, at 610 West Third Street near its intersection with Newtown Pike. Erika designs and builds tables, benches, sculpture, garden accessories—such as gates and trellises—and lighting fixtures, which often include hand-blown glass shades. Tony specializes in innovative architectural metalwork, like railings, balconies, furniture, fire screens, kitchen hoods, vanities, lighting, and furniture. Both use a variety of techniques that range from traditional blacksmithing with a hammer, forge, and anvil to sleek fabrication with high-tech equipment. Whatever the combination of techniques, every piece made by these artists is unique and handmade at a high level of craftsmanship—a welcome respite in this world of mass production. The work in their gallery is for sale but also serves to help visitors see the range of possibilities in terms of materials and forms. Commissions are welcome. The gallery is open between 9 a.m. and 5 p.m. Monday through Friday or by appointment. Call (859) 396-7118 for more information. To see portfolio images, take a look at ironhorseforge.com and erikastrecker.com.

Despite being central Kentucky's second-largest tourist attraction (the largest is the Kentucky Horse Park), Lexington children's museum, the *Explorium,* is something of a hidden treasure. It is hidden to adults because we might assume it's not for us. Think again. I found myself replanning the design of my shower stall after playing in the "bubble area," where you stand in a funny little booth and pull a giant vertical bubble completely around you, while watching it all in a fun-house mirror. Being confronted with "kid" information is also humbling. The ever-changing display areas range from cultural exhibitions about the Ukraine to a hands-on exhibit about how animation works. One educational area is a walk-through human heart, a series of sculpted and painted plaster chambers representing ventricles and auricles, all vibrating to the constant beat of our most powerful muscle. This megaheart was designed (and made, in part) by medical illustrator Rick Gersony. This museum is an all-day treat at the price of $8 per person; children under 1 admitted free. Hours are 10 a.m. to 5 p.m. Tuesday through Saturday and 1 to 5 p.m. Sunday. The museum is located downtown, in Victorian Square, a complex of renovated 19th-century commercial buildings at the corner of Vine and Broadway. Call (859) 258-3253 for more information (explorium.com). If you have kids, be sure to call or stop by the *Lexington Children's Theatre* at 418 West Short Street, also by Victorian Square. Get a schedule of plays and special events at (859) 254-4546; lctonstage.org.

The *Atomic Cafe* (859-254-1969; atomiccafeky.com), located in an old corner building near downtown at 265 North Limestone (across Third Street from Transylvania University), is definitely a hot place to eat. Guinness on tap and a huge basket of spicy sweet-potato chips are reasons enough to go. The whole menu is Caribbean, ranging from a savory chicken pot pie to spicy lime shrimp. In good weather there's outdoor patio seating. Indoors, the cafe tends to be loud and lively. Island murals cover the walls from floor to ceiling. Dinner only, Tuesday through Saturday.

Just blocks away is the *Kentucky Theater* (214 East Main; 859-231-7924; kentuckytheater.com), a true living treasure of the city and an architectural gem to boot. The main theater was built in 1922 in Italian Renaissance style, complete with highly ornamental ceiling and massive velvet stage curtain. In 1929 the adjacent State Theater was built in a Spanish style—clouds are painted on the dreamy blue sky ceiling. A fire in 1987 nearly condemned the buildings. But ten years later a restored Kentucky was open to the delighted and now faithful public. There is also an ongoing effort to fully restore the theater's original Wultitzer Organ. It's a real pleasure to see a film or a concert in the space, but what makes the theater a living treasure is its devotion to showing art films, documentaries, animated shorts, and midnight flicks, like *The Rocky Horror Picture Show* or *Eraserhead*. Monday nights are devoted to the live taping of the *Woodsongs Old-Time Radio Hour,* an internationally syndicated live folk music program the public is welcome to attend and become the live audience at a price of usually only $6.50, except for special shows (woodsongs.com). Several times a year look for fabulous concerts organized by the Troubadour Concert Series—big names in the theater's gorgeous, almost intimate setting (troubashow.com).

Ashland, the Henry Clay Estate was originally the home and 600-acre farm of Henry Clay, 19th-century statesman (U.S. Senator, Speaker of the

House of Representatives, Secretary of State, peace commissioner, and presidential candidate). The Italianate mansion itself has the status of a National Historic Landmark. Admission is $10 for adults, $5 for students, and free for children age 5 and under. The most interesting room is an octagonal library with a vaulted, domed ceiling, reportedly designed by Benjamin Latrobe, who also designed the U.S. Capitol in Washington, D.C. Even if you choose not to go indoors, the serpentine paths through the grounds and handsome gardens are a pleasure to walk. Clay named the place Ashland because the estate grounds were, and still are, covered with majestic old ash trees. The gardens are formal, 18th-century parterre style, and are lovingly maintained by the Garden Club of Lexington. You can also get a box lunch (seasonally) at the *Ginkgo Tree,* open from 11 a.m. to 4 p.m. daily late April through October, weather permitting. The garden is open dawn to dusk daily, year-round. House tours are given from 10 a.m. to 4 p.m. Monday through Saturday and from 1 to 4 p.m. Sunday. The house is closed in January and on Monday, November through March. Ashland is located at 120 Sycamore Road, off Richmond Road. Call (859) 266-8581 or visit henryclay.org for more information.

true blue

Kentucky became the 15th state in 1792.

When *Alfalfa Restaurant* opened in the early 1970s, it was probably one of thousands of health-food cooperatives that operated on limited budgets and lots of heart. It has survived and flourished as one of Lexington's most cherished eateries. Although it is not purely vegetarian, the restaurant has always catered to the vegetarian and health-conscious population. Whole grains, vivid flavors, internationally inspired recipes, potent desserts, imported beers, and cinnamon coffee keep us coming back. There's live music nightly by your table, ranging from jazz flute to Irish bouzouki. Alfalfa is located at 141 East Main, next door to the Downtown Arts Center. Hours are 11 a.m. to 2 p.m. Monday through Saturday, and for dinner from 5:30 to 10 p.m. Wednesday and Thursday, 5:30 to 11 p.m. Friday and Saturday, and 9 a.m. to 2 p.m. for a beloved Sunday brunch. Call (859) 253-0014 or visit alfalfarestaurant.com for specials and information.

Located near the campus of the University of Kentucky, *Joe Bologna's* (859-252-4933; joebolognas.com) has been a favorite Lexington hangout since the early 1970s, and not just for students. In the early 1990s it moved across the street from its original location to a restored church building at 120 West Maxwell Street—the bar is sacrilegiously located right where the altar used to be, and televisions are everywhere. Joe B's is the place to go for pizza and other Italian dishes. You must order the famous breadsticks, served in a sinful pool of garlic butter. For a dinner that's a bit more expensive, but much more Italian, try *Giuseppe's Ristorante Italiano.* Go south out of town on Nicholasville Road ½ mile beyond Man o' War, and look for the sign on the left. A great wine list dominated by Chianti is featured. Call (859) 272-4269 for reservations, a recommended practice, or visit giuseppeslexington.com.

Almost directly across Nicholasville Road at 225 Waveland Museum Lane is the *Waveland State Historic Site* (859-272-3611; parks.ky.gov/parks/historicsites/waveland) a grand Greek Revival mansion that was built in 1847 by Joseph Bryan, the grandnephew of Daniel Boone. Guided tours cost $7 and are offered year-round (except January when it is closed), Monday through Saturday between 10 a.m. and 5 p.m. and on Sunday from 1 to 5 p.m. You'll see all aspects of life on an antebellum plantation, from the smokehouse and icehouse to the servants' quarters and some remarkable period furnishings. The most intriguing object is a hickory ladderback chair that originally came from the home of Daniel Boone's parents in Pennsylvania. The chair was tied to the side of a packhorse in 1779 to make a seat for two-year-old Rebecca Boone Grant, Daniel's niece, as her family traveled to Kentucky from North Carolina. The building underwent an extensive renovation in 2000 and is in excellent condition.

Although *Raven Run Nature Sanctuary* (5888 Jacks Creek Road; 859-272-6105; lexingtonky.gov/index.aspx?page=276) is just outside of town, it has the ability to make you feel as if you're deep in Appalachian wilderness. From downtown take Richmond Road (also Main Street) east out of town and turn right onto Highway 25 (across from Jacobson Park). Go approximately 3½ miles to Jack's Creek Pike and turn right (at Judy Ray's Grocery Store). Go about 5½ miles on Jack's Creek Pike, and Raven Run is located on the left. A large chain-link fence and a sign mark the entrance. The sanctuary's 470 acres include a perfect little piece of the region's most dramatic geologic feature—the Kentucky River limestone palisades—and the remarkable diversity of native wild plant species unique to it. Raven Run is open daily year-round (except for major holidays) for hiking along its 8 miles of trails. Just sign in at the nature center and bring your own water. Along the trails you'll discover remnants of 19th-century structures like stone chimneys.

The sanctuary's nature center has a number of hands-on exhibits that kids will love. Make sure to ask about current programs, which include sessions on the life cycles and identification of butterflies and dragonflies, bird watching, tree-identification, night hikes to view nocturnal animals and learn owl calls, map and compass navigations, and so forth. Spend some time there and you'll see why Lexingtonians, especially children, love their nature sanctuary.

The other natural area owned by the Lexington Fayette County Urban Government, Parks and Recreation Department is *McConnell Springs* at 416 Rebmann Lane (859-225-4073; mcconnellsprings.org). It's not near town, it's in town, a 26-acre pocket of preserved natural space inside an industrial area just inside New Circle Road. To get there, get onto Old Frankfort Pike and watch for signs on the south side. It's open daily from 9 a.m. to 5 p.m. year-round. There are two miles of very well-maintained hiking trails that wind through farmland with stone fences and wooded areas, and past several unusual natural springs. The site was first settled in 1775 by William McConnell and is said to be the site where Lexington was named. A gunpowder mill here supplied powder for the war of 1812. After the mill closed, the land changed hands five times, finally coming to the Cahill family. The stone foundation at the farm site once supported a large 1920s-era dairy barn. In 1958 the land was sold to the Central Rock company, which tore down the buildings and started mining rock and gravel. The Friends of McConnell Springs bought the land in 1994 and conserved it as a natural area.

trueblue

The Vest-Lindsay Home in Frankfort was the boyhood home of U.S. Senator George Graham Vest, credited with the immortal phrase "Dog is man's best friend."

The most amazing features of the preserve are the two springs. The waters of the Blue Hole emerge from underground through the limestone bedrock from a wide area of southwest Lexington. The name comes from the prismatic blue effects caused by its unusual depth of 15 feet into a conical basin filled by the springs. The Boils get their name from the energetic surging of water into the spring after heavy rains. The pressure is great enough that the fountain-like columns may reach two feet tall. The Boils are cold, with an average temperature of 55 degrees Fahrenheit. Both the Boils and the Blue Hole are artesian springs—wells or springs that force water to the surface due to subsurface pressures.

When the waters reach the final sink, they disappear underground into a cavelike formation for a third of a mile before surfacing again at Preston's Cave and eventually reaching Elkhorn Creek. An exposed window like the Final Sink is characteristic of the Karst topography that underlies much of this area. Sinkholes are also a common feature of Karst systems, formed when surface soil is carried away from below as cracks in the limestone bedrock enlarge. A major evolution of the Final Sink took place just after the property was acquired. Part of the soil bank at the back right of the main sinking point collapsed and formed a deep, vertically walled shaft. This new sink began to enlarge rapidly and threatened some of the trees overlooking the sink. Measures were taken to stop or slow the erosion, but, as many local farms can attest, the natural processes of the springs always win.

The other superstars of the site are the majestic 250-year-old Bur oak trees dating from the era before much human intervention when the bluegrass region was predominantly an open savannah, open fields of thick native grasses with a few interspersed trees. You can occasionally get the sense of a savannah on some of the older horse farms where ancient trees dot pasture. Imagine large cats like cougars lounging on massive branches and waiting for a herd of elk or deer to stop for shade.

For an unusually intimate look at the workaday world of thoroughbred training, plan to tour *The Thoroughbred Center* (now owned by Keeneland Race Course), 3380 Paris Pike. From downtown Lexington take North Broadway out of town, which becomes Paris Pike (or US 68 and US 27). After a few miles, look for the horse center on your right. Since 1969, when this business was started, it has been one of the most prestigious privately owned thoroughbred training centers in the world. More than 1,100 stalls are leased to individual horse owners, who supply their own trainers and riders.

The tour takes you through a barn, by the rail where you can talk to a trainer, and into the sales pavilion, where you'll be amazed at the complexity of yet another aspect of the business—horse sales. Tours take one and a half hours and cost $15 for adults, $8 for children. They're given at 9 a.m., 10:30 a.m., and 1 p.m., Monday through Friday, plus on Saturday April through October. November 1 through March 31, only the 9 a.m. tour is available (or by appointment). Call ahead because tour space is limited (859-293-1853; thethoroughbredcenter.com). Either before or after the tour, stop by the extensive tack shop, where you may luck into an opportunity to watch leather workers in action.

From The Thoroughbred Center, drive north to Paris along US 68, "Paris Pike" as it's known locally. This beautiful route represents an innovative approach to highway planning. With numerous accidents along its narrow, curving path, this busy road had a deadly reputation, but it was also lined by mature trees, dry-laid rock fences, and some of the area's finest horse farms. Highway planners and preservationists battled for years over how to improve the road without destroying its character. Their compromise is a four-lane highway that runs through carefully preserved scenic setbacks; the rock fences were moved and rebuilt.

In the late 18th century, the ***Duncan Tavern,*** at 323 High Street, was in its heyday. Major Joseph Duncan built the huge inn out of native limestone on this spot in 1788, four years before Kentucky was a state. Everything else in town was built of logs, so the tavern was an eye-catcher as well as

---

Freedom and the Spirit of Invention

On the corner of Tenth and Vine Streets is a bronze historical marker recognizing the birthplace of Garrett Morgan, African-American inventor of the tri-color traffic signal, forerunner of the present traffic light, and a gas mask design that became the basis for one used during World War I. Among his many awards was the first grand prize of the Second International Exposition of Safety and Sanitation in 1914. In addition to the highway marker, there is a permanent exhibit on Garrett Morgan on display at the Hopewell Museum, 800 Pleasant Street.

Also recognized on the marker is Morgan's childhood school, Branch School, located in the neighborhood of Claysville, adjacent to the marker. Claysville was one of the early black settlements that sprang up after the Civil War when newly emancipated slaves needed a place to live, work, and structure their lives as free citizens. Garrett Morgan's maternal grandfather, Rev. Garrett Reed, was one of the early settlers in the little community.

a social catchall. Originally there was a ballroom, a bar, a billiards room, dining rooms, kitchens, and bedrooms. Daniel Boone slept there. So did frontiersman Simon Kenton.

Today the Duncan Tavern and Anne Duncan House is a historic site owned by the Kentucky Society of the Daughters of the American Revolution (DAR), which has acquired enough period furniture and significant artifacts to fill the huge building gracefully. Much of the original large furniture was built on-site. Its tradition as a tavern is maintained by keeping it active as a party place: People can rent the Duncan Tavern for parties and receptions. The DAR hosts small events in the original dining room and serves meals on a long, cherry, boardinghouse-style table, valued at $30,000. Normally the tavern and genealogy library are open to visitors Tuesday through Saturday from 10 a.m. to noon and from 1 to 4 p.m. Tours are given Tuesday through Saturday at 1:30 p.m. Admission to the tavern is $8 for adults; $6 for senior citizens; $2 for children ages 6 to 12; free for children under 6. Admission to the house is $3 for adults and free for children and students. Call (859) 987-1788 or visit kentuckydar.org/duncantavern.htm for more details.

Learn about area history at the **Hopewell Museum** (859-987-7274; hopewellmuseum.org), in a proud little building at the corner of Eighth and Pleasant Streets. Admission is free, and hours are Wednesday through Saturday from noon to 5 p.m. and Sunday from 2 to 4 p.m. Closed in January. Just up the street is the **Nannine Clay Wallis Arboretum,** 616 Pleasant Street, at the headquarters of the Garden Club of Kentucky (859-987-6158; garden clubky.org/arboretum/). A "study guide" for tree identification is available. Admission is free, and hours are Monday through Saturday from 10 a.m. to 6 p.m. and Sunday from noon to 6 p.m.

Bourbon County has more than 85 horse farms, but very few allow visitors. One exception is **Claiborne Farm,** home and burial place of the celebrated Triple Crown winner Secretariat, which generously welcomes visitors by appointment only. Call (859) 233-4252 or (859) 987-2330 or visit clairbornefarm.com. From downtown Paris go south on Highway 627 (also called Winchester Road) beyond the edge of town. Watch for the farm entrance on your left.

Cane Ridge Meeting House Shrine is the site of some powerful events and the source of some wild stories. Follow Main Street (US 68) north from downtown Paris and go east on US 460 to Highway 537 North.

Take the latter for 5.4 miles and look left (north) for the shrine. Said to be the largest one-room log structure in North America, the church is impressive.

Two events make this church significant. The first was the Cane Ridge Revival, which took place August 6–12, 1801. It was the nation's largest revival during a period of big ones. Between 20,000 and 30,000 people attended. Preachers stood on platforms, stumps, and hay bales all over the fields talking simultaneously to thousands of people for seven days and six nights. As the story goes, women's hair stood straight out and crackled like fire; people spoke in tongues, shook, danced, laughed, and sang, and were moved every which way by the Holy Spirit. The excitement ended when the food ran out. The second event occurred in 1804 when Cane Ridge preacher Barton Warren Stone led the people away from the Presbyterian Church and started a new movement that became the Christian Church (Disciples of Christ), the denomination that now owns and manages the shrine. In 1957 an enormous limestone superstructure was erected to protect the log church. Later a museum was built nearby. From April through October the whole place is open Monday through Saturday from 9 a.m. to 5 p.m. and from 1 to 5 p.m. on Sunday. Donations are encouraged. Call (859) 987-5350 or go to caneridge.org.

Roll up your sleeves and choose your own produce at either of these two Paris area farms. Call ahead to see what's ripe and to ask whether you should bring your own containers. **Reed Valley,** 239 Lail Lane (859-987-6480; reedvalleyorchard.com), features blueberries, blackberries, nectarines, raspberries, peaches, pears, and apples. And **Marshalls' Strawberries,** 325 Austerlitz Road (859-987-6502), features—guess what—strawberries.

Downtown **Georgetown** is chock-full of history. It's also a good place for a walk. Pick up a **Walk Through Time** tour brochure from the Georgetown/Scott County Tourism Commission office at 399 Outlet Center Drive (502-863-2547; georgetownky.com) or at various locations around town, and take a stroll along this pretty Main Street where architecture spans more than 200 years. Many buildings have interesting legend and lore attached—such as the statue of justice on the courthouse that is rumored to come to life and roam the streets every Halloween. **Fava's Restaurant,** established in 1910 on East Main Street (502-863-4383), is a true diner in the old style (fast becoming extinct in Kentucky), where you can eat breakfast, lunch, or dinner

Sentenced to a New Life

One building you can't overlook in downtown Georgetown is the *Old Scott County Jail Complex* at Main and Water Streets. When it was built in 1892, this massive Victorian-style building was acclaimed as the "jewel" of Kentucky jails and offered the latest amenities, such as electric lights and indoor plumbing. A hundred years later, when the county built a new Justice Center, the old jail seemed archaic and gloomy inside by modern standards. Some wanted to tear it down, but a small group of local citizens and artists thought this former jewel might be creatively recut. Since the late 1990s, Scott County Arts Consortium has been working to transform the historic jail and attached jailer's house for use as a community arts and cultural center. By applying for grants, soliciting memberships and donations from local citizens, sponsoring art shows, house tours, suppers, silent auctions, and locally famous bake sales (the group includes some awesome cooks), they've overcome the naysayers and put a new copper roof on the jailer's house, renovated the porch, and developed a phased plan to rehabilitate the structure. If you'd like to find out more about this project (or those bake sales), call the consortium at (502) 570-8366 or check scottcountyartworks.org.

between 6:30 a.m. and 9 p.m. from Monday through Saturday. Or, have three o'clock coffee and argue local issues with politicians and merchants.

If you're interested in antiques, look in any direction. In a state as obsessed with old stuff as Kentucky, any town that dares call itself the Antiques Capital of Kentucky better be able to back up that claim with something substantial. Georgetown does, with five malls all within easy walking distance of the courthouse. If it's old, you probably can find it at the *Central Kentucky Antique Mall* at 114 East Main Street (502-863-4018; antiquemalls.com), or the *Georgetown Antique Mall* at 136 West Main Street (502-863-1891; georgetownkyantiquemall.com). A list of antiques dealers is available at georgetownky.com/shop.html. Just west of Georgetown Antique Mall at 124 West Main Street is *Heirlooms and Gretchen's* (502-863-2538; heirloomsandgretchens.com), where the Heirlooms crew does picture framing, custom leaded- and stained-glass work, and what they call "family heirloom bears." Say your grandmother had a fur coat, but moths have damaged it over the years. You can take what's left to Heirlooms, and they'll transform it into lovable Mama, Papa, or Baby bears.

The old buildings on Georgetown's Main Street have seen other changes in recent years. When the post office moved from Main and Mulberry to a new suburban building, many residents were concerned about the fate of the stately limestone building that had housed the post office since the early 1900s. They were thrilled when the county purchased the building as a home for the *Georgetown and Scott County Museum.* The museum features a variety of displays about local history, from bourbon to ballpoints, with special programs on local history every month. The marble-floored lobby of the post office has been left pretty much intact. Museum hours are 9 a.m. to 4 p.m. Monday through Friday, 10 a.m. to 4 p.m. Saturday. Admission is free. Call (502) 863-6201 or visit georgetownky .com/attrac.html.

From downtown Georgetown take US 25 North out of town and watch for signs to *Cardome Centre* (502-863-1575; cardomecenter.com), a property that has played a significant role in Kentucky history for hundreds of years. After having been a major hunting ground for Choctaw, Mingo, and Shawnee Indians, it was one of the first areas deeded and settled west of the mountains. It was home to a number of early prominent white families during the 1800s, including James F. Robinson, a Kentucky governor, who gave the place its name, Cardome, after the Latin phrase *cara domus,* or "dear home." The Sisters of Visitation, a cloistered sect, bought Cardome in 1896 and ran an academy there until 1969. Now Cardome belongs to a private owner. The original academy and monastery buildings include a science classroom and a "dream house," where the senior girls were finally allowed to have outside visitors and even to smoke. Cardome's pride and joy is the school chapel, which features some gorgeous woodwork, Romanesque vaulted ceilings, stained-glass windows, and a classic bell tower. The whole property can be rented for huge company picnics, or smaller areas can be used for weddings, seminars, meetings, and so forth.

Adjacent to Cardome is an unusual work in progress, "the official Kentucky-Japan Friendship Garden," *Yuko-En on the Elkhorn.* The garden was envisioned by members of the Scott Education and Community Foundation as a way to commemorate the 10th anniversary of the sister city relationship between Georgetown and Taharo-cho, Japan. Plants and rock native to Kentucky are used in accordance with Japanese gardening principles. So, in place of bamboo, there is a large grove of native cane. The spare Zen rock garden employs large pieces of naturally sculpted Kentucky limestone. In the Savannah Gardens, there are upper and lower waterfalls cascading down natural limestone outcrops into reflecting pools lined with walls built like central Kentucky's famous dry-laid stone fences. The high canopy of American maple trees hovers almost protectively over the delicate little Japanese maple in the Stroll Garden in which the land has been resculpted to represent the rolling bluegrass region in miniature. Visitors are welcome to stroll through this unique landscaping gem anytime year-round. There are six acres to explore—by Japanese standards, that's almost endless.

Moonshine and Wood Carvings

You'd better sit down for this one: The father of bourbon whiskey was a Baptist preacher. According to legend, the good Reverend Elijah Craig ran a distillery, a hemp rope walk, and a paper mill (the first in the state). A fire swept through a building where barrels were being stored, and being something of a tightwad, Reverend Craig decided to put new corn whiskey into the charred barrels despite the damage. The color of the whiskey changed, the flavor mellowed, and a tradition was born. Eventually this new sour mash was named bourbon because large quantities were made in nearby Bourbon County. Baptists, don't despair. In the late 18th century, Baptists were not as concerned with temperance. Drunkenness among preachers was prohibited, but drinking was not. In fact, clergy often were paid in whiskey. Gambling, dancing, and going to barbecues, on the other hand, were considered serious crimes.

Elijah Craig's sundry enterprises were all built near the *Royal Spring,* a steady water source gurgling up from under a huge bed of limestone, discovered in 1774. Georgetown was built around the spring, and the city still gets its water from it. A small park around the spring is the site of an 1874 log cabin built by a former slave, Milton Leach, and a 1997 wooden statue of Elijah Craig by Georgetown artist Sandy Schu. This is no typical wood carving; it was created using a chainsaw from a tree still rooted in the park grounds. Other examples of Schu's noisy yet surprisingly detailed work can be seen throughout the area. He created the buffalo on display at Cardome Centre, north of downtown. His 20-foot eagle inspires golfers at the 12th hole of Kearney Hill Links golf course in Lexington. For more information about Royal Spring and other Georgetown attractions, call *Georgetown/Scott County Tourism* at (502) 863-2547 or go to georgetownky.com.

The address is 700 Cincinnati Pike. For more information call Scott County Education and Community Foundation at (502) 863-8039. Visit yuko-en.com. Guided tours can be organized around various topics—Japanese culture, the Elkhorn Creek corridor, or wildlife conservation. There are ongoing programs for regional students in environmental education.

While a Japanese garden may be a new idea in Georgetown and Scott County, growing things certainly isn't. Across US 25 from Cardome is *Bi-Water Farm* (502-863-3676; biwaterfarm.com), one of a bumper crop of Scott County farm markets. Bi-Water, run by the Fister family, features flowers and herbs as well as homegrown vegetables. The farm's Autumnfest runs several weekends in the fall with hayrides, a corn maze, and other family activities. On Newtown Pike, look for *Evans Farm Orchard* (502-863-2255; evansorchard.com), which features a petting zoo and tomatoes, squash, and other hot-weather veggies in the summer and dozens of apple varieties in late summer through fall. *Amerson Farm Orchard* (502-863-3799; amersonfarms.com) on the US 62 bypass also features vegetables and apples along with delicious apple cider slushies. So, summer through fall, this is a great place to load up on farm-fresh food. All are open on weekends; weekday hours vary.

Through all of its varied projects since 1989, *Shooting Star Nursery* is accomplishing the goals of educating people about preserving the world's biodiversity and promoting renaturalization in Kentucky and elsewhere. The nursery itself supplies more than 3,000 species of nursery-propagated native plants for gardening, landscaping, and restoring damaged lands such as strip mines and tired farmland. The nursery's botanists spend lots of energy doing consultation for those involved in ecological restoration and education. (See, for example, the native prairie grassland plantings at the Shaker Village at Pleasant Hill.) Their website, shootingstarnursery.com, is in itself an excellent resource. It explains that natural landscaping provides lost habitat and protects natural resources, but also that it is extremely important not to dig plants from the wild as the practice further endangers native species. Descriptions are thorough and the photos are lovely. You can, for example, order a collection of plants that form a native perennial hummingbird garden, complete with suggested landscaping layout. Or order enough native grass and wildflower seed to restore an entire farm to its pre-1700 botanical condition. Plants described on the website can be mail-ordered directly from Shooting Star. Otherwise you are welcome to visit the nursery by appointment. They are open to the public on a drop-in basis for retail sales twice a year, in May and September. Call (502) 867-7979 or (866) 405-7979 or check the website for exact dates and times. To get there, take US 460 out of Georgetown to the west (3.7 miles from the I-75 exit) and watch for Soards Road on the left-hand side. The nursery is on the left. The address is 160 Soards Road, Georgetown.

One of the best-selling family sedans in America, the Camry, as well as Avalon sedans and Sienna minivans, are made in Georgetown at *Toyota Motor Manufacturing, Kentucky, Inc.,* on Cherry Blossom Way (exit 129 from I-75). Hourlong guided tours of the plant are given at 10 a.m., noon, and 2 p.m. Monday through Friday, with an additional tour at 6 p.m. on Thursday, by reservation. Call (800) 866-4485. No shorts, cameras, purses, or children under first grade are allowed. You'll don a hard hat and safety goggles and ride an electric tram through the stamping, body weld, and assembly areas of the plant. The plant is a big—about eight million square feet under one roof—bright, and noisy place, all the more mind-boggling when you consider that nearly 400,000 vehicles and 500,000 engines are made here each year. Plant tours usually get booked far in advance, but you can stop by and look at the cars and manufacturing exhibits at the visitor center any time between 10 a.m. and 4 p.m. Monday through Friday (toyotageorgetown.com).

In the Beginning

In the beginning there was *Harrodsburg.*

A friend of mine swears that it takes a Harrodsburg resident, in any conversation, less than four minutes to bring up the fact that the genesis of the American West is Harrodsburg, Kentucky. On June 16, 1774, James Harrod and his company took a great leap of faith and of foot when they chose to settle the fertile strip of land between the Kentucky and Salt Rivers, the "Big Spring"—more than 250 miles of wilderness and mountains away from the nearest Anglo-Saxon settlement to the east.

Today Harrodsburg sports a full reproduction of the 1775 fort in the *Old Fort Harrod State Park,* at the intersection of US 68 and US 127, a good place to begin your exploration of one of the state's significant historic areas.

Soooooeyyy!!!

If you leave town going northeast on US 68, toward Lexington, you will pass Harrodsburg High School, affectionately known as "Hog Town." This nickname harks back to the late 1820s, when hogs outnumbered county residents two to one, and on the hill where the school stands now were huge hog corrals, sales rings, and auction blocks that served the whole region. The official high school sports mascot was a pioneer with a coonskin cap, but the proud rallying cry was Soooooeyyy!!! (Self-deprecating humor is healthy, especially for the adolescent soul.)

(Oddly, the reproduction fort is not exactly sited where the original stood.) Inside the park's entrance is the *Mansion Museum,* featuring Civil War artifacts, and the *Lincoln Marriage Shrine,* a redbrick building that protects the log chapel where Abraham Lincoln's parents "got hitched." Inside the fort's walls, people in period costumes demonstrate pioneer crafts during the summer. The fort is open to the public year-round, and from March 16 to November 30 the museum is also open. Hours vary by season. Admission is $5 for adults and $3 for kids. Call (859) 734-3314 or visit http://parks.ky.gov/parks/recreationparks/Fort-Harrod/default.aspx. For general information on Harrodsburg, check harrodsburgky.com.

Follow Chiles Street south to Kentucky's first row house, circa 1800, known as *Morgan Row,* after the builder Joseph Morgan. The street is named after Morgan's son-in-law, John Chiles, who ran a famous tavern on the site. In front of Morgan Row, Uncle Will of Wildwood, a prominent Mercer County farmer, is said to have been cited for speeding in his one-horse buggy. When Uncle Will went to pay his ticket, he paid double the amount, telling the clerk in a voice loud enough for the whole courthouse to hear, "I'm paying you double 'cause I plan to leave the way I came." Today Morgan Row houses, among other things, the *Harrodsburg Historical Society Museum* and office (859-734-5985; rootsweb.com/~kymercer/hhs/).

Another of Harrodsburg's claims to fame is *The Beaumont Inn.* The massive brick Greek Revival building, constructed in 1845, was once a finishing school called the Greenville Institute, then Daughter's College, and later Beaumont College. It was converted into an inn in 1919 by Annie

Bell Goddard and her husband, Glave. The inn has remained in the family and is now managed by Annie Bell's great-grandson, Chuck Dedman. The dining room serves very traditional Kentucky-style meals that include dishes such as two-year-old cured country ham (smoked and cured by the proprietor himself), fried chicken, corn pudding, and Robert E. Lee Orange-Lemon Cake. Be ready for a feast! The antiques-filled sleeping quarters suggest the extravagance of the Old South, with a few modern conveniences. A swimming pool, tennis courts, and a gift shop are also on the premises. The **Old Owl Tavern** has become a popular watering hole and features fine wines, spirits, and draft beer as well as more casual lunch and dinner menus. Reservations are advisable for meals and lodging. Closed late December though early March. Call (859) 734-3381 or (800) 352-3992 or visit beaumontinn.com.

Acting as a business-savvy alchemist, the city of Harrodsburg transformed an unsightly lot where an old building burned down in the first block of South Main Street into a city park, called **Olde Towne Park,** which includes a stage for civic events and a 14-foot-high by 35-foot-wide sculptural wall/water fountain, The fountain sculpture is a lyrical representation of the historic limestone palisades that line the Kentucky River on the eastern border of Mercer County. This work is made of nearly 700 large, high-fired ceramic tiles, all molded or directly sculpted by hand, featuring high-relief plants, vines, reptiles, and rocklike textures for the falling water to play over. For more information call (859) 734-6811.

The umbrella tables in the park by the fountain are very popular lunch spots. And if they're not too busy two doors down at **La Fonda Restaurant,** 121 South Main Street (859-734-0033), the waiters will actually serve your meal in the park. This little restaurant is very popular for its genuine Mexican dishes (the *chiles rellenos* are unusually good) for its reasonable prices, and, in a mostly dry or "moist" county, beer. You get the pleasant feeling that the chefs are making the food that they love. Open every day for lunch and dinner.

One of the most unique historical buildings in Mercer County is the **Old Mud Meeting House,** built in 1800 by members of the Dutch Reformed Church. As early as 1781 a group of Dutch settlers immigrated here and formed a community where they spoke Dutch and worshipped as they did in the Old World. The church they built became known as the Mud Meeting

House because massive timber walls are chinked with clay, straw, twigs, roots, and gravel. The handsome structure, constructed "for the sole Benefit & use of the said Reformed Church forever," has long outlasted its little congregation. The church was restored to its original form in 1971. To visit the site, drive south from town on US 127 to the junction of US 68 (Moreland Avenue) and turn right. Follow US 68 until you reach Dry Branch Pike; turn left and look for the historical marker. Getting there can be confusing. Here's an even better idea: Call the Historical Society office at (859) 734-5985 to arrange a guided tour.

Shaker Village of Pleasant Hill is one of central Kentucky's most significant historic sites. It is located 8 miles east of Harrodsburg off US 68. The whole restored village is a museum featuring 30 original Shaker buildings and more than 2,700 acres of manicured farmland (about half of what the Shaker community farmed in its prime). "The United Society of Believers in Christ's Second Appearance" was originally founded by an English Quaker woman, Mother Ann Lee, who came to America in 1774 and claimed to be Christ incarnate (this time as a woman) to herald the millennium preceding the total destruction of Earth, as prophesied in the Book of Revelation. The most publicized doctrine of the sect was that Believers should remain pure by avoiding "the World" (non-Shakers) and all its ways, including the "disorderly" state of matrimony. Instead of procreating, the Shakers adopted orphans and received converts, who were plentiful during America's "Great Revival" period of Protestant faiths in the early 19th century. Shakers also avoided "the World" by remaining economically self-sufficient; their products were always of the highest quality, from seeds to silk, and continue to influence modern design. The Shakers' utopia at Pleasant Hill lasted more than 100 years, until the death of the village's last resident in 1923.

The village admission fee enables you to take a self-guided tour through the buildings, which, like Shaker furniture, are renowned for their graceful, functional aesthetic simplicity. (The song "Simple Gifts" is associated with the Shakers.) In recent years, this village has expanded its interpretation of historic farming techniques. Draft horses and oxen are used for traction in the gardens of heirloom vegetables and to power an impressive collection of period equipment. Blacksmithing, sorghum growing and making, and seed propagation and sales are among the agricultural practices demonstrated. Be sure to visit the interpretive center, where an excellent video and other exhibits provide insight into the Shakers and their tenure at Pleasant Hill. The village offers fine Southern dining and overnight accommodations in original buildings.

A wonderful development at Shakertown is the system of trails for hiking, mountain biking, horseback riding, and Lampton Carriage travel. Ask at the lodging desk for a map pamphlet and gate keys. Some essential features of central Kentucky's geography, flora, fauna, and 19th-century history are made vividly accessible as you travel these trails. You'll see remnants of Shaker structures like bridges, dams, and mills for grinding flour, extracting flaxseed oil, and fulling wool for textiles. The trails bring you close to some wonderful examples of the dry-stacked rock fence for which the area is famous. In the springtime the wildflowers are stunning, especially on the trails that wind into creek valleys. Two native grass and flower prairies have been reestablished on the property and although they are small, you will get a rare glimpse into how the landscape looked to native hunters and to Daniel Boone.

Horse enthusiasts are welcome to bring their trusty mounts with them on this vacation. Overnight equine guests may be boarded, for a small fee, in facilities with handsome paddocks and fully equipped stalls, with an available tack room while owners tuck themselves into village lodgings. Ask about special "Bed and Bridle" packages. Call (800) 734-5611 for more information, special programs, and reservations (shakervillageky.org).

The Shakers traded goods with "the World" in large part by river. The road built by the Shakers in 1861 still accesses one of the most spectacular stretches of the Kentucky River, known as **The Palisades,** where high Ordovician limestone bluffs change color with the time of day. Go east about ⅛ mile from Shakertown's entrance and turn right where a sign indicates river excursions. Shakertown offers one-hour trips on a paddle-wheel boat called *The Dixie Belle.* From the boat you have a perfect view of **High Bridge,** the first cantilever bridge in the United States,

trueblue

John A. Roebling, designer of the famous bridges in Cincinnati and Brooklyn, New York, also designed a suspension bridge for the Kentucky River at the site where High Bridge now stands. After the financial panic of 1857, the project was abandoned; his exquisite stone piers were torn down in 1929, never having been used.

One Well-Used Cavern

Just behind High Bridge on the Jessamine County side in Wilmore is the mouth of a fabricated cavern that is huge—32 acres of limestone rooms, 130 feet underground. The 30-foot-high corridors were originally created by the Kentucky Stone company between 1900 and 1972 as it mined commercial-grade limestone. The Civil Defense Department used the space for the storage of food and equipment during the bomb-shelter era, the Campbell Soup Company once filled the floors with loam and grew mushrooms for soup there, and local hearsay is that the secretive Free Masons continue to conduct rites in the unused, unlighted recesses of the mine. In 1979, when Bill Griffin bought the mine to use for underground commodity storage, engineers advised him to drain the water from an underground spring in order to control humidity. It was going to be a big expense. One day Mr. Griffin glibly commented to his daughter, "Well, why don't we just bottle the stuff and sell it off?" Everyone laughed, but by 1990 the family-run business, High Bridge Springwater, had sold over two million gallons of bottled spring water. It now dominates the local market as bottled water becomes increasingly common in households with unfiltered cisterns and in those with unsavory, chlorinated city water. To find out how to get a taste, visit highbridgesprings.com or call (888) 547-6971.

a miracle of engineering at the time of its completion in 1877. High Bridge stretches 1,125 feet and stands 280 feet high; it is still the highest two-track railroad pass in North America.

For a dizzying view of High Bridge, follow US 68 east across from Shakertown, toward Lexington. The road begins to wind dramatically as it descends into the river gorge, crosses the Kentucky River on Brooklyn Bridge, and begins another curvy climb. At the top of the hill, take Highway 1268 into Wilmore, then turn right onto Highway 29 and drive to the little community of High Bridge. There are places to park so you can walk to the end of the underside of the criss-crossing bridge structure. Wait for a train. It's a goofy thrill to feel the frequent trains passing over your head. Notice too the confluence of the Kentucky and Dix Rivers. The Kentucky is the big, usually brown, slow-moving river, while the Dix is often a clearer green. If you were down on the water, you'd also notice that the Dix River's water is much, much colder. Less than a mile away, the river is being released from the base of the Dix Dam which forms Herrington Lake. Often, in the summer, the colliding air temperatures form a low, flat layer of fog, just 3 feet high, right over the water's surface, so that people in boats appear to be floating heads. Swimming in that 48-degree water can stop your heart.

Beginning at the Kentucky River and traveling north on US 68, turn west (or left) onto Highway 33 and follow the signs to *Irish Acres Antiques* (859-873-7235; irishacresgallery.com) in *Nonesuch* (population 343), a "downtown" composed of the smallest freestanding voting building you'll ever see and a cluster of houses, one of which has the greatest number and variety of purple martin houses known to humanity (the owner must be a frustrated urban housing planner). Irish Acres Antiques is a not-to-be-missed 32,000-square-foot antiques gallery and tearoom founded by Bonnie and Arch Hannigan and now run by their daughters Emilie and Jane. Two floors of what was once the Nonesuch School are gracefully crammed with antiques, which range from affordable early American primitives to pricey Asian art, 15th-century Chinese lacquered boxes, and 19th-century French country furniture. Hours are 10 a.m. to 5 p.m. Tuesday through Saturday.

The old basement cafeteria has been converted into a whimsical, elegant tearoom called *The Glitz.* Amid a fantasia of lights, grapevines, iridescent paper, and silver cherubim, you can enjoy a lavish four-course meal for $21.50 plus tax. It's a good place to take your time and not the best place to take your kids. Reservations are required. Lunch is served from 11 a.m. to 2 p.m., when the gallery is open. Gallery hours are 10 a.m. to 5 p.m. Tuesday through Saturday. Irish Acres and The Glitz are closed January through mid-March. They reopen on St. Patrick's Day (surprise!). Call (859) 873-6956.

Get back onto Highway 33, which winds through lush horse-farm country, to *Versailles* (pronounced ver-SALES). You can also get to Versailles by way of US 60 or 62, once one of the largest buffalo trails in the United States. From the landscaping and architecture in town, one senses an aura of the wealth and deliberate pace of the Old South. Downtown Versailles is full of well-preserved old Federal and Beaux Arts homes, beautiful churches, and antiques stores. People come to Kentucky from all over the country to towns that were early settlements in search of information about their ancestors. Like the Mercer County Public Library in Harrodsburg (859-734-3680; mcplib .info), the *Woodford County Historic Society Museum* (859-873-6786) has an excellent library of genealogical data that is free and available for anyone's use. The museum is housed in what was formerly the Big Spring

Church, circa 1819, at 121 Rose Hill. Hours are Tuesday through Saturday from 10 a.m. to 4 p.m.

For the toy train enthusiast, Versailles offers a once-in-a-lifetime opportunity to pore over the collection of Wanda and Winfrey Adkins, who have converted an old (1911–32) Louisville and Nashville (L&N) railroad station into the *Nostalgia Station Toy Train Museum,* located at 279 Depot Street, a one-way street on the east side of Main. The Adkinses, who do repairs and will find rare parts, can tell you just about anything there is to know about model trains and antique cast-iron and mechanized toys. Before meeting the Adkinses, I didn't realize that there are modern versions of the 1950s locomotives, boxcars, switches, coal cars, and crossing lights that we played with every Christmas. Wanda likes to point out a wind-up Mickey and Minnie Mouse hand-pump car, one of L&N's forgotten "cheap" toys from the 1930s when the company was struggling, and a regular engine and coal car that cost at least $32. Hours are Wednesday through Saturday from 10 a.m. to 5 p.m. and Sunday from 1 to 5 p.m. Admission to the museum grounds and displays is free. Admission to the museum is $3.50 for adults, $3 for senior citizens, and $1.50 for children. Call (859) 873-2497 for more information or bgrm.org/nostalgiastation.

For enthusiasts of full-size railroad artifacts, follow US 62 west to the *Blue Grass Railroad Museum Inc.* in Woodford County Park. On weekends from May through the end of October, you can take a 5½-mile train ride on the Old Louisville Southern Mainland through quintessential bluegrass country, including a hawk's view of the Kentucky River palisades, Wild Turkey Distilleries, and Young's High Bridge. The museum is an actual train car with historic railroad displays. A recent addition to the collection is an original L&N railroad bay-window caboose. From June 3 through October 29, Saturday and Sunday, trips are at 2 p.m. (arrive 15 minutes early). Admission is $11.50 for adults and $9.50 for kids ages 2 to 12. For special events, call (859) 873-2476 or (800) 755-2476 or visit bgrm.org.

Boyd Orchard, 1500 Pinckard Pike, Versailles (859-873-3097; boyd orchards.com), is a farm where you can pick your own strawberries, apples, and pumpkins, each in its own season. The setting is lovely and practical. Call ahead to see what is ripe and the current hours.

"Here's to Old Kentucky, The state where I was born, Where the corn is full of kernels and the Colonel's full of corn" goes an old Kentucky toast.

The abundant corn crops of early Kentucky settlers played an important role in the creation of bourbon whiskey, as did, undoubtedly, its appreciation by Southern gentlemen. When, how, and by whom bourbon was first made remains a matter of debate that may never be settled (Georgetown claims it was Baptist minister Elijah Craig; nearby Bourbon County credits Jacob Spears). There's no disagreement, however, that by the early 1800s whiskey making had evolved into a fine art in bluegrass country. Elijah Pepper started making whiskey near Versailles in 1797. In 1812, in search of a more abundant water supply, he moved his operation to a spot along Glenn's Creek. Today, whiskey is still made at the site of Pepper's early distillery, under the name *Labrot & Graham, The Bourbon Homeplace* (7855 McCracken Pike; 859-879-1812; www.woodfordreserve.com).

The property has been renovated as a showplace of the "old ways" of making premium bourbon whiskey. The bulky old stone buildings strung along the creek, the complex aromas from the mash tank, the 25-foot-tall copper stills (unique in modern American distilling), and the lively presentations by the tour guides make this a premium tour, which ends with a taste of bourbon ball candy at the "bar" in the visitor center. Opened on April 9, 2014, after a major renovation, the visitor center offers a panoramic view of the distillery grounds, a new tasting room lined with copper stools, and a fireplace with copper detail. Check out the tabletops in the visitor center and tables in the tasting room—all crafted using reclaimed wood from a barn on the distillery property. Coffee tables in the main area of the visitor center are constructed from a fragrant cypress vat once used at the distillery.

By the way, the bourbon distilled on the day you visit won't be available in a bottle for about seven years. Several tour options are offered. Given seven days a week, the $10 Bourbon Discovery Tour explains the history of bourbon, the five sources of flavor, the bottling process and more. At tour's end, guests age 21 and over can sample award-winning craft bourbon. Offered Wednesday at 2:30 p.m., the two-hour $30 National Landmark Tour explores the history of Woodford Reserve as well as the history and architecture of the property and its importance to Kentucky heritage. The Corn to Cork Tour lasts two hours and explains all aspects of producing bourbon. Offered Tuesday and Thursday at 2:30 p.m., the $30 tour accepts a maximum of six guests. Call to see if reservations are required for the tour of your choice.

The distillery is about 6 miles from Versailles (so far out that it has its own lake as a source of water in case of a fire). If you're in Versailles, take US 60 toward Frankfort, turn left onto Grassy Spring Road, then right on McCracken Pike. Or take Elm Street out of downtown Versailles.

Continue on Highway 1659 past the distillery, then turn left (west) on Highway 1964 and right onto Germany Road, then follow the signs to the 374-acre **Buckley Wildlife Sanctuary,** which offers an appropriately private and meditative way to explore the wooded Kentucky River Gorge. You can hike on loop trails between ¼ mile and 2 miles long, and there's a bird blind that keeps you concealed while birds come within view (or camera range). You're likely to see everything from warblers to wild turkeys; some people come solely for the hummingbirds. There's an interesting exhibit center, a gift shop, and various events. As a sanctuary should be, it's a peaceful, beautiful place. Admission is $4. Hours are Wednesday through Friday from 9 a.m. to 5 p.m. and on weekends from 9 a.m. to 6 p.m. The nature center is open from 1 to 6 p.m. on weekends. The sanctuary is closed in January and February. Call (859) 873-5711 for event information.

For another worthwhile excuse to take a drive, visit the restored **Jack Jouett House,** circa 1797. This home was built by folks who believed, like Mies van der Rohe, that "God hides in the details." From Versailles go 5 miles west on McCowans Ferry Road, and turn on Craig Creek Pike. Jack Jouett, the original owner, was a legendary Revolutionary War hero who rode all night to save Gov. Thomas Jefferson from the British. His son, Matthew Jouett, became a well-known portrait artist. Tours are free April through October. Tours can be arranged throughout the year by reservation. Open Monday 10 a.m. to noon, Friday noon to 5 p.m., Saturday 10 a.m. to 5 p.m., and Sunday 1 p.m. to 5 p.m. The house is closed November through March. Call (859) 873-7902. Check jouetthouse.org for special events like the Frontier Day festival or the Matthew Jouett Art Show and Sale.

From Versailles take US 62 north toward **Midway,** named so because it is exactly midway between Frankfort and Lexington. At the Nugent Crossroads, where US 62 intersects

trueblue

Frank and Jesse James's mother, Zerelda Cole, once lived in the Offutt-Cole Tavern, located at the intersection of US 62 and Highway 1981 between Versailles and Midway.

Old Frankfort Pike, you will see the old *Offutt-Cole Tavern* building. The building was constructed in the 18th century and has been a tavern, an inn, a stagecoach stop, and a tollhouse. Part of the building contains what may be one of the oldest log structures in the state. One of the old inn's most famous tenants was Zerelda Cole James, the mother of the infamous Frank and Jesse. Zerelda was born in the building and lived there with her grandfather, who ran a tavern at the site called the Black Horse Inn. Various businesses have occupied the building in recent times, although at press time it sat empty. You can still park and look around the outside of this charming old structure.

Midway was the first town in Kentucky built by a railroad company. The tracks are both centerpiece and divider of the tiny downtown. These days it is a quaint college town full of antiques shops, beautiful historic homes, and a few surprises.

One such surprise is an operative, century-old, hydropower grain mill on the South Elkhorn Creek. The *Weisenberger Mill* is the oldest continuously operating mill in Kentucky and one of the few in the nation to remain in the same family. In 1866 a German steamboat and mill specialist named August Weisenberger bought the mill that had been built on the site in 1818. He revamped the entire system and began grinding all manner of grain at the rate of 100 barrels a day. His great-grandson, Philip J. Weisenberger, and Philip's son, Mac, have modernized some of the methods and now grind about 3,000 tons of grain a year. The Weisenbergers introduced the use of the mill's electricity-making capacity by having Kentucky's alternative energy whiz, Dave Kinlock, rebuild the mill's hydropower turbines and add an efficient generator. Now most aspects of the business are water powered, even the computers. Although visitors are not allowed inside the work area, you can walk around the property. Everything at Weisenberger mills is sold by the package in the front office (the 50-pound bags are a very good bargain). As an avid bread maker, I can attest to the excellent quality of the products. Call (859) 254-5282 or go to weisenberger.com for more information. The mill is open Monday through Friday from 8 a.m. to 4:30 p.m.; Saturday 9 a.m. to noon.

From Railroad Street, turn east on Winter Street (US 62), veer to the right at the Corner Grocery, and go about ¼ mile. You will find yourself at the *Holly Hill Inn,* an 1830 Greek Revival house that has been home to fine dining for more than 20 years. In 2000 the inn also became home to Ouita and Chris Michel, who came well prepared to add their own special touches to the Holly Hill tradition. Both are graduates of the Culinary Institute of America and have cooked at fine restaurants in the Lexington area. Their Holly Hill Inn serves dinner Wednesday through Saturday beginning at 5:30 p.m., as well as Sunday brunch from 11 a.m. to 2 p.m. The dinner menu changes monthly and the brunch menu changes weekly, but you can be sure of two things: Whatever comes out of Ouita's kitchen is going to be delicious and creative, and whenever possible, it will be made with locally grown produce, Kentucky-raised beef, lamb, and pork, and fresh seafood. A four-course dinner—your choice of appetizer, entree, and dessert—is offered for a fixed price of $40 per person. Brunch is $18, and lunch is served Friday and Saturday from 11 a.m. to 2 p.m. Call (859) 846-4732 or visit hollyhillinn.com for reservations.

Quita and Chris Michel also are owners of **Wallace Station,** an unusually excellent deli at 3854 Old Frankfort Pike, just outside of Midway. Open daily 8 a.m. to 8 p.m., Wallace Station offers wonderful carry-out food, including innovative sandwiches on fresh baked bread. Desserts are made by scratch by Quita Michel at her Midway School Bakery using real butter, eggs, Weisenberger Mill flours, nuts, and vanilla. No mixes or filler. The place is a real favorite with locals and travelers alike. Call (859) 846-5161 with questions or check out wallacestation.com.

In the late 1800s Kentucky was the third-largest grape and wine producer in the United States. Prohibition, however, uprooted not just the vines but also the industry. Cynthia Bohn is among a new generation of vintners working to help grapes make a comeback in the Bluegrass State. At her **Equus Run Vineyards,** 35 acres located on Moores Mill Road, off US 62 between Midway and Georgetown, she has renovated a tobacco barn into a wine-making facility and added a taste of fun to the whole experience. Virtually every month there's some kind of special event—a concert, a barbecue, or an open house. Any day, visitors are invited to go fishing or bring a picnic to enjoy amid the flower gardens or by the old gristmill along the banks of Elkhorn Creek. There's even a life-size art horse, *Vegetariat,* part of Lexington's Horse Mania community art event, as well as other Horse Mania equine sculptures on the grounds. And, of course, there are acres of vineyards, a tasting room, and a gift shop, where Equus Run wines sell for

$10 to $15 a bottle. Regular operating hours are 11 a.m. to 7 p.m. Monday through Saturday, Sunday from 1 to 5 p.m. from April through October. Winter hours are Monday through Saturday 11 a.m. to 5 p.m. and Sunday 1 to 5 p.m. Call for information or a schedule of special events (859-846-9463 or 877-905-2675; equusrunvineyards.com).

Danville is a handsome little college town just south of Harrodsburg. From town take US 127; from Shakertown take Highway 33 through Burgin. Drive or walk around Danville and the Centre College campus to admire the architecture. For arts and cultural events, check the gallery and schedule of performances at the Frank Lloyd Wright–style *Norton Center for the Arts* (859-236-4692; nortoncenter.com) on campus.

Right across West Walnut Street, a place of simple beauty awaits to nourish your inner spirit. McDowell Park, the lawn of the Presbyterian church, is the setting for *Pathway of Peace: The Danville Labyrinth Project.* A marker explains: you are entering sacred space. A meditative tool, the labyrinth is an ancient path of prayer. Unlike a maze, its single path leads to the center. This labyrinth is based on the one in the cathedral at Chartres, France. Pause and relax. Walk at your own pace. You may pass other people quietly. Once you reach the center, stay as long as you like. Exit by retracing your steps. The centuries-old idea of the labyrinth takes on a special Kentucky beauty here. Envisioned and funded by an interdenominational group of local citizens, the Danville labyrinth was created by Robert Ferre, an internationally known mason. The large stone blocks that form the 43-foot circular foundation are made of sandstone quarried in McCreary County, Kentucky, with the pathway etched into the beautiful stone. Shaded by the park's huge trees, this is a pleasant place to find your own contemporary meaning in an ancient idea.

trueblue

Because of its many 19th-century houses and old-fashioned charm, Danville was chosen as the location for the 1956 film *Raintree County* starring Elizabeth Taylor and Montgomery Clift. My uncle Ive Poynter was an extra as a soldier in the film, as were many other area folks.

You know an Italian place is good when there's always a customer at the counter reading an Italian newspaper. *Freddie's Restaurant* (140

Stanford Street; 859-236-9884) serves quick, primo cuisine for lunch and dinner Monday through Saturday.

The hospital in Danville was named for a local medical hero, Ephraim McDowell, who performed the first successful removal of an ovarian tumor in 1809. Something should be named for his patient, Jane Todd Crawford, who survived the surgery without the aid of antisepsis or the comfort of anesthetic. The site of the operation, the *Ephraim McDowell House and Apothecary* at 125 South Second Street, has been accurately restored and is open Monday through Saturday from 10 a.m. to noon and 1 to 4 p.m., Sunday from 2 to 4 p.m. From November through February it is closed Monday. Admission is $8 for adults, $5 for senior citizens, $3 for students ages 13 to 18, $2 for children ages 5 to 12. Call (859) 236-2804 or visit mcdowellhouse.com.

Across the street is *Constitution Square State Park,* a reproduction of the state's first courthouse square and the site of the first post office in the West, circa 1792. All the buildings are log replicas, and most have recorded interpretations (kids like to push the buttons and run when the voice begins to drone). The lawn is a good place for a downtown picnic, and dessert is right across the street at *Burke's Bakery,* 121 West Main (859-236-5661). Burke's is in its fourth generation of owners and customers and makes good, old, sweet pastries for times when you just don't want whole grains and carob powder. Open Monday through Friday 7 a.m. to 6 p.m., Saturday 7 a.m. to 5 p.m., and Sunday noon to 4 p.m.

Since 1950 Danville's *Pioneer Playhouse* has been offering audiences live theatrical performances (and dinner) under the stars. Its claim to fame is being the oldest summer stock theater in the state and having "the most unique outdoor theater history in America." Founded and run by Eben C.

true*blue*

The Kentucky School for the Deaf in Danville was established in 1823 with only three pupils. It was the first state-supported school of its kind in the nation. Today, a large number of its graduates go on to attend college or technical school and join the workforce.

true*blue*

John Travolta, Lee Majors, and Jim Varney are among the actors who once performed summer stock at Pioneer Playhouse in Danville.

Henson (1923–2004) and his wife, Charlotte, the playhouse is now being run by Charlotte and their children: Holly, a comedian; Robby, cinematic director; Eben, businessman; and Heather, novelist. Everything on the complex "campus" is cobbled together creatively and economically from salvaged materials so that the effect is charming full-scale folk art. For example, the amphitheater is paved with brick Henson reclaimed from one of Danville's historic buildings, the Ephraim McDowell apothecary shop. Overhead are two standard-issue streetlights that serve as house lights; the stage lights are C-clamped all along the lights' cross bars. Every structure has a quirky story.

Every two weeks a new play is produced from mid-June until late August. The plays are primarily romantic comedies, "rib-ticklers," as Charlotte puts it, performed by actors from New York and from the region. Showtime is 8:30 p.m., Tuesday through Saturday. Southern "comfort" dinner food is served at 7:30 p.m. Dinner and show are $28 for adults, and show only is $15 for adults. Dinner and show are $15 for children ages 12 and under; $9 for show only. A real treat with dinner is hearing Charlotte Henson play guitar and sing folk songs. For information and reservations call (859) 236-2341 or (859) 236-2747; pioneerplayhouse.com. The playhouse is at 840 Stanford Road, just on the edge of town. Follow the clearly marked signs from downtown.

It takes a lot of brass to envision being home to a national festival and for at least one weekend of the year, Danville has more brass than just about any place else. Danville attracts some 40,000 people and dozens of bands from around the world to its *Great American Brass Band Festival* in mid-June. The festival celebrates the old-time joy of brass bands and the role of band music in community life. For information about the festival (a full four-day weekend of everything from Sousa to Civil War songs), call (859) 319-8426; gabbf.org.

A number of acclaimed visual artists call Danville home. At the *Jones Visual Arts Center at Centre College,* you can see the blown-glass creations of Stephen Rolfe Powell. Powell, a Centre College professor (and self-proclaimed pyromaniac), is recognized as a master hot-glass blower. His glass vessels (some weighing up to 30 pounds) are known for their vivid colors, elegant form, and fascinating texture (created by the thousands of beads of color integrated into the surface). The arts center is open by appointment; call (859) 238-5735 or visit centre.edu. A small gallery inside the art center exhibits rotating shows as well as student work.

Exhibits of local and regional art, gifts, and coffee in a clean, well-lighted place are in store for you at Danville's **Community Arts Center** (401 W. Main Street; 859-236-4054; communityartscenter.net). The handsome *beaux arts* building was formerly home to the region's federal government offices. Three galleries offer rotating shows—you may see the stunningly complex still-life paintings of Danville artist and Centre College professor Sheldon Tapley or quirky folk art miniature houses by a local unknown. Classes in dance, drama, and visual arts are offered regularly. The coffee is always good and everyone is welcome. Open Monday through Friday 10 a.m. to 6 p.m., Saturday 10 a.m. to 4 p.m., evenings during special events. Admission to exhibits is free. Admission to Lisi's Art Lab is $1 per child, which includes supplies. Children must be supervised while in the lab. Lisi's Art Lab is a creative space for kids of all ages and is open whenever exhibits are open.

Just a few more miles east on Highway 300 brings you to the **Isaac Shelby Cemetery State Historic Site.** Shelby became Kentucky's first governor in 1792 after having earned a reputation by fighting in Lord Dunmore's War and in the Revolutionary War. He won the gubernatorial race again 16 years later and victoriously fought the British (again) in the War of 1812. In 1818 he and Andrew Jackson were responsible for the negotiations with the Chickasaw Indians to purchase the land to the west of the Tennessee River for Kentucky, an area now known as the Jackson Purchase. This state-owned site is where his farm, Traveler's Rest, was and where he and his family are buried.

Near Forkland at 257 Penn's Store Road in Gravel Switch, **Penn's Store** may be the oldest continuously operated one-family-owned store west of the Alleghenies, and it looks like it. Everyone falls in love with the wise, tumbledown appearance of the general store, which was opened in 1852 by Dick Penn. The original building burned, and this replacement is more than 100 years old. In the winter, the little potbellied stove is stoked up hot, and at least three men are playing checkers on a barrel in the middle of the room at all times. (It takes two to play and one to shake his head and chew on his toothpick.) In the summer there's no better place in the world to have a Dr Pepper than on Penn's front porch, where you can hear the creek rumble by. The store is usually open Saturday 11 a.m. to 6 p.m. and

Sunday 2 to 6 p.m. from April through September. From October through March, it is open Saturday 11 a.m. to 5 p.m. and Sunday 1 to 5 p.m. But before you go, be sure to call to make sure Penn's is open. The store notes that its times are "country hours—give or take a few minutes." The store phone number is (859) 332-7706, website is pennsstore.com. From Forkland continue on Highway 37 south to Highway 243, turn right, then right again just after crossing a concrete bridge. When you see the store by the creek, cross the new bridge.

Leaving Danville to the west, Main Street becomes US 150 (or 52) and leads to the historic town of *Perryville.*

On Perryville's main street is an area known as *Merchants' Row,* a small row of renovated buildings that house antiques and gift shops, a pizza place, a dry goods store, and an active saddlery. Moving away from creature comforts, proceed in an appropriately somber spirit to the *Perryville Battlefield State Historic Site.* Go north on Highway 1920 for 3 miles and follow the signs. Eighty thousand men fought for one bloody day at this site on October 8, 1862, when Confederate soldiers in search of water accidentally encountered Union troops who were guarding nearby Doctor's Creek. More than 7,500 soldiers were killed, wounded, or missing by sunset. This battle was the largest ever fought on Kentucky soil and, when the Confederate general Braxton Bragg retreated into Tennessee after the battle, there was no real hope left that Kentucky would ever join the Rebel states.

"The Knobs"

If you leave Junction City on Highway 37 south, you will suddenly enter "the knobs," a narrow belt of fairly isolated, wooded hills that encircles the bluegrass region. (Rock lovers: The creeks here are loaded with geodes.) In the heart of this alluring terrain is a little town called Forkland, where there's a good country festival the second weekend of October at the *Forkland Community Center.* Notice the huge, round piece of sandstone in the yard. It measures 51 inches in diameter, is 18 inches thick, and probably weighs more than a ton. What in tarnation is it? No one knows. Sandstone is never used for grinding grain, so a millstone is out. Archaeologists say it's not prehistoric. The best guess is that it was a "hemp brake," a heavy rock rolled by hand or by oxen over hemp stalks to break the fibers apart for making rope.

There's a small museum (859-332-8631) with artifacts and battle displays on the 270-acre grounds. A walking tour introduces visitors to important landmarks. There is also a driving tour of the area; ask for maps. The best time to visit is on the weekend closest to October 8, during the massive annual reenactment of the battle, when people in full period costume, with weapons and horses, stage the long, gory combat. The park is open daily from April through October from 9 a.m. to 5 p.m. and by appointment the remainder of the year. Admission is $3.50 for adults, $2.50 for children over age 6. The park is open from daylight to dark. Visit the website for more information, perryvillebattlefield.org. The town of **Stanford** is about 13 miles south of Danville on US 150. There's a charming restored railroad depot used as a community meeting center.

The ***William Whitley House State Historic Site*** is southeast of Stanford on US 150 at 625 William Whitley Road. Famous "Indian Fighter" William Whitley built the elegant brick house in the mid-1780s, making it one of the oldest brick buildings west of the Alleghenies. It was called "a guardian of the Wilderness Road" because it stood next to the important overland route and served as a place of refuge for white travelers. The high upper windows and barred lower windows, the gun ports, and a hidden staircase were built as precautions against attacks.

Whitley's big contributions to Kentucky (and American) culture were building the first racetrack in the state and running the horses counterclockwise, a practice he encouraged to rebel against the British custom of racing clockwise. Having served as a colonel in the Revolution, Whitley was passionately anti-British. Whitley died in the 1813 Battle of the Thames River after he supposedly killed the great chief Tecumseh. Tours of the house are given May 1 through October 31 from 9 a.m. to 5 p.m. Wednesday through Saturday and 11 a.m. to 5 p.m. on Sunday. For further information, check parks.ky.gov/parks/historicsites/William-whitley or call (606) 355-2881.

Downtown **Lancaster** is a small but bustling central square around which you will find a number of antiques malls and boutiques. One of several worth checking is **Lancaster Homes and Holiday** at 124 Eisenhower Court. The mother- and daughter-owned wholesale and retail company offers designer home accessories, jewelry, and holiday trimmings. Visit lancasterhomeandholiday.com or call (859) 885-0300 for more information. The ***Garrard County Jail Museum***, at 208 Danville Street (gcjail.tripod.com;

A Teetotaler with a Mission

Just north of Lincoln County and east of Boyle County is Garrard County, birth-place of a radical antiliquor activist often neglected by history books. From Lancaster take US 27 north to Highway 34 and go east to its junction with Fisher Ford Road to find *Carry A. Nation's birthplace* at "the jumping-off place," as local folks call it. The house was built about 1840, and Carry was born there in 1846. In 1900, after a short, disastrous, and life-changing marriage to a severe alcoholic, Carry single-handedly wreaked havoc on the saloon at the Hotel Casey in Wichita, Kansas, and, consequently, spent seven days in jail, her first of more than 30 jail sentences on similar charges. I've seen fearsome pictures of Ms. Nation in her prime: hatchet in one hand, Bible in the other, purse to the front, and a glare that would make any bartender's blood run cold.

859-792-9452), is an interesting building featuring local historic artifacts, including the noose and hood of the last man hung in the county. Admission to the jail museum is free and the jail is open to the public from noon to 4 p.m., Monday through Friday. Tours are given any time during the afternoon by appointment. Built in 1873 in the Italianate style, the jail closed its doors on prisoners in 1986 for the last time. But it has been said that numerous ghosts still haunt its sad halls. A local historic home that is open for tours is *Pleasant Retreat,* at 656 Stanford Road, the 1804 home of Gov. William Owsley, after whom the 96th county was named. Tours are by appointment only. The house is closed from December through March. Admission is $9 for adults and $4 for children ages 6 through 18. By request, tours can focus on genealogy, architecture, or quilts and wallpaper.

Tradition Meets Invention

An old jail, a lot of used furniture, 12,000 locks, and a cemetery—that is what *Nicholasville* has to offer. Go almost due south of Lexington, via US 27, then take the business loop into downtown Nicholasville. Write or make a quick stop at the Jessamine County Chamber of Commerce office at 508 North Main Street, Nicholasville 40356 (jessaminechamber.com; 859-887-4351), for a list of the many antiques malls and maps for walking the historic district. The *Old Jail,* 200 South Main Street, is actually interesting, though it would not have been a good place to spend the night after committing a crime. There are no regular tours of the restored 1870 building. It is now rented as a place for meetings and socials.

Without doubt, the most fascinating site to visit in town is the *Harry C. Miller Lock Collection,* at 1014 South Main Street inside Lockmasters Inc. (859-887-9633; lsi-lockmasters.com). From the time he was a locksmith's apprentice at the age of 12 to the years he traveled the world developing locks for the State Department's classified materials, Harry Miller collected an astounding variety of locks in order to study their designs. The oldest lock in the collection is Arabic and dates to 1303. A lock removed from the Oval Office during Lincoln's presidency and a key to the Capitol's 16-ton doors are in the collection. Many of the locks were invented by Miller himself; he holds some 54 lock patents. Some locks have been donated to the Smithsonian, but the rest are on view in the Lockmasters Security Institute for free Monday through Friday from 8 a.m. to 5 p.m.

The first commercial wine grape operation in the United States was established in sloping fields along the Kentucky River more than 200 years ago by Jean Jacques Dufour. Prohibition in the 1930s led to the closure of many of the vineyards. In recent years there has been a renewed interest in viticulture in the Bluegrass State and our mild climate and rich soil is promising success for contemporary projects. One example is the *Chrisman Mill Vineyards and Winery,* just outside Nicholasville, at 2385 Chrisman Mill Road (859-881-5007). Denise and Chris Nelson planted their first vines in 1997 with the goal of making all their wines from Kentucky-grown fruit. With 1,000 vines producing nine varieties of grapes and fruit from 12 additional growers, Chrisman Mill has won over 200 wine competition awards. Tours and tastings are offered Thursday through Saturday from 11 a.m. to 5 p.m. A tapas and dessert menu is also available during those hours. The winery also has a gift shop.

Head south of town on US 27 for 5 miles to 6614 Danville Road to the *Camp Nelson Heritage Park,* (campnelson.org; 859-881-5716) a large Union supply depot and recruitment center. Founded in 1863, Camp Nelson was the preeminent recruiting and training ground for African-American soldiers. More than a thousand slaves were "impressed" to construct the camp, its roads, and its railroads, and many of the same men subsequently enlisted. Any Kentucky slaves who enlisted were immediately freed. Later, their families were also freed and allowed to live nearby in a refugee camp. Despite the army's attempts to administer the camp, many people died of exposure and disease. The army even joined forces with evangelical abolitionists to provide schools at the camp. One such missionary was Rev. John Gregg Fee, who, shortly after his work at the camp, formed an integrated school in Berea that later became Berea College. When all of Kentucky's slaves were freed in 1865, Camp Nelson served as an issuing station for emancipation papers, and the next year the site was designated the *Camp Nelson National Cemetery.* If you drive another 2 miles south of the supply depot site, you can visit the actual cemetery, where some 4,000 Civil War soldiers are buried (campnelson.org).

campnelson

A group of local citizens has created a foundation to restore and preserve Camp Nelson. You can view the progress of restoration of the Oliver Perry House, an 1855 house that was appropriated for military use during the Civil War. The group also sponsors numerous reenactments and living-history events at Camp Nelson throughout the year. For more information call (859) 881-5716.

To go any farther east, you have to get across the Kentucky River, and there is no bridge. From Nicholasville take Union Mills Road (Highway 169) down to the river's edge and wait for the ferry. In 1785 the Virginia Assembly granted the *Valley View Ferry* a "perpetual and irrevocable franchise." Let me emphasize the word *perpetual.* More than 200 years later, the little boat is still carrying anyone and anything that needs to cross between Madison and Jessamine Counties at the mouth of Tates Creek. This ferry is Kentucky's oldest recorded business continuously in operation. Originally, workhorses pulled the ferry across; later a motor was connected to the ferry's paddle wheel and the boat was guided between fixed cables. Now a motorized ferryboat can carry three cars at a time. Recently the governments of Jessamine, Madison, and Fayette Counties decided to purchase and jointly operate this sole functioning ferry on the Kentucky River. Operating hours are Monday through

trueblue

A sequence of the movie *Flim Flam Man,* starring George C. Scott and Sue Lyon, was filmed in Valley View, near the present-day ferry.

Friday from 6 a.m. to 6 p.m., Saturday and Sunday from 8 a.m. to 8 p.m., except when it is closed due to high or turbulent water. There is no charge to use the ferry, but it's a good idea to check the running status in advance by calling (859) 258-3611 (press "1" after the first traffic message) or check lexingtonky.gov/index.aspx?page=662.

When you arrive on the east bank, keep driving and you'll soon be in **Richmond,** home of Eastern Kentucky University and very much a university town, full of restaurants, bars, hotels, and shops. For the stargazer, the **Hummel Planetarium** at 521 Lancaster Drive on campus is totally cosmic. This is the 12th largest planetarium in the nation, and it feels even larger as you crane your neck in the dark dome to catch a view of the galaxy 9.3 billion miles away from Earth. Public shows are offered Saturday at noon and 1:30 p.m. Call (859) 622-1547. To get there from I-75, take exit 87 onto the Eastern Bypass. Follow the signs to Kit Carson Drive and the planetarium (planetarium.eku.edu).

Local history comes to life at **Irvinton House Museum,** 345 Lancaster Avenue. This Federal-style house has been restored and filled with furniture, clothing, and other artifacts reflecting local history. There are no rope barriers in the rooms. The idea is to make it feel as if you're visiting the family; they have stepped out for a few moments. The guided tour fills you in on the histories of the wonderful vintage clothing, furniture, and rare artifacts from nearby Fort Boonesborough that are on display, many items donated by local citizens. The museum features one of only seven remaining Revolutionary War uniforms. The house is open 9 a.m. to 5 p.m. Monday through Friday, and the tour is free. From May through September, there are Saturday hours from 10 a.m. to 2 p.m. Call (859) 626-1422 for more information. The Richmond Visitors Bureau is located at the rear of the house, so you can find out about other area attractions before or after your tour of the house.

One of those attractions is **White Hall State Historic Site,** accessible from I-75 (exit 90) or directly from Richmond at 500 White Hall Shrine Road. Take US 421/25 and follow the signs to the restored home of one of Kentucky's best-loved big mouths and influential abolitionists, Cassius Marcellus Clay, the "Lion of White Hall." The White Hall building is well fortified in part because Clay's ideological and political opponents were not beyond attempts at physically sabotaging the basement press where he produced his radical paper, the *True American* After a failed political career, Clay served under President Lincoln as minister to the court of Czar Alexander II in St. Petersburg, Russia, then retired and lived bankrupt at White Hall until his death in 1903. Park grounds are open April 1 through October 21, Monday through Saturday from 9 a.m. to 5 p.m. and Sunday noon to 4 p.m. Mansion tours are offered Wednesday through Saturday from 10 a.m. to 3 p.m. and Sunday from noon to 4 p.m. From November 1 through March 31, the mansion is closed to the public except for a Victorian Christmas the first two weekends in December. Call (859) 623-9178 or visit parks.ky.gov/parks/historicsites/White-Hall. Admission is charged.

Berea is a nationally well-known folk arts-and-crafts center located just south of Richmond in southern Madison County off I-75. Stop by the Welcome Center, 3 Artist Circle (berea.com; 859-986-2540), for brochures about all the crafts businesses. You'll find more than 30 craftspeople—chair makers, potters, leather makers, blacksmiths, stained-glass artisans, weavers, spoon makers, basket weavers, quilters, and on and on—whose studios and salesrooms are open to the public.

The place to start is the *Kentucky Artisan Center* (859-985-5448; kentuckyartisancenter.ky.gov), just off I-75 at exit 77 at 200 Artisan Way. This center is designed to showcase the diversity of Kentucky craftsmanship in one stop, much as West Virginia's Tamarack Center spotlights that state's handmade heritage. The primary forum of the center is a large gallery

Native Americans in Kentucky

You've probably heard that Native Americans did not have permanent habitations in Kentucky because it was a commonly owned hunting ground. Not true. Thirty-five hundred acres in southeastern Clark County were occupied, farmed, kept clear, and hunted by Shawnee. Archaeologists are in search of the Shawnee village called Eskippakithiki, meaning "blue lick place" because of salt-sulfur springs in or near the present-day town of Oil Springs. This relatively permanent settlement was established around 1718 and was occupied by as many as 200 families, according to legend and to a 1736 census taken by French Canadians. By 1754 the village was probably abandoned as the Shawnee moved north across the Ohio River, where many other Shawnee lived. Later, the structures burned and the cornfields returned to a wooded state. Some historians believe that the name Kentucky came from an Iroquois name for this particular area, *kenta,* which means "level," and *aki,* which indicates location, or "place of level land."

that exhibits and sells the work of artists and craftspeople from the state. Also for sale are Kentucky-made food items, music, and books by and about anyone associated with the state. The Artisan Center also contains a cafeteria-style restaurant. Hours are 8 a.m. to 8 p.m., seven days a week, except Thanksgiving, Christmas, and New Year's Day. There are three annual outdoor fairs—in spring, summer, and fall—that feature members of the *Kentucky Guild of Artists and Craftsmen,* a juried organization. The following are samples of the many crafts studios you can visit in Berea: Warren May is the state's best-known dulcimer maker. Dulcimers are graceful, Appalachian, wooden string instruments played flat on the lap, usually to accompany vocals, often in a minor key. This is an instrument many Americans probably had never heard of before Jean Ritchie. *Warren A. May's Woodworking Shop* (110 Center Street; 859-986-9293; warrenamay .com) is open Monday through Saturday from 9 a.m. to 5 p.m. At *Churchill Weavers* (100 Churchill Court; 859-986-3127; thechurchillco.com), you can walk through the loom house and see master weavers hard at work creating shawls, throws, and blankets.

From Chestnut Street (also called KY 21 or Lancaster Road), turn into Old Towne on Lester Street. On the same side of the road as the turn onto Lester, you'll notice the *St. Clare Catholic Church* at 226 Chestnut Street. The architecture of the church building, completed in 2003, is what I would call "truth-in-materials" style—raw wood, unaltered concrete, brick, all in a spare clean space. If you walk into the church you will immediately see a sculptural baptismal font. The baptismal pool is octagonal and is lined with deep blue, handmade cross-shaped tiles, some of which have a line of gold leafing that reflects in the water. The outer form of the piece is clad with hundreds of chestnut oak leaves made of patinated and textured copper. The upper pool is a massive bowl. St. Clare herself belonged to the Franciscan order, a nature-oriented sect; the design of the baptistery pays homage to that history by appearing as if it had been sitting in the forest for ages and is completely covered with jewel-like leaves. Many of the other furnishings and ceremonial objects were made by regional artists, like the crucifix made by sculptor Jeanne Dueber, the communion chalice and plate made by a Berea potter, and the altar and other liturgical furniture made by a local woodworker who milled lumber from a giant tree that was felled on the exact site where the new church stands. You can visit the church weekdays or by special appointment (or during mass!). Call (859) 986-4633 or visit stclareberea.org.

An elegant place for fine regional foods and downtown lodging at 100 Main Street is the **Boone Tavern Hotel and Restaurant** (859-985-3700 or 800-366-9358; boonetavernhotel.com), owned and run by Berea College. It's open daily for all meals. Berea College is a highly acclaimed liberal arts college that serves talented, low-income students from southern Appalachia. Students pay no tuition but work 10 to 15 hours a week at any of 138 college-owned businesses, which include the Boone Tavern and studios for pottery, weaving, woodworking, broom making, and other crafts. The student-made crafts are sold at the **Log House Craft Gallery** at 200 Estill Street. The Log House Craft Gallery phone number is (859) 985-3225, and website is berea.edu/student-crafts/log-house-craft-gallery.

trueblue

Of Kentucky's 120 counties, 38 are completely dry (of alcohol sales, that is), 38 are wet, and 49 are moist. The Alcoholic Beverage Control uses the term "dry" to mean that all sales of alcoholic beverages are prohibited. The term "wet" means that sales of alcoholic beverages are permitted. The term "moist" means that dry counties have one or more cities that have voted to allow alcoholic beverage sales.

Fort Boonesborough State Park is on the beaten path and pretty self explanatory. From I-75 take exit 95 on Highway 627 and follow the signs to 4375 Boonesboro Road. The reconstructed fort is at the site of Kentucky's second settlement, established in 1775 by Boone and Richard Henderson when they worked as surveyors for the Transylvania Company. Interpreters at the park dress in period clothing and demonstrate pioneer crafts, such as making lye soap. The park also offers a campground, swimming pool, beach, and more. The park grounds and campgrounds are open year-round. Call (859) 527-3131 or visit parks.ky.gov/parks/recreationparks/Fort Boonesborough.

If you continue north on Highway 627 toward **Winchester,** you may want to veer to the left (west) 3½ miles after crossing the bridge onto Old Stone Church Road and see the lovely little church by the same name. This was supposedly the first church established west of the Appalachian

Mountains. It still has an active congregation, but they don't mind visitors as long as you don't leave trash.

In 1925 the **Leeds Theatre** was probably the most popular place in Winchester because it had one of the town's first air conditioning systems. The theater operated as a movie house until 1986, when it closed in a dilapidated condition. A citizens group, the Winchester Council for the Arts, raised enough money to give the place a facelift, and in 1990 it reopened as the **Leeds Center for the Arts.** Along with local productions, this reborn entertainment palace features national arts performances from dance to jazz concerts. Write the center at 37 North Main Street, Winchester 40392, call (859) 744-6437 or (888) 772-6985, or visit leedscenter.org for information on upcoming performances.

Though the telephone has radically altered our society and world, it is seldom commemorated. Winchester's **Pioneer Telephone Museum** is one of a kind. The collection of antique phones, phone booths, switchboards, and memorabilia was long housed in a phone company maintenance building. In 2000 the whole collection was moved to Winchester's **Bluegrass Heritage Museum,** at 217 South Main Street. The museum, created by a combination of citizen activism and city/county support, is located in a stunning Roman- esque Revival building that served as the Guerrant Clinic from 1927 to 1971. Dr. Guerrant's offices were located in the building until 1989. The museum focuses on local and regional history, including agriculture, transportation, and Native American and pioneer heritage, according to curator Sandy Stults. Call (859) 745-1358 for hours and more information (bgheritage.com).

The clinic building was donated by Wallace and Lana Guerrant, who operate **Guerrant Mountain Mission Bed and Breakfast** at 21 Valentine Court in what was the nurses' home for the clinic. There are two nicely self- contained units, one with a Jacuzzi and one with a fireplace and balcony with a view of the courtyard fountain. You can have breakfast anywhere, even in bed! Call (859) 745-1284 for more information.

If you are driving near the Mount Sterling Plaza on the bypass, stop at Arby's. Please don't eat. Just get out of the car and look for a rather abrupt grassy knob. That's not a Maya Lin earth sculpture, but the **Gaitskill Mound,** an Adena burial mound dating to between 800 BC and AD 700.

In downtown **Mount Sterling** there is an artifact from the 1950s. **Ber- ryman's Tastytreat,** open since 1951 on East Main Street, is a full-fledged

Kentucky's Re-Covered Bridges

Almost any time of the year is a good time to take the winding road KY 1262 off US 60 between Georgetown and Frankfort to the small community of Switzer. There, at the center of a small country park, the **Switzer Covered Bridge** spans Elkhorn Creek. It's a picture-postcard scene, this wooden beauty with sawtooth entrances, flanked by trees, and atop stone foundations on each side of the creek.

Switzer looks like a part of the landscape, and it has been since 1855. But if you had made that winding drive, as I did, in March 1997, you would know that Switzer's presence is nothing short of a miracle.

In March of that year, the worst flooding in more than a century hit central Kentucky. The waters of the Elkhorn swelled and pushed downstream with enough force to lift the Switzer Bridge right off its foundation. Had it not been for a modern concrete span just down the creek, Switzer would have been washed away into oblivion. Instead, it hit the concrete bridge and crumpled into the creek like a folded cardboard box. There were more than a few teary-eyed central Kentuckians standing on the banks in the days after the flood.

But Switzer, one of just 13 covered bridges remaining in a state that once boasted 400, was too precious to be lost. Through a community and state effort, the bridge was lifted, removed, and, ultimately, rebuilt, with new materials added to what could be salvaged. The bridge that spans Switzer today is not exactly the same as it was, but it's close enough.

Switzer isn't the only central Kentucky covered bridge to be "re-covered" in recent years. **Colville Covered Bridge,** which crosses Hinkston Creek near Millersburg, was damaged by flooding in 1999. This bridge, too, was removed, repaired, and reinstalled. You can now drive though this "timbered tunnel." To get to Colville, take Highway 1893 west off US 68, go about 3.1 miles, then turn right at an unmarked road lined by stone walls.

vintage take-out ice cream stand famous for its chili hot dogs. Berryman's is open from 7 a.m. to 9:30 p.m. daily. It closes for the winter in mid-November. Its annual reopening in early March is a sign to area residents that spring has arrived. For information call (859) 498-6830.

For more area information, stop by—or write—the Mount Sterling Chamber of Commerce, 126 West Main Street, Mount Sterling 40353 (859-498-5343; mtsterlingchamber.com). Ask about October Court Days, a big trading festival reminiscent of earlier times when each county held court once a month in a central location so the more remote farmers didn't have to come to town more often. During this four-day extravaganza, approximately 130,000 people crowd into the town of 6,895.

Just uphill from the Bell House at the corner of Broadway and High Street at 48 West High Street is *Ascension Episcopal Church,* a beautiful little church with walnut paneling, exquisitely carved wood, exposed beams, and stained-glass windows thought to be the first to cross the mountains (by oxcart!). The doors are open during the day so visitors can drool at this 1877 gem. For more information, call (859) 498-3730 or visit ascensionmt sterling.org.

If you're a history buff, be sure to drive by *Morgan Station,* the site of the last Indian raid in Kentucky. Daniel Boone's cousin, Ralph Morgan, built the big stone house east of Mount Sterling at 3751 Harpers Ridge Road.

Mount Sterling is sweet-tooth heaven. Make a molasses run (but not as slowly as molasses itself runs) to *Townsend's Sorghum Mill,* at 11620 Main Street (also US 460) in Jeffersonville, south of Mount Sterling. Go any time of year because they always have pure sorghum syrup (and occasionally maple syrup) on hand, but in September and October you can watch them process cane. The Townsend family has been raising cane for 150 years. Although they use tractors to do the real work, at festivals they bring out the mule team to demonstrate the old-fashioned way of harvesting cane. Call Judy and Danny Townsend at (859) 498-4142, townsendsorghummill.com, or plan to come by after 4 p.m.

The ultimate dessert is chocolate—real food for real people. If you are a chocoholic, you might be in mortal danger upon entering *Ruth Hunt Candies.* The aroma of liquid chocolate, sweet cream, and roasting nuts will cause lightheadedness in even the strong of heart. Everything is handmade and very fresh. Just like in the old days, you can ask the clerk for a quarter pound of pulled cream candy, a half pound of caramel and bittersweet chocolate balls, and a handful of hot cinnamon suckers, and they'll reach into the big, colorful bins for the goods.

This operation is small and friendly enough that Larry Kezele, the owner, may have time to show you the whole production process. Ruth Tharpe Hunt started the business in 1921 after her bridge buddies encouraged her to go public with her candy making. The Blue Monday Sweet Bar is a dark chocolate with pulled cream in the center and is perhaps the most famous of the company's products. The candy bar was named by a traveling minister who was eating Sunday dinner at the Hunts' and claimed that he needed candy to get through those blue Mondays. Look for Larry and his staff dressed like Blue Mondays in parades. The company, located at 550 North Maysville Road, is open Monday through Saturday from 9 a.m. to 5:30 p.m. and Sunday from 1 to 5:30 p.m. Call (859) 498-0676 if you need more information or if you are jonesing and need an order FedExed now. Their website is ruthhuntcandy.com. (If you're in Lexington, Ruth Hunt has a new store at 213 Walton Avenue; 859-268-1559.)

City Lights

More than 95 percent of the bourbon whiskey made in America is made in Kentucky, and most of it comes from this area. *Wild Turkey Distillery* (of Boulevard Distillers and Importers Inc.) is a place to get a fascinating bourbon education. From Lawrenceburg take US 62 east of town until it splits with Highway 1510. Bear right, go downhill, and watch for the visitor information center on the right. (Note the high train trestle spanning the Kentucky River. Young's High Bridge is a single-span, deck-over cantilever 281 feet high and 1,659 feet long, the last of its kind.)

The Wild Turkey Distillery has been operating continuously since the mid-1860s, except during Prohibition, when nearly all distilleries were shut down. During World War II this facility made only surgical alcohol. Federal law states that for whiskey to be called straight bourbon, it must be manufactured in the United States, of at least 51 percent corn, and stored at 125 proof or less for at least two years in new, charred, white-oak barrels. Char caramelizes the wood, which gives the bourbon its rich color and flavor. The corn is ground, cooked, and cooled. The distillers add rye for starch, then barley malt, which converts the starch to sugar (unlike moonshiners, who simply dump cane sugar in the corn mash). Yeast is added, and when the fermented mash is

true blue

Lawrenceburg, county seat of Anderson County, was named for 19th-century U.S. Navy captain James Lawrence, who is credited with coining the phrase "Don't give up the ship."

steamed from below, whiskey vapor rises to the top where it is condensed into liquid form. The whiskey is distilled again, put in barrels, and aged for four to twelve years. It's tasted at every stage, and meticulous production records are kept for every batch. Tours for $5 are available Monday through Saturday between 8 a.m. and 4 p.m. Tours are offered Sunday between 11 a.m. and 3 p.m. from April through November only. Call (502) 839-4544 or visit wildturkeybourbon.com.

From Lawrenceburg take US 127 north into **Frankfort,** the state capital. At the corner of Capital Avenue and Second Street at 100 Capital Avenue is an ornate Queen Anne–style house with gingerbread trim, the official Frankfort Visitor Center (502-875-8687 or 800-960-7200; visitfrankfort.com). Because the city's layout is confusing, a map is good headache prevention.

Directly across Capital Avenue from the visitor center is **Rebecca-Ruth Candy Inc.,** at 112 East Second Street. Chocolate and candy addicts will love the tour of one of Kentucky's oldest houses of sweet repute. In 1919 Rebecca Gooch and Ruth (Hanly) Booe quit teaching and went into business making candy. Ruth's grandson, Charles Booe, carries on the tradition today.

Tour the production area to see pipes running full of liquid Dutch chocolate and churning vats of sugar and thick cream. Some candies are made completely by hand on the original 1919 marble slab. Rebecca-Ruth sells hundreds of varieties, including delicate mints, crunchy chocolate turtles, fudge galore, and variations on the theme of the bourbon ball. The store is open Monday through Saturday from 10 a.m. to 6 p.m. and Sunday from noon to 6 p.m. Tours of the factory and museum are given Monday through Saturday between 10 a.m. and 5:30 p.m. (excluding the lunch hour, noon to 1 p.m.). Tours cost $4 per person and are free for children age 5 and under. Tours include free chocolate. Call (502) 223-7475 for a tour schedule or a free catalog (rebeccaruth.com).

The **Thomas B. Clark Center for Kentucky History** is the definitive high-tech repository of documents, photos, and all manner of important archival material concerning the history of our commonwealth. View such things as Daniel Boone's original survey note, in his handwriting. For years the Kentucky Historical Society had dreamed of having a permanent, state-of-the-art facility for research and education, and this impressive 167,000-square-foot facility was the dream-come-true and then some. The center, at 100 West Broadway, is in downtown Frankfort, next to the railroad tracks on the corner of Broadway and Ann Street. History Center hours from March through December are Wednesday from 10 a.m. to 4 p.m., Thursday from 10 a.m. to 8 p.m., and Friday and Saturday from 10 a.m. to 5 p.m. Admission of $4 for adults and $2 for children also includes the Old State Capitol and the Kentucky Military History Museum. Call 502-564-1792 for information about changing exhibits and special events at the center (history .ky.gov).

Just across and down a block on Broadway you'll find numerous interesting shops. There are several antiques malls with everything from antique linens to cannonballs. ***Poor Richard's Books,*** at 233 West Broadway Street, carries a mix of new and used tomes (including some hand-printed at Larkspur Press in Owen County). Call (502) 223-8018 or visit poorrichards.indiebound.com. A few doors away is ***Completely Kentucky,*** at 237 West Broadway Street, which, as its name implies, carries products made in the Bluegrass State. Call (502) 223-5240 or visit completelykentucky.com. Outside of Berea, stores that specialize in regional crafts and other indigenous products are surprisingly few, and Completely Kentucky has variety in both items and price range.

true**blue**

Kentucky towns bear an international array of names. Kentucky has a Moscow, Athens, Cairo, Dublin, London, Manila, Paris, and Warsaw.

From wonderful and affordable cherry kitchen tools and foods to fine raku pottery and handmade jewelry to whimsical metal yard "critters," you're sure to find something of interest.

One of Frankfort's newest attractions is actually old—a resurrected bit of Civil War history (and in-town forest) called ***Leslie Morris Park on Fort Hill.*** There were two Civil War earthwork forts on the hill, Fort Boone and New Redoubt. In 1864 Confederate general John Hunt Morgan's raiders attacked Fort Boone, but local citizens successfully defended the city. You can take a self-guided walking tour (begin at the Fort Hill visitor center in the Old Capitol Annex, 100 Broadway). It's a moderately strenuous trek up Old Military Road, but the reward is a chance to see the walls of Fort Boone and earthworks of New Redoubt, as well as a commanding view of downtown Frankfort.

About 8 miles north of Frankfort is ***Canoe Kentucky*** (7323 Peaks Mill Road; 502-227-4492 or 888–CANOEKY; canoeky.com). Canoe Kentucky offers a variety of excursions on a dozen Kentucky waterways, but it is the one in Canoe Kentucky's own backyard, Elkhorn Creek, that is most dear to the company's heart. Take an excursion and you'll soon understand why. This long and winding waterway—which flows for more than 100 miles through parts of six counties—played an important role in the settlement of the bluegrass area. Poet Walt Whitman, whose soldier brother was encamped in Kentucky in 1863, wrote of "the vale of the Elkhorn." Whether your interest is historic sites, fishing (some sections are great for catching bass), picnicking, or just a quiet-at-your-own-pace getaway, Canoe Kentucky can suggest a good paddle route. If you want to learn all about the Elkhorn, its history, its wildlife, and the need to protect it in light of rapidly encroaching development, or if you want to try a more unusual aspect of canoeing, such as winter canoeing, Canoe Kentucky is the one to go up (or down) the creek with. Prices vary depending on length and type of excursion. Kayaks are also available. A half-day guided experience costs $150. Office hours are Wednesday through Friday, 9 a.m. to 5 p.m., Saturday and Sunday 9 a.m. to 6 p.m.

From Frankfort go west on I-64 or US 60 to Shelbyville. In 1825 Julia Tevis founded **Science Hill,** a girls' school at 525 Washington Street in downtown **Shelbyville,** because she believed young women needed an education in math and science, not just needlepoint and etiquette. During its 114-year operation, Science Hill was known as one of the best preparatory schools in the country. Etiquette, however, never lost its essential place. A former student remembers this story about Miss Julia Poynter, the last principal of the school: The mother of a "town boy" had a party in her home. One of the students thanked the hostess by saying, "I enjoyed myself thoroughly." Miss Julia reprimanded the girl, saying, "You do not go to a party to enjoy yourself, you go to enjoy others. Tell your hostess that you enjoyed her party."

true blue

The first successful transplant of a human hand was performed in Louisville, Kentucky, in 1999.

Today, **Science Hill Inn** is a popular lunch spot featuring down home country cooking, including hot water biscuits, cornbread, creamy soups, and Kentucky country ham. The restaurant is open Tuesday through Saturday for lunch from 11:30 a.m. to

2:30 p.m. and for Sunday brunch from 11:30 a.m. to 2 p.m. Contact Science Hill Inn at (502) 633-2825; sciencehillinnky.com.

Today the fully restored Science Hill complex houses the **Wakefield-Scearce Galleries** (502-633-4382; wakefieldscearce.com), which are full of elegant English (plus a touch of Asian, American, and European) furniture, silver, china, rugs, paintings, and other decorative objects. Much of the furniture is antique, and the reproductions are beautifully made. The quality is high, as are the prices. Whether or not you can afford the decor, these museum-like galleries provide room after room of visual and tactile delight. Hours are 10 a.m. to 5 p.m. Monday through Saturday.

There are several other charming shops along Washington Street. Needlepoint enthusiasts won't want to miss **The Needle Nest,** 702 Washington Street (502-633-4701; needlenestky.com), which carries an extensive selection of patterns, fabric, thread, and accessories.

There is a cluster of antiques stores downtown, all within walking distance of one another. The Ruby Rooster is at 514 Main Street. Paisley Pig Antique Mall is at 528 Main Street. And Country Cottage Collectibles is a block away at 137 Frankfort Road (also US 60). It's a good town for walking and browsing.

Follow US 60 (or, if you're in a hurry, take I-64 West) to **Louisville,** largest city in the state and home of the world-famous **Kentucky Derby.** The greatest two minutes in sports are also part of the greatest 24 hours in fashion. For a week before the Derby, everyone and everything is dressed to the nines—houses are repainted, yards are relandscaped, hair is coiffed, and bodies are clothed in the latest styles, no matter the cost or the weather. For Kentuckians the Derby marks the beginning of early summer and, therefore, the first day that it's acceptable for women to shed their dark winter garb and wear white again. Fashion sometimes follows need and sometimes it leads. Several years ago we had a bitter cold, rainy Derby Day, but the dresses were already purchased, and hats were garnished. Women simply wore thermal underwear under sleeveless gowns, and men, for once, were happy to keep on their coats and ties.

trueblue

Although the mint julep is now associated with the Kentucky Derby, the early meaning of the word *julep* or *julap* is associated with a medicinal drink taken to combat "fevers arising from night air and hot climates."

The Kentucky Derby is run the first Saturday in May at Churchill Downs Race Track at 700 Central Avenue (502-636-4400; churchilldowns.com). The gates open at 8 a.m., and you can join the party on the infield or wander the paddock area for $50—standing room only or bring your own chair or blanket. Racing begins at 11:30 a.m., but the Run for the Roses isn't until 6:04 p.m. Dress however you want, and keep your eyes peeled for celebrities. Churchill Downs also hosts thoroughbred racing during a Spring Meet, which runs from the end of April to the beginning of July, and a Fall Meet, from late October through late November.

If you're planning to be seen at the Derby and want to be on the cutting edge of fashion, you may want to check out the annual pre-Derby fashion show held in mid-April at the *Kentucky Derby Museum* on the grounds of Churchill Downs. Celebs and local media personalities model the latest in hats and clothes, setting a precedent for the masses. Any time of year the Kentucky Derby Museum is an interesting stop. Naturally, the exhibits feature the Derby's history, but there are others concerning the whole thoroughbred industry. Winter hours (December 1 through March 15) are 9 a.m. to 5 p.m. Monday through Saturday, noon to 5 p.m. Sunday. Summer hours (March 15 through November 30) are Monday through Saturday 8 a.m. to 5 p.m. and Sunday 11 a.m. to 5 p.m. The museum opens at 8 a.m. on the Sunday following the Kentucky Derby. Also on-site is the Finish Line Gift Shop and The Derby Cafe. Call (502) 637-1111 or visit derbymuseum.org.

trueblue

Zachary Taylor grew up and is buried in Louisville.

Far from the madding crowd, but not far from Churchill Downs, are several peaceful sites. The most surprising is just inside the I-264 loop between Poplar Level Road and Newburg Road: the *Beargrass Creek State Nature Preserve* (502-458-1328). The best way to get there is to turn onto Illinois Avenue off Trevilian Way (behind the Louisville Tennis Center), then park in the lot next to the *Louisville Nature Center,* where you'll find informative exhibits and a friendly staff. There's a bird blind viewing area behind the building. Trails in the preserve are well defined, though not marked, so pick up a map at the center. No dogs or bicycles are allowed. The preserve encompasses 41 acres and has a remarkably diverse community of flora and

Fascinating Facade

One of Louisville's most fascinating house tours isn't really a house; it's just the front of a house. Like a piece of a movie set, the front of the **Charles Heigold House** sits forlornly in Thurston Park, off River Road east of downtown Louisville. If this were a movie, it would be a historical drama, set in the mid-1800s, when Heigold, a German immigrant and stonemason, decided to carve his political feelings in stone—on the front of his house. "The Union Forever, All Hail to This Union, Let It Never Desolve It" is among the sayings and figures elaborately carved into the facade in exuberant fashion. The rest of the house was razed when the street on which it originally stood became part of the city landfill. Luckily, city officials decided to save this face for visitors and future residents to ponder and enjoy.

fauna. Because it's smack-dab in the middle of the city, it is constantly in use for environmental education. So if you placed all your bets badly at the track, here's a balm. This lovely spot is open daily from sunrise to sunset, and there's someone at the nature center Tuesday through Saturday, 9 a.m. to 4 p.m. (louisvillenaturecenter.org).

The park is named after Beargrass Creek, which empties into the Ohio River just above the famous *Falls of the Ohio,* a rocky series of rapids over a 3-mile descent, which stopped early travelers on their way south. Beargrass Creek proved to be a place to rest and to develop a strategy for getting around the falls. In 1778 George Rogers Clark set up a military and civilian camp nearby, on Corn Island. Floods on the island caused the settlers to move to the mainland (somewhere between what are now Twelfth and Rowan Streets), where they started building the city of Louisville. Since the installation of the Portland Canal and the McAlpine Dam (easily seen from town near the Northwestern Parkway and Twenty-seventh Street), the Falls of the Ohio is an exposed coral reef, a fossil bed over 350 million years old. Some 600 fossil species can be seen; 400 species have never been seen anywhere else. To get a good look at the fossils, cross the river into Clarksville, Indiana, park at Riverside Park, and walk near where the Fourteenth Street railroad bridge and five dam gates meet the shore. From I-65 take exit 0 and follow the signs. There is an interpretive center (812-280-9970; fallsoftheohio.org) open Monday through Saturday from 9 a.m.

to 5 p.m. and Sunday from 1 to 5 p.m. Admission is $5 for adults, $2 for students and children.

The *Portland Museum* (502-776-7678; goportland.org) features exhibits illustrating 200 years of the city's river history. One of the most enthralling items is an old newsreel of the great 1937 Ohio River Flood. A few exhibits are located in the Beech Grove antebellum home. Admission is $7 for adults, $6 for seniors, $5 for children, and free for children age 5 and under. Hours are Tuesday through Friday from 10 a.m. to 4:30 p.m. From I-64 take the Twenty-second Street exit, turn right, and go to 2308 Portland Avenue. It's a good idea to call ahead.

Jefferson County has restored and opened to the public a grand-style Greek Revival brick house, circa 1835, known as the *Farnsley-Moreman House.* With an extremely high front portico that haughtily faces the river, the house represents a showy attitude prevalent in prosperous river cities in the 19th century. In the 1860s this house sat at the center of what was the largest farm in the county at the time. If you visit Riverside (as the property is now known), you'll see period antique furnishings and historically authentic kitchen gardens in addition to exhibits reflecting life on the river as far back as 4,000 years. (It is considered the best view of the Ohio River in Louisville.) Call (502) 935-6809 or check riverside-landing.org for information on special events. Normal hours are Tuesday through Saturday from 10 a.m. to 4:30 p.m., Sunday from 1 to 4:30 p.m. The house is closed on Sunday from December through February. Grounds are open sunrise to sunset year-round. Admission is $6 for adults, $5 for seniors, $3 for children ages 6 to 12, and free for children age 5 and under, or $15 for the whole family. To get there, head west on Gene Snyder Freeway (you can access this from I-64 and I-65), and stay on the "greenbelt," as it's called, until you reach Lower River Road. Then just follow the signs. The house is 7410 Moorman Road, at the intersection of Lower River and Moorman Roads.

In 1810 John and Lucy Fry Speed had a Federal-style mansion built based on a design by Thomas Jefferson. *Farmington* has octagonal rooms, hidden stairs, and orderly gardens. Abraham Lincoln visited this home of his friend, Joshua Speed, for six weeks in 1841 during a temporary break in his relationship with Mary Todd, his future wife.

Originally the house was in the center of a 552-acre hemp plantation. Now it's on 18 acres, all of which are carefully restored and maintained in keeping with its early-19th-century history. You can visit it Tuesday through Saturday from 10 a.m. to 4:30 p.m., Sunday from 1:30 to 3:30 p.m. The address is 3033 Bardstown Road. Call (502) 452-9920 for more information.

Another spectacular Federal-style structure, which has been exquisitely restored, is the 1900 Ferguson Mansion, 1310 South Third Street, now home to the **Filson Club Historical Society** (502-635-5083; filsonhis torical.org). The society has a nationally renowned genealogy library and extensive manuscript, photography, and museum collections. Stop by between 9 a.m. and 5 p.m. Monday through Friday or 9 a.m. to noon Saturday. Next to Beargrass Creek Park is the **Louisville Zoological Garden,** at 1100 Trevilian Way, home to more than 1,300 animals. The zoo has

trueblue

In 1893 a pair of Louisville sisters penned the kindergarten greeting song, "Good Morning to You," which later became the most-sung song in the world rewritten as "Happy Birthday to You."

a Gorilla Forest, Lorikeet Landing, Glacier Run, and other animal exhibits. The zoo also offers train rides, a Conservation Carousel, ropes adventure course, splash park (in warmer weather), petting zoo, and playground. It is open daily year-round. Admission is $15.95 for adults and $11.50 for seniors and children ages 3 to 11. Call (502) 459-2181 for current hours or check louisvillezoo.org.

From the zoo take Newburg Road to Eastern Parkway, and go west to Third Street; turn right and you're on the University of Louisville campus. The **Speed Art Museum** at 2035 South Third Street (502-634-2700; speed museum.org) is a small but outstanding museum not to be missed at any cost. The permanent collection includes works from all periods, including some distinguished medieval, Renaissance, and Dutch masterpieces, and a broad representation of contemporary art. The museum also maintains a stimulating schedule of traveling exhibitions. The Speed Art Museum is currently closed for construction of a $50 million expansion. The grand opening is scheduled for 2016. Under the project, a new 60,000-square-foot North Building will double the museum's overall square footage and nearly triple gallery space. Other additions include a state-of-the-art space for large special exhibitions, new contemporary art galleries, a family education welcome center, indoor and outdoor cafe, a museum shop, and a multipurpose pavilion for lectures, performances, and entertaining. An exciting addition will be the new Elizabeth P. and Frederick K. Cressman Art Park and Piazza for the display of sculpture.

During the summer, more culture is in store at the corner of Fourth and Magnolia Streets in Old Louisville's Central Park. The Kentucky Shakespeare Festival performs free, high-quality, live Shakespeare productions from June through August. The oldest free Shakespeare Festival in the nation, Kentucky Shakespeare can seat more than 1,000 audience members at the C. Douglas Ramey Amphitheatre, which is wheelchair accessible. Curtain time is 8 p.m. Tuesday through Sunday. Call (502) 574-9900 for current schedules or check kyshakespeare.com.

Indoor theater is always happening in this town. Consult the *Louisville Courier Journal* for performances by the myriad little theaters, and check the schedule at **Actors Theatre,** 316 West Main Street. In addition to producing a surprising variety of plays all year (except during July and August), Actors has become nationally known for the Humana Festival of New American Plays in March and April. Shows in the festival are booked early, so get the schedule and make reservations by calling (502) 584-1265 or check actorstheatre.org.

Main Street is art street in Louisville. The glass structure with the big whimsical sculpture is the **Kentucky Center for the Arts** at 501 West Main Street. The center hosts a little of everything, including the Louisville Opera, ballet, orchestra, theater for all ages, and a series of national and regional performers. Call (502) 584-7777 or (800) 775-7777; kentuckycenter.org. Two blocks west, at 715 West Main Street, the **Kentucky Museum of Art and Craft** (502-589-0102; kmacmuseum.org) features the work of some of the state's finest craftspeople. Hours are 10 a.m. to 5 p.m. Tuesday through Saturday and 11 a.m. to 5 p.m. Sunday. The **Zephyr Gallery,** at 610 East Market Street (502-585-5646; zephyrgallery.org), is another place worth exploring. This art cooperative never fails to hang imaginative shows.

The **21C Museum Hotel,** at 700 West Main, is a renovated luxury hotel as well as a museum of international contemporary art collected by the owners, Laura Lee Brown and her husband Steve Wilson. The 21C Museum collects and exhibits solely contemporary art of the 21st century in a wide range of media. The artwork is exhibited throughout the hotel, with the main atrium/lobby serving as the primary gallery—it is here that a series of guest curators organize engaging, intelligent, even pioneering exhibitions of contemporary art. The collection includes artists such as Tony Oursler, Yinka Shonibare, Kara Walker, and Red Grooms. The hotel consists of five historic tobacco and bourbon warehouses combined and reconfigured into a clean-lined, minimalist, contemporary structure that occasionally reveals its architectural memories—exposed brick walls and massive wooden beams overhead.

The 90 rooms include high quality modern amenities such as 42-inch HDTV screens standard in each room, Wi-Fi connections, and classic pewter mint julep cups. It's worth noting at this point that Brown and her family control the Brown-Forman liquor corporation. In addition to their support of contemporary art on the national and international scale, Brown and Wilson have been longtime supporters of regional arts projects and institutions. For more information, call (502) 217-6300 or (877) 217-6400 and see 21cmuseum hotels.com/Louisville. Watch for the big red penguins, which have a way of appearing and disappearing around the hotel. One time I opened my hotel room door to find a pesky plastic penguin standing outside.

The restaurant at 21C, **Proof on Main,** features regional ingredients, like Kentucky striped bass and locally grown produce, in American-style dishes "with Tuscan influences." They're open weekdays for lunch and daily for dinner and late-night offerings (until midnight and 1 a.m.). Closed Sunday. Of course, you'll dine with art. For reservations call (502) 217-6360; proofonmain.com.

Another not-to-be-missed arts attraction is **Glassworks,** located in a renovated commercial building at 815 West Market Street. Here you can see the art of glassmaking in numerous forms, from glassblowing to the creation of stained glass and architectural glass. A Walk-In Workshop invites guests to find their inner artist and create glass art. The class uses cold glass fusing so no hot glass blowing is necessary. Projects include nightlights, bowls, vases, jewelry, suncatchers, and more. Prices range from $12.50 to $135. Children must be 12 or older to cut glass. A suncatcher/ornament project that uses smooth rounded glass nuggets and special glue can be done by children ages 2 to 12. Self-guided studio tours are given Monday through Friday from 10 a.m. to 3 p.m. and cost $5.75 for adults and $4.75 for seniors and students. Guided tours are offered on Saturday at 11 a.m., 2 p.m., and 3 p.m. and cost $7.75 for adults and $6.75 for seniors and students. There's no charge to see the changing glass exhibits in the main floor gallery. Call (502) 584-4510 for more information or visit louisvilleglassworks.com.

With the 2004 opening of **Flame Run Gallery and Studio,** Louisville is on its way to becoming a hot spot for hot glass. At 828 East Market, the studio is just blocks away from Glassworks (above). The 12,500-square-foot space is primarily a functional hot shop, but there is also a gallery that showcases changing exhibitions of studio glass art. The gallery is open Monday through Friday from 10 a.m. to 4 p.m., Saturday from 10 a.m. to 5 p.m., by appointment, and by chance at other times. When the glassblow-

trueblue

Louisville is second only to Boston in number of registered historic sites.

ers are working in the shop, you're welcome to observe the activity. Special tours can be arranged for groups. They offer classes in all aspects of hot glass, from blowing to kiln casting or sand casting to making paperweights; they also rent shop time. For more information, call (502) 584-5353 or visit flamerun.com.

The next stop is for kids. The **Louisville Science Center,** 727 West Main Street, is a big, colorful, hands-on place orchestrated for discovery. The selling point for adults is the IMAX theater, a four-story screen surrounded by speakers; the experience blows your confidence in logic to pieces. "It's just a movie," you tell yourself as you clutch the nearest person's arm to keep from falling. Call the museum at (502) 561-6100 or (800) 591-2203 for show times and admission charges (kysciencecenter.org).

In case you didn't notice, there's a 120-foot baseball bat at Main and Eighth Streets. The erect bat is a beacon for the **Louisville Slugger Museum** (502-588-7228 or 877-775-8443; sluggermuseum.com). Baseball fans of all ages will love the museum and tour of the world's largest manu-facturing plant of baseball bats. (Over one million are made there annually.) There's a full-size dugout, a replica of Orioles Park, a replica of a northern white ash forest, and exhibits tracing the history of the game and its most famous brand of bat. Despite being called the Louisville Slugger, for 22 years the bats were actually made across the Ohio River in southern Indiana. In 1996 the manufacturing plant returned to Louisville. Guided factory tours are offered daily and begin at 9 a.m. with the last tour of the day departing an hour before closing time. Check the museum website for daily hours, which change according to the season. Admission is $12 for adults, $11 for seniors, and $7 for children ages 7 to 12. Admission includes a free souvenir mini-bat after the factory tour. Directly across from the Louisville Slugger Museum, is the *Frazier International History Museum* (829 West Main Street; 502-753-5663; fraziermuseum.org). The city's three-story museum is primarily devoted to American military history and related artifacts and weaponry. Some notable items in the permanent collection include Daniel Boone's family Bible, Geronimo's bow, and President Theodore Roosevelt's "big stick." In addition to traditional displays, history is presented in lively reenactment performances by elaborately costumed actors in several parts of the museum. There are also interactive multimedia presentations and frequently screened films in the internal theater. Not a fan of arms? Pacifism is given its due, too. There is, for example, a fascinating display of World War I photos by a pacifist soldier named Andre Jeunet. Carrying a simple folding camera, Jeunet captured more than 200 images of the war depicting everyday life as a foot soldier and documenting his travels to the Balkans and Greece as a participant of the Salonica campaign. The museum is open Monday through Saturday from 9 a.m. to 5 p.m. and Sunday from noon to 5 p.m. Admission is $10.50 for adults, $8.50 for seniors, $7.50 for children ages 14 to 17, $6 for children ages 5 to 13, and free for children 4 and younger. As a nice nod to educators, teachers in Kentucky and Indiana receive free admission.

Kizito Cookies (502-456-2891; kizito.com) wins a prize for the most unusual method of dessert distribution. Elizabeth Kizito started her business by carrying baskets of scrumptious chocolate cookies through the downtown streets on her head during lunch hours. (She still sells from her head basket at ball games, parades, and special occasions.) She is from Uganda, where it's commonplace for folks to keep their hands free by means of this balancing act, but in Louisville, she's become famous for it. These days she has a retail store at 1398 Bardstown Road, where you can buy coffee, cookies, and muffins while looking over a colorful selection of African earrings or small carvings from Kenya and wonderful baskets from Uganda. Hours are 7 a.m. to 5 p.m. Tuesday through Friday, 8 a.m. to 5 p.m. Saturday.

If you're looking for fragments of almost anything imaginable, pay a visit to *Joe Ley Antiques* at 615 East Market Street. Joe Ley's place is two acres under one roof full—and I mean full—of antique treasures. For

Tattoos—While You Wait (Is There Any Other Way?)

A little-known cultural reference library of sorts is found in the halls of *Tattoo Charlie's,* a dermagraphic extravaganza. Tattoo art has come a long way since bones and charcoal or needles in a cork. For the uninitiated, you can watch consenting clients being decorated by a certified tattoo technician wielding an electric needle that looks and sounds like a dentist's drill. Prices range from $25 for a single music note, for example, to more than $3,000 for a series of full-color illustrations. Even if you aren't personally interested in a tattoo, check out the tattoo design gallery and museum featuring photos, tattoo machines, and other memorabilia. Then there are hundreds of photographs and slides of customers displaying actual tattoos, no matter where they are. No appointment necessary. Call (502) 366-9635. Open daily from 10 a.m. to midnight. Located at 7904 Preston Highway (tattoocharlies.com).

architects and home-restoration folks, this is an endless toy shop. Stained glass, chandeliers, mantels, carousel horses, stuffed moose, fine silver—you name it, it's here. Hours are Tuesday through Saturday from 8:30 a.m. to 5 p.m. Call (502) 583-4014. Also check joeley.com. Want more? Head down to *Architectural Salvage* at 618 East Broadway Street for more of the same. This place is crammed full of mantels, hardware, stained glass, doors, wrought iron, and on and on. Call (502) 589-0670 if you care to ask specifics or visit architecturalsalvage.com. I recommend the browsing method myself. Or for the whole gamut, stop by the *Crazy Daisy Antique Mall* at 1430 Mellwood Avenue. The mall is open Monday through Saturday from 9 a.m. to 5 p.m., Sunday from noon to 5 p.m. Call (502) 560-1335 or visit crazydaisyantiquemall.com.

On the mezzanine level of the Seelbach Hilton Louisville, at 500 Fourth Avenue, is the *Oakroom,* Kentucky's first and only AAA Diamond restaurant. Awards (of which there are many) aside, the truth is that the chefs use fresh local ingredients (Amish free-range chickens, wild morel mushrooms, pungent Trappist monk–made cheese, still-dripping-with-dew fruits and vegetables, etc.) to very creatively conjure palate-tingling, eye-popping-gorgeous dishes. The restaurant is in the hotel's 1907-era gentlemen's billiard hall—the aesthetic is still powerfully present in the carved lion's head columns, ornate molding, dark wood beam ceiling, and brass chandeliers. They offer 1,200 wines and a huge collection of Kentucky's many bourbons (also used in many of the dishes). Call (502) 807-3463 to make reservations (recommended). They are open Tuesday through Saturday from 6 to 10 p.m. and Sunday for an elegant Champagne Piano Brunch between 10 a.m. and 2 p.m. (theoakroomlouisville.com).

Bardstown Road has long been home to countless artists, musicians, playwrights, and people of diverse backgrounds. Over the years that cultural richness has grown and now includes many of Louisville's most popular and successful small businesses. For international cuisine and an usually wide selection of vegetarian dishes, try *Ramsi's Café on the World* (1293 Bardstown Road; 502-451-0700; ramsiscafe.com). While you wait for your table, be sure to walk next door to a pair of favorite and very complementary local businesses, *Carmichael's Bookstore* (1295 Bardstown Road; 502-456-6950; carmichaelsbookstore.com) and *Heine Brothers' Coffee.* (There are seven locations in town—this one is at 1295 Bardstown Road; 502-456-5108; heinebroscoffee.com). Don't worry about missing your reservation at Ramsi's because the host is happy to retrieve you when your table is ready. Across the street from Ramsi's are the *Baxter Avenue Filmworks* (1250 Bardstown Road; 502-459-2288; village8.com/Baxter_home), a small set of movie theaters tucked into the middle of town that show the usual blockbusters as well as a variety of foreign films, documentaries, and indie art films.

If you want to stay in town but escape briefly, head to *Cherokee Park,* off Eastern Parkway east of downtown, for bicycling, jogging, and picnicking. Or take Third Street south to *Iroquois Park* and admire a nearly 200-year-old forest. Louisville has some of the most beautiful public parks found anywhere, thanks to foresight on the part of city leaders. In 1891 Louisville hired Frederick Law Olmsted to design and construct the city's park system. Olmsted is known as the father of landscape architecture; his other credits include New York's Central Park, Biltmore Gardens, and the 1893 Chicago World's Fair. When Olmsted retired in 1895, his stepson, John C. Olmsted, completed the Louisville plan. In all, the Olmsteds created 16 Louisville parks between 1891 and 1935. Although a 1974 tornado took its toll, citizens rallied in the late 1980s to conserve and, where necessary, restore the parks' beauty.

To explore the world in all its infinite detail is a lifelong process demanding your every sense. But not every sense is challenged equally by those of us who have the use of all human senses. The blind can access nearly any information that seeing people can if they have the tools, and some of their senses, like touch and hearing, are sharpened by intensive use. The **American Printing House for the Blind,** established in 1858, is the world's largest and oldest publisher and manufacturer of education aids for visually impaired people. The printing house has recently opened a museum of rare artifacts relating to the history of technology developed for the blind—from the tactile language of Braille to the audio recording of almost any text that exists in the world. This museum is one of the most important and unique sites in Louisville. Free tours are given Monday through Thursday at 10 a.m. and 2 p.m., and you can browse the museum before or after. The museum is open from 8:30 a.m. to 4:30 p.m. Monday through Friday and from 10 a.m. to 3 p.m. Saturday. For more information call (800) 223-1839. The printing house and museum is located at 1839 Frankfort Avenue (aph.org).

Abbeys and Art

What was once an abused tract of tired farmland is now **Bernheim Forest Arboretum and Nature Center,** a 10,000-acre native forest protected since 1928. Available in this legacy of "the knobs" are hiking, picnicking, limited fishing, unlimited daydreaming, and a self-education in the nature center's museum or in the arboretum, where an enormous variety of ornamental plants are grown in meticulously labeled, manicured beds. I used to skip high school in the spring to make an annual pilgrimage here, armed with my bicycle and a sketch pad. The forest is open from 7 a.m. to sunset daily. The visitor center, art gallery, and nature shop are open from 9 a.m. to 5 p.m. daily. Call (502) 955-8512 for information. Bernheim Forest is right next to the intersection of I-65 (exit 112) and Highway 245. Admission is free weekdays, $5 per vehicle on weekends (bernheim.org).

While traveling, Mark Twain was asked by the luggage inspector if he had anything besides clothing in his suitcase. Twain said no, but I guess he looked suspicious because the man opened his case anyhow and found a fifth of bourbon whiskey. "I thought you had only clothes!" the man roared.

Run, Rooster, Run!

If you're going toward Bardstown from the west on Highway 245, not stopping at *Rooster Run General Store* (502-348-8753) is like being in Memphis and skipping Graceland. The store, formerly called Evans Beverage Depot, was the only place in Nelson County in the late 1960s that sold alcohol. One day a man had too many drinks, and his wife showed up with fire in her eyes, stood in the Depot door, and snarled his name. When the drunk man sped obediently to her side, someone remarked, "Well, would you look at that old rooster run." Such is the history of town names in our state. I still wonder whether the name had anything to do with the fact that the next town over is called Hen Peck. Whatever the truth may be, Joe Evans put the place on the map by selling over a million Rooster Run caps to truck drivers and celebrities alike.

"Ahh," Twain answered, "but that's my nightcap." Twain's drink of choice had to be bourbon, and it had to be from the limestone hills of Kentucky, which provide the water that gives Jim Beam and other regional bourbons the distinctive flavor that makes them the best in the world. For a crash course in whiskey mash, take a free tour of the *Jim Beam American Stillhouse* (502-543-9877; americanstillhouse.com) at 526 Happy Hollow Road in Clermont. Hours are 9 a.m. to 5 p.m. Monday through Saturday, noon to 4:30 p.m. Sunday.

Bardstown is dense with well-advertised, historically significant treasures, such as *My Old Kentucky Home State Park* and house of John Rowan. Rowan invited his cousin from Pittsburgh, Stephen Foster, to visit in 1852, and shortly afterward, Foster wrote the tune that is now our official state song. The mansion and gardens are open from 9 a.m. to 5 p.m. daily year-round. Admission is $7 for adults, $5 for seniors, and $3.50 for children. From early June through Labor Day, the famous musical, *The Stephen Foster Story,* is performed outdoors. You can't miss the signs. Call (502) 348-3502 for more information or check parks.ky.gov/parks/recreationparks/old-ky-home.

Near the park on Highway 49 at 1311 Gilkey Run Road is *Heaven Hill Distilleries,* touted as the largest family-owned distillery in the country. Three tours priced from $5 to $35 include a lesson in bourbon making and a visit to the bottling operation. This distillery makes Heaven Hill, Elijah Craig, and Evan Williams. Open 10 a.m. to 5 p.m. Tuesday through Saturday and, from March through October, also on Sunday from noon to 4 p.m. Call (502) 337-1000 or visit bourbonheritagecenter.com.

Two on-the-beaten-path restaurants in town are **Old Talbott Tavern,** the oldest western stagecoach stop in America, circa 1779, which also has bed-and-breakfast lodging in the old inn at 107 West Stephen Foster Avenue (502-348-3494; talbotts.com), and **My Old Kentucky Dinner Train** (502-348-7300; kydinnertrain.com), where you dine in vintage 1940s dining cars pulled by old diesel-electric engines on a two-hour ride to Limestone Springs and back.

At the corner of US 62 West, also called Stephen Foster Avenue, and Fifth Street at 310 West Stephen Foster Avenue is the **Saint Joseph Proto-Cathedral.** The cathedral, circa 1823, is the oldest west of the Alleghenies and contains a collection of paintings given by the French king Louis Philippe, Francis I, King of the Two Sicilies, and Pope Leo XII. Here's what impressed me: Six solid tree trunks, lathed and plastered, were transformed into the building's huge Corinthian columns. St. Joseph is open every day. Guided tours are given April through October from 9 a.m. to 5 p.m. Monday through Friday, Saturday from 9 a.m. to 3 p.m., and Sunday from 1 to 5 p.m. You can tour on your own November through March. Admission is free, but donations are encouraged. Call (502) 348-3126 or visit (hardstown .com/~stjoe).

Behind the cathedral at 114 North Fifth Street is **Spalding Hall,** circa 1826, a large brick building that was originally part of Saint Joseph College,

Who Really Invented the Steamboat?

Pay your respects to John Fitch, the unhappy inventor of the steamboat in 1791. Then listen to the Earth rumble when Robert Fulton turns over in his grave—wherever he's buried, may he rest in some peace. John Fitch was not born in Bardstown, but he died here after a lifetime of work on steam navigation and a lifetime of struggle with inventor James Rumsey, who, like Fulton, claimed to have been the first to apply it successfully. After failing to get sponsors, comparable to today's lusted-after research grants, Fitch came to Nelson County, built steamboat models, and tested them in local streams. *John Fitch's grave* in the square is marked by a small steamboat replica.

and later Saint Joseph Prep School. Two adjoining museums housed here are the **Bardstown Historical Museum** and the **Oscar Getz Museum of Whiskey History,** both free. Displays range from items like Jenny Lind's cape and Jesse James's hat to an original 1854 E. G. Booz bottle, which inspired the word booze, and a Carry Nation exhibit. Hours from May through October are 10 a.m. to 5 p.m. Monday to Friday, 10 a.m. to 4 p.m. Saturday, and noon to 4 p.m. Sunday. From November through April the museums open at 10 a.m. and close at 4 p.m., except on Sunday, when they are open from noon to 4 p.m., and Monday when they're closed. Call (502) 348-2999 for information or visit whiskeymuseum.com.

Think about the basis of homesteading—self-sufficiency. Now apply the concept to the visual arts and you will begin to appreciate Jim and Jeannette Cantrell. The **Bardstown Art Gallery,** at 214 West Stephen Foster Avenue, is a fine-art gallery, a framing shop, pottery and painting studios, a hand-set printing press operation, an office, a home, and a small book-sales business, which boasts one of the country's most comprehensive collections of Thomas Merton's writings. That both Cantrells have a love of high quality is apparent in everything from Jim's treatment of light and reflections in his oils to Jeannette's hand-set letterpress gallery announcements. Jeannette curates group and solo shows in addition to displaying Jim's originals in oil, watercolor, pen and ink, and anything else that catches his eclectic eye.

It was by accident that Jeannette became a Merton expert. One of the monks at the nearby abbey asked if she wouldn't mind selling a few of Merton's books to tourists. She started with a few copies of *Seven Storey Mountain,* and now she carries a respectable line of Merton's out-of-print writings, valuable limited editions, related scholarly works, and cassettes of Merton himself reading from his works or just talking about such subjects as Rilke's poetry, silence, art, and beauty. Hours at the Bardstown Art Gallery are officially "By Chance or By Appointment," but since the Cantrells live in the building, someone is usually there from 10:30 a.m. to 5 p.m. Tuesday through Saturday. Contact the Cantrells by calling (502) 348-6488. They have two web addresses: bardstownartgallery.com and thomasmertonbooks.com.

To visit Thomas Merton's residence, the **Abbey of Gethsemani,** oldest Cistercian monastery in the United States, follow US 31E south from Bardstown, veer left at Culvertown onto Highway 247, and watch for Trappists' signs. From the heart of Italy around AD 500, Saint Benedict developed a set of rules to help monks in a spiritually based community follow the example of Christ as closely as possible. These Trappist monks take vows to renounce the capacity to acquire and possess goods, to obey the house rules and the abbot's advice, and to remain celibate. Silence is encouraged but not required. "Enclosure," I've been told, "is enforced not so much to keep laypeople out as to keep the monks in." But these monks do indulge in some wandering. Thomas Merton, quintessential ascetic, aesthete monk from this abbey, was known to go "out" to lecture, to meet with other spiritual people, and occasionally to hear jazz. While visiting the abbey, I met a monk who travels to Owensboro for the barbecue festival. No matter what else you think, their life choice is radical.

Merton the Monk

Perhaps no one in Kentucky has done more to translate the personal journey of the spirit into a universal dialogue of understanding than Trappist monk, author, and poet, Thomas Merton. Born in Paris (France, not Kentucky), Merton traveled throughout Europe as a child with his parents, both of whom were artists. After graduating from Cambridge and later from Columbia, Thomas joined the Trappist order of monks, the most ascetic of the Roman Catholic monastic orders, at the Abbey of Gethsemani in the hills outside Bardstown. At his quiet retreat Merton immersed himself in prayer, mediation, and writing. His many books, essays, and articles address a breadth of issues with intensity and grace, including pacifism, race relations, world peace, and meditation. In his later work, Merton used his insight and wisdom to encourage an interfaith dialogue between the East and West, even traveling to meet with the Dalai Lama and to learn from Buddhist monastic orders. It was on one of these journeys in December of 1968 that Merton was tragically electrocuted by a faulty fan while in his bathtub. There is lingering suspicion that his death was not accidental. Merton's unflinching insistence on the universality of spiritual experience caused him to be both loved and despised during his lifetime—many Christians believed his work with other faiths to be blasphemy. Although the voices of discontent have quieted over the years, Merton's insights have continued to shape discussions of faith into the present day.

To learn more about Thomas Merton's life and works, visit the **Merton Center** at Bellarmine University, 2001 Newburg Road, Louisville, where his many photographs, drawings, and writings are preserved. The center is open from 8 a.m. to 5 p.m. Monday through Friday. The center is closed on all major holidays, including the university's spring break, so call ahead (502-452-8100).

Economic survival is perhaps the greatest difference between early and modern cloisters. The 76 resident monks make and sell fruitcakes, bourbon fudge, and three kinds of Port Salut Trappist cheese, a pungent, creamy, French-style aged cheese. Everyone takes part in all aspects of the work, from making cheese to doing dishes to answering the phone or laying sewer pipes. The slogan *Ora et Labora* means "prayer and work," but they don't have "all necessary things" on their 2,000-acre farm. They use hired help to raise the beef cattle and to do some construction and maintenance. Health care, for example, is sought in the secular world, including modern services such as weight-loss centers. To learn more about the abbey's farm products or to place an order, call (800) 549-0912 or use the website, gethsemanifarms.org.

Laypeople are welcome to join in parts of life at the abbey. Mass is always open to the public, if you can make it at 5:45 a.m. on weekdays (the monks will have been awake for hours by then), and there are a variety of other prayer services and vespers throughout the day. Sunday Mass is at 10:30 a.m. in the main chapel, a long, narrow, modern building where the choir's chant reverberates as if produced in outer space. Hospitality is historically part of the living monastic tradition. Saint Benedict instructed that the guest represents Christ and is to be welcomed and cared for by the community. Anyone is welcome to make a retreat at the Abbey, in the words of Merton, "to entertain silence in the heart and listen for the voice of God—to pray for your own discovery." Abbey retreats are silent, unstructured, and undirected (speaking is permitted in designated areas). Gethsemani has a retreat house with 30 rooms (with private bathrooms and air-conditioning) that can be reserved for personal or group retreats. Women are welcome during the first and third full weeks of each month (that's Monday to Monday), and men can make retreats during the second and fourth weeks. Call far in advance at (502) 549-3117. For a group day visit, call (502) 549-4129. For more information, write Abbey of Gethsemani, 3642 Monks Road, Trappist 40051 or visit monks.org.

If you drive south from Bardstown on US 31E, you will arrive in the tiny town of **New Haven.** Downtown on Main Street the old train depot now houses the **Kentucky Railway Museum,** where you can hop a train to Boston—that's Bawston, Kentucky—11 miles away on the old Louisville & Nashville Railroad's former Lebanon Branch. Members of the museum completely restored an L&N steam locomotive (No. 152) and the streamlined

No. 32 of the former Monon, made in the late 1940s. When these babies pump by, you feel your heart making reply. From March through December trips run between 10 a.m. and 4 p.m. on weekends, when the museum and gift shop are also open. In the summer there are excursions daily, except Monday. For exact fares, times, and dates, contact the Kentucky Railway Museum, P.O. Box 240, New Haven 40051-0240, or call (502) 549-5470 or (800) 272-0152 or check kyrail.org.

trueblue

Marion County is located at the geographic center of Kentucky.

To visit one of the state's most famous and picturesque whiskey distilleries, take US 52 east from New Haven, or Highway 49 south from Bardstown, to Loretto; then take US 52 east until you see the sign on the left for *Maker's Mark Distillery.* Like the process, the facility is old. In 1953 Bill Samuels Sr. bought the shabby country distillery where folks were accustomed to filling their own jugs straight from casks of whiskey in the Quart House. Now Maker's Mark is known around the world for its supersmooth bourbon (nicknamed "Kentucky champagne"). The distillery is open year-round from 9:30 a.m. to 3:30 p.m. Monday through Saturday. Also from March through December, the distillery is open on Sunday from 11:30 a.m. to 3:30 p.m. Tours and bourbon tastings cost $9 per adult. For more information, call (270) 865-2099 or visit makersmark.com.

In Loretto take Highway 49 north, then veer right at a fork in the road onto Highway 152. You'll soon see the sign for *Loretto Motherhouse.* The Sisters of Loretto, founded in central Kentucky in 1812, was one of the first American religious communities of women. The sisters moved here in 1824 from Little Loretto at nearby St. Charles. Near the entrance of the grounds is the restored cabin, circa 1808, of Father Charles Nerinckx, founder of the order. Going toward the cemetery you'll see one of the country's first outdoor Stations of the Seven Dolors, installed in 1911. On the east side of the drive, you'll see *Knobs Haven Retreat,* a center at which folks can reserve space for taking a serious, personal retreat. For rates and further information, write Director, Knobs Haven, Nerinx 40049, or call (270) 865-2621; lorettocommunity.org.

Next to the main church and convent, circa 1860–63, you'll notice a group of abstract sculptures in various media. This is the work of Jeanne

Dueber, nun and artist in residence at Loretto. Her studio is in ***Rhodes Hall Art Gallery,*** at the north end of the driveway. Her work is amazing in its variety and feeling, and her exploration of form is almost religious. Large, refined abstract sculptures in wood, resin, metal, and paper fill the big rooms. A large willow, struck by lightning, has been transformed into a powerful piece called *Tempest*, in which Dueber strategically added heads and arms of a man and a woman in such a way that they seem to be sliding away from each other while reaching toward each other. Many pieces are playful, like a series on Pelé, the soccer star, or an academic charcoal drawing of a heavy, drooping nude woman entitled *Homage to Gravity*. Pieces about Prometheus, ecstasy, companionship, and yoga positions accompany overtly religious work such as crucifixes for churches. If she's working in the first-floor studio and isn't too busy, tell her what you think. You can visit the gallery daily from 9 a.m. to 5 p.m. To buy a piece, just put your money in the slotted box by the stairs—a self-service fine-art gallery. Write Jeanne Dueber, Rhodes Hall, Nerinx 40040, or call the Loretto Motherhouse, (270) 865-5811, ext. 2068.

Another retreat center located near New Haven and the Abbey of Gethsemani is ***Bethany Spring*** (115 Dee Head Road; 502-549-8277; bethanyspring.org), sponsored by the Sisters of Charity of Nazareth. Private or directed spiritual retreats are offered to adults of all faiths and cultures. There are three housing options available. The Main House can accommodate up to eight people and includes a home-cooked dinner nightly and simple fare made available for other meals. The cottage for couples, called Emmaus, is a simple and lovely retreat spot for two with a kitchen where guests cook their own meals. The retreat is open year-round and rates start at $65 per person.

For more local lodging head south on Highway 49 into ***Lebanon*** and check into the ***Myrtledene Bed and Breakfast*** at 370 North Spalding Avenue. The house is an 1833 formal brick affair with a colonial columned portico. Famous Confederate raider Gen. John Hunt Morgan used Myrtledene for headquarters in 1862, and a year later, when he returned with the intention of destroying Lebanon, it was from here that he waved the white flag of truce. During his stay, Morgan rode his horse into the front door of Myrtledene and up the front steps; the hoof prints survived well into the 20th century. A room with full breakfast costs $95 a night. Call (270)

Turtleman Hometown Honors Critter Catcher

Air bubbles mark the spot on the murky pond where Ernie Brown Jr. has slipped underwater to capture the elusive snapping turtle. Watching intently from the sidelines, Neal James urges, "Be careful, buddy." Just as watchers begin to worry that the turtle might have won the wrestling match, Ernie splashes to the surface, triumphantly holding the turtle by the tail. Shouting his trademark Indian yell, Ernie declares it, "Live action!"

Folks in his Kentucky hometown of Lebanon (pop. 5,587) share the story of their native son who has come to be known as Turtleman. A new museum exhibit recently opened to satisfy the curiosity of travelers who want to know more about the Animal Planet star in the *Call of the Wildman* series. It all goes back to Ernie's dirt-poor childhood when the oldest of four children of Lola and Ernie Brown Sr. grew up in the Kentucky backwoods. Watching his uncle and father, the youngster learned to catch turtles with his bare hands. At the age of 7, Ernie caught his first snapping turtle.

Before long, Ernie became known as a critter catcher. Answering the calls of people whose homes or property had been invaded by pesky animals, Ernie has caught and relocated countless turtles, bats, snakes, porcupines, skunks, raccoons, foxes, venomous spiders, armadillos, turkeys, beavers, flying squirrels, and other animals with his bare hands. The payment for his services is usually whatever country folk can afford—homemade jam, canned tomatoes, pumpkins, fresh-baked pie, couple of chickens, rocking chair, handshake, thank-you hug, or bit of change for gas money.

Hitting the airwaves in November 2011, the Animals Planet's *Call of the Wildman* follows the adventures of Turtleman, his faithful canine companion Lolly—found wandering the streets looking for shelter during an ice storm—and his right-hand man Neal. But Turtleman hasn't escaped wrangling pesky animals without injury. A museum mannequin is dotted from head to toe with "band aids" recounting past hurts. Turtleman estimates he's been injured about 35 times in his critter career. Rolling up his sleeve to bare his twin feather tattoos symbolizing his belief that hopes and dreams and wishes do come true, Turtleman said he encourages everyone to pursue their goals—no matter how impossible they seem. "I'm living proof you can do it."

For more information: Contact the Lebanon Tourism & Convention Commission at (270) 602 0021; visitlebanonky.com.

692-2223 for reservations. Also check the website, myrtledene.com. By the way, Union soldiers from the 1862 Battle of Perryville are buried in *Lebanon's National Cemetery.*

Since Lebanon is out of the way, you might be happy to know that the little town boasts a classy eating establishment at 157 West Main Street called *Henning's Restaurant* (270-692-6843). In addition to occupying a handsomely restored building in the historic district, the restaurant offers homemade soups, entrees, breads, and desserts, recommended by the locals. The restaurant is open Monday through Friday from 9 a.m. to 5 p.m.

The Cedarwood Restaurant at 660 East Main Street (270-692-4474; cedarwoodrestaurant.com) features family-style meals, including fried green tomatoes and fried dill pickles. The restaurant's chili cheese fries—French fries covered with chili con carne and cheddar cheese—are popular.

Although there were once more than 400 covered bridges in Kentucky, there are now only 13. The *Mount Zion Bridge* (referred to in some quarters as the Beech Fork or Mooresville Bridge), in the northwest corner of Washington County, is the only remaining example of two-span Burr Arch construction and, at 102 feet, is the longest in the state. It was almost lost recently before the county restabilized the piers, and it may yet be moved to a more accessible location. For now, the easiest way to see it is to get off the Blue Grass Parkway at exit 34 and go south on Highway 55; at Mooresville take Highway 458 north and watch for the bridge on the left spanning the Beech Fork Creek. The bridge is closed to traffic, but you can walk through it.

Like nearby *Hodgenville* (covered in the South-Central Kentucky chapter), central Washington County is a repository of sites and stories connected to Abraham Lincoln. Abe's parents, Thomas Lincoln and Nancy Hanks, were from this area, and several of their family buildings are restored or replicated. For details go by the *Lincoln Homestead State Park* at the intersection of Highways 438 and 528, just 5 miles north of Springfield off US 150 at 5079 Lincoln Park Road. An 18-hole golf course has been built on old Mordecai Lincoln's land, and I'll bet he's rolling over violently in his grave. The park also has several log structures, such as the original Berry Home, where Nancy Hanks lived when she and Thomas were courting. While the golf course is open year-round, the museum is seasonal; it's open May through September Thursday through Sunday from 10 a.m. to 5:30 p.m.

and on weekends only in October. The cabin is closed November 1 through April 30. Ask at the park for a map of the Lincoln Heritage Trail. For more information call (859) 336-7461 or visit parks.ky.gov/parks/recreationparks/ Lincoln-homestead.

In downtown *Springfield* notice the *Washington County Courthouse* on Main Street (859-336-5425). Built in 1816, it is the oldest courthouse still in use in Kentucky. Records in the files, including the marriage certificate of Abraham Lincoln's parents, date back to 1792. If court isn't in session, look at copies of this and other documents hanging on the walls. It's open from 8:30 a.m. to 4:30 p.m. Monday through Friday and from 9 a.m. to noon Saturday.

In 1822 Father Samuel Wilson, a Dominican priest in Springfield, asked young women of the parish to dedicate their lives to Christian education. One of those who answered the call was Maria Sansbury. A year later she and eight other women opened St. Magdalen Academy in a converted building on the banks of Cartwright Creek. As Mother Angela, Maria is considered the founder of the first order of Dominican Sisters in the United States. In 1891 their school became Saint Catharine Academy, and in 1920 the sisters established a teachers college. The academy has long been closed, but the college survives today as Saint Catharine College, a two-year liberal arts institution (859-336-5082; sccky.edu). The *Saint Catharine Motherhouse* (859-336-9303), 2 miles west of town on US 150, is under renovation, but visitors are welcome. Not too far away on US 52, about ½ mile off US 150, is the *Saint Rose Proto-Priory.* Founded in 1806, this was the first Catholic educational institution west of the Alleghenies. Students included Jefferson Davis, who would become the president of the Confederacy. Tours of the priory are by appointment; call (859) 336-3121.

More Good Lodging in Central Kentucky

Ask about lower-priced weekend specials and other special rates.

BARDSTOWN

Beautiful Dreamer Bed & Breakfast
440 East Stephen Foster Avenue
(502) 348-4004 or
(800) 811-8312
bdreamerbb.com
A new home built in classic Federal style, across from My Old Kentucky Home.

Hampton Inn Bardstown
985 Chambers Boulevard
(502) 349-0100 or
(800) HAMPTON
Newer motel with pool.

Jailer's Inn
111 West Stephen Foster Avenue
(502) 348-5551 or
(800) 948-5551
jailersinn.com
Renovated 1819 historic limestone jailhouse, with Jacuzzi suites and one humorously decorated "cell room."

BEREA

The Doctor's Inn
617 Chestnut Street
(859) 986-3042
doctorsinnofbereaky.com
Luxurious B&B accommodations in an elegant colonial style mansion.

DANVILLE

Golden Lion Bed & Breakfast
243 North Third Street
(859) 583-1895
thegoldenlionbb.com
Beautiful home with an excellent genealogy library on the Jones name.

FRANKFORT

The Meeting House
519 Ann Street
(502) 226-3226
themeetinghousebandb.com
1849 Civil War–era home located in the historic district.

GEORGETOWN

Jordan Farm
4091 Newtown Pike
(502) 863-1944 (evening) or (859) 321-5705 (day)
jordanfarmbandb.com
Bed-and-breakfast in a carriage house on thoroughbred horse farm. It has a fishing lake!

HARRODSBURG

Beaumont Inn
638 Beaumont Inn Drive
(859) 734-3381
beaumontinn.com
Since 1919, the Beaumont Inn has been welcoming guests as Kentucky's oldest family-operated bed and breakfast inn. Beaumont offers beautiful rooms with modern comforts in three historic buildings, as well as a fine-dining restaurant.

LEXINGTON

Gratz Park Inn
120 West Second Street
(800) 752-4166
gratzparkinn.com
A historic downtown hotel complete with a ghost or two.

Swann's Nest at Cygnet Farm
3463 Rosalie Lane
(859) 226-0095
swannsnest.com
Distinctively appointed suites and rooms on a thoroughbred farm near Keeneland Race Course.

LOUISVILLE

The Brown Hotel
335 West Broadway
(502) 583-1234 or
(888) 387-0498
brownhotel.com
A 1920s landmark with an
excellent restaurant, home
of the legendary Hot
Brown sandwich. Find the
recipe on the website.

**DuPont Mansion Bed
and Breakfast**
1317 South Fourth Street
(502) 638-0045
dupontmansion.com
Elegant 1884 Italianate
house with marble
mantels and period
furniture.

Galt House
140 North Fourth Street
(502) 589-5200
galthouse.com
Overlooking the Ohio
River.

Seelbach Hilton
500 South Fourth Avenue
(502) 585-3200 or
(800) 333-3399
seelbachhilton.com
A luxurious Beaux Arts
showplace in the heart of
downtown.

NEW HAVEN

Sherwood Inn
138 South Main Street
(502) 549-3386
Bed-and-breakfast in a
restored railroad hotel
next to the Kentucky
Railway Museum.

PARIS

**Country Charm Historic
Farmhouse Bed and
Breakfast**
505 Hutchinson Road
(859) 988-1006
countrycharm.net
Bed-and-breakfast with
one room or suite in the
main house and a three-
bedroom stand-alone
cottage.

**The Treehouse at
Stoner Creek Bed and
Breakfast**
131 Taylor Avenue
(859) 987-6251 or cell
(859) 707-0369
treehouseatstonercreek
.com
Bed-and-breakfast right
downtown in an unusual
creekside house. Canoes
and pontoon rides are
available to guests.

RICHMOND

The Bennett House
419 West Main Street
(859) 623-7876
bennetthousebb.com
Romanesque-style house,
on the National Register of
Historic Places.

SPRINGFIELD

**Maple Hill Manor Bed
and Breakfast**
2½ miles east out of
Springfield on US 150
(Perryville Road) at 2941
Perryville Road
(859) 336-3075 or
(800) 886-7546
maplehillmanor.com
An antebellum Greek
Revival mansion, circa
1851, restored with
Jacuzzis and porch grills
with every room.

VERSAILLES

Montgomery Inn
270 Montgomery Avenue
(859) 251-4103
montgomeryinnbnb.com
Large restored Victorian
home with numerous
Jacuzzis and electric
fireplaces. Gourmet
breakfast is featured; 10
guest suites.

WINCHESTER

**Guerrant Mountain
Mission Bed and
Breakfast**
21 Valentine Court
(859) 745-1284

House on Belmont B&B
331 Belmont Avenue
(859) 745-0850
houseonbelmont.com
Renovated, elegant 1872
home in downtown.
Fireplace, Jacuzzi.

More Fun Places to Eat in Central Kentucky

BEREA

Boone Tavern Restaurant
100 Main Street
(800) 678-8946
boonetavernhotel.com
Elegant dining with award-winning "Kentucky Proud" cuisine.

BURGIN

The Village Inn
501 East Main Street
(859) 748-5943
villageinn.com
If you like country cooking, this is your place. Locals who have moved away are drawn back like moths to flame.

CYNTHIANA

Biancke's Restaurant
102 South Main Street
(859) 234-3443
bianckes.net
Open 7 a.m. to 9 p.m. Monday through Saturday and 9 a.m. to 2 p.m. Sunday. It's the spot where everyone goes—teenagers on prom night, local grandmas and tile setters, and visitors alike. Great homemade pies.

FRANKFORT

Gibby's
204 West Broadway
(502) 223-4429
eatatgibbys.com
Open Monday through Saturday 10:30 a.m. to 9 p.m., closed Sunday. Hot Italian entrees, pasta, fresh gourmet salads, sandwiches, soups, and ice cream.

Jim's Seafood
950 Wilkinson Boulevard
(502) 223-7448
jimseafood.com
Seafood while you watch the Kentucky River out the window.

Serafini Broadway at the Saint Clair
pedestrian mall at 243 West Broadway Street
(502) 875-5599
serafinifrankfort.com
Lunch Monday through Friday 11 a.m. to 3 p.m. Dinner Monday through Saturday 4:30 to 10 p.m.

HARRODSBURG

Kentucky Fudge Company and Cafe
225 South Main Street
(859) 733-0088
kentuckyfudge company.com
An 1865 pharmacy serving floats, fudge, and ice cream.

Old Owl Tavern
638 Beaumont Inn Drive
(859) 734-3381
bcaumontinn.com
Casual fine dining with 70 different bourbons to choose from.

LEXINGTON

a la lucie
159 North Limestone (downtown)
(859) 252-5277
alalucie. com
Possibly the best restaurant in Lexington. Excellent, creative nouvelle cuisine in a glamorous and tightly packed space. Reservations are recommended.

Natasha's Bistro & Bar
112 Esplanade
(859) 259-2754
bistro.beetnik.com
Eclectic international cuisine with an attached boutique selling items from Slavic cultures and live entertainment on weekend nights.

Parkette Drive-In
1230 East New Circle
Road
(859) 254-8723
theparkette.com
Drive-through? No, a real
drive-in, with sign, service,
and menu much the same
as when it opened in
1952. A new '50s retro
dining room has been
added. Slide into a seat
and relive those happy
days.

Planet Thai
2417 Nicholasville Road
(859) 373-8269
planetthai.net
Linen napkins, moderate
prices, plentiful vegetarian
options, fabulous flavors,
enough said.

Ramsey's Diner
151 West Zandale Road
(859) 259-2708
4391 Harrodsburg Road
(859) 219-1626
4053 Tates Creek Road
(859) 271-2638
and 3090 Helmsdale
Place
(859) 264-9396
ramseysdiners.com
Down-to-earth menu of
"classy comfort food"—
even Brussels sprouts and
crawfish.

LOUISVILLE

Lilly's
1147 Bardstown Road
(502) 451-0447
lillyslapeche.com
Upscale bistro and
gourmet-to-go with
award-winning chef.

Queen of Sheba
2804 Taylorsville Road
502-459-6301
queenofsheba
louisville.com
Authentic Ethiopian
cuisine. Traditionally
served by tearing off a
piece of Ethiopian flat
bread, scooping the food
with it and placing it in
your mouth. However,
the restaurant is happy
to serve entrees with
silverware.

Vincenzo's
150 South Fifth Street
(502) 580-1350
vincenzositalian
restaurant.com
Fine Italian cuisine by
Agostino Gabriele.
Winner of more than 20
awards. Check out the
website for photos and
names of some of its
diverse clientele, including
Hillary Clinton, Usher,
Muhammad Ali, and Al
Pacino.

MOUNT STERLING

**Melini Cucina Italian
Ristorante**
908 Indian Mound Drive
(859) 497-7066
melinicucina.net
Owned by a fabulous
cook born and raised
in Italy. Ham calzone,
spinach and veggie
calzones, Melini stromboli,
and baked lasagna. Select
Italian wines. Open daily
for lunch and dinner.

NEW HAVEN

Sherwood Inn
138 South Main Street
(502) 549-3386
Dinner served
Wednesday, Friday, and
Saturday.

PARIS

Paradise Cafe
731 Main Street
(859) 987-8383
Reasonably priced lunch
and dinner in the world's
tallest three-story building
(yes, it's in the *Guinness
Book*!).

WINCHESTER

Hall's on the River
1225 Athens-Boonesboro
Road
(859) 527-6620
hallsontheriver.com
Hall's is famous for
seafood entrees and
take-home foods like beer
cheese.

Eastern Kentucky

Most of North America is inhabited by a wild soup of dissenters' descendants, but what makes eastern Kentucky different is the mountains.

The Appalachian Mountains are a long, beautiful line of steep, nearly impregnable rock that has always tended to keep outsiders out and insiders in. Although the Appalachian culture initially strikes outsiders as foreign, visiting can have the strong allure of a homecoming, in part because your roots may be in European cultures that are better preserved here than anywhere else in the big melting pot. The isolation also has caused eastern Kentuckians to live close to the land, close to one another, and to survive self-sufficiently. As you meet people, listen to the language of this region, the beautiful phrases loaded with humor, knowledge of quirky human nature, and sensitivity to the cycles of the natural world.

There are opportunities in this region to expose yourself to very fine traditional craftsmanship by meeting individual artists or craftspeople and by visiting craft cooperatives where knowledge and tools are being shared with those who want to take the baton. Music and dance, for which

AUTHOR'S FAVORITE PLACES IN
EASTERN KENTUCKY

Bad Branch State Nature Preserve
near Whitesburg
(502) 573-2886
naturepreserves.ky.gov/nature
preserves/pages/badbranch.aspx

Carter Caves State Resort
Park Olive Hill
(606) 286-4411 or (800) 325-0059
parks.ky.gov/parks/resortparks/carter
-caves/default.aspx

Furnace Mountain
Write for information to the Abbess
Box 545
Clay City 40312
furnacemountain.org

Lilley Cornett Woods Skyline
(606) 633-5828
naturalareas.eku.edu

Mine Portal Number 31
Lynch
(606) 848-1530
portal31.org

Mountain Homeplace
Paintsville
(606) 297-1850
mountainhomeplace.com

Red River Gorge
(contact Natural Bridge State Resort
Park) Slade
(606) 663-2214
redrivergorge.com

Seedtime on the Cumberland
music festival in early June at
Appalshop
Whitesburg
(606) 633-0108
seedtimefestival.org

mountaineers have always been admired, have developed in fascinating ways and play an important role in the life of this region. Festivals and community dances, which are always open to visitors, are good events to attend if you want to get an authentic taste of the music here. In addition to music, the mountains themselves can soothe the soul.

I have a wonderful recent memory of traveling through the mountains at the end of a long, hot day and stopping on a bridge where a "passel" of people had gathered. Below, by the side of a wide brook, a small revival was in progress. Babies were being passed from lap to lap, and people of all ages were sitting in folding chairs by the little stage, clapping and singing. A sweet hymn in an irresistible minor key rising just above the constant tumble of the water calmed me and opened my eyes to the changing mountains, rosy in the last light of the setting sun. Even in the heat of summer, a mist gathers in the folds and hollows of the land and baptizes everyone equally, even passersby.

Through the Gap

Dr. Thomas Walker was hired by Virginia's Loyal Land Company to go west in search of fertile settling land. In 1750, when Walker found the only natural route west, a divide he named Cumberland Gap, he built a small cabin to claim the territory, mapped the route, and went home. You can visit a replica of Walker's crude cabin at the **Dr. Thomas Walker State Historic Site** on Highway 459 off US 25E just southeast of Barbourville (606-546-4400; parks.ky.gov/parks/historicsites/Thomas-walker). Though Walker and his group missed reaching the bluegrass region by just a few days of traveling, they did succeed in blazing a trail through the mountains for more than 300,000 pioneers to roll toward a new life in the West. The house and grounds are open year-round.

The 20,000 acres of **Cumberland Gap National Historic Park,** off US 25E south of Middlesboro (nps.gov/cuga), include the 800-foot natural break in the Cumberland Mountains through which Native Americans and, later, Daniel Boone and other settlers entered Kentucky. Go to Pinnacle Overlook and you can see three states, as well as the twin tunnels that go 4,600 feet through the mountain to connect Kentucky and Tennessee. Seventeen years in the making, the tunnels finally opened in 1996, replacing a stretch of US 25E so treacherous that it was known as Massacre Mountain. Near the overlook is **Fort McCook,** which was built by Confederate troops to guard the passage.

trueblue

Between 1750 and 1783, some 12,000 settlers had entered Kentucky through the Cumberland Gap.

More than 55 miles of hiking trails wind through the park, but one of the most interesting is the **Ridge Trail** on Brush Mountain, which runs the entire length of the park from the Pinnacle Overlook to a site on the far eastern side of the park called White Rocks, where, on a clear day, you can actually see the Great Smoky Mountains. Early pioneer records note that the 600-foot-high white limestone rock face was an important landmark.

Other great hiking destinations include an area called *Indian Rocks,* where Native people used to fashion flint tools (there are still remnants of their work), and the *Goose Nest Sink,* a massive sinkhole created when part of a cave ceiling collapsed. Civil War sentries viewed the valley from this spot, where now you can look down into the canopies of 100-foot-high trees. The Sand Cave is an extraordinarily beautiful and humbling space, a wide cave with a one-and-a-half-acre sand floor next to a 100-foot-high waterfall. One popular stop on the trail is the *Hensley Settlement,* a restored cluster of farms and houses inhabited from 1903 until 1951. To drive, take the Brownies Creek Road from Cubbage, or take a shuttle from the visitor center in Middlesboro, which is open daily from 8 a.m. to 5 p.m. For all park information, stop by the center during business hours, or call (606) 248-2817. Write to the Cumberland Gap National Historic Park for campsite reservations and so forth at P.O. Box 1848, Middlesboro 40965.

On the second floor of the visitor center at the national park is the Southern Highland Craft Guild's retail gallery, *Cumberland Crafts* (606-242-3699; southernhighlandguild.org). The guild is a highly competitive juried craft organization that showcases about 250 artists from southern Appalachia. All the work is handmade and includes pottery, glass, fiber, paper, quilting, wood, metals, jewelry, and more. Artist demonstrations are often available. Gallery hours are seven days a week from 9 a.m. to 5 p.m. Much of the Wilderness Trail that early settlers used was paved to become US 25E. But the rerouting of motorized traffic between Middlesboro and Tennessee through the modern Cumberland Gap Tunnel, which opened in 1996, is enabling the original trail to be restored so visitors can have a better sense of what the area looked like in the 1700s. Middlesboro is just north of the Gap, outside the national park, in a circular basin that was probably formed between 30 million and 300 million years ago by a large meteor that disintegrated or was blown back into space upon impact. Another possibility is that the depression was formed by the collapse of an underground cavern, since no meteor fragments have been found.

Coal fragments, chunks, and seams, on the other hand, are everywhere and at the heart of the recent history of the area. The *Bell County Chamber of Commerce* (606-248-1075; bellcountychamber.net) at 189 North Twentieth Street is housed in a building faced with 40 tons of bituminous coal.

Next door is *The Coal House Museum,* (cityofmiddlesborokentucky.org), a little open-air collection of mining artifacts—old mine train cars, headlamps, drill bits, and photos. Ask about the *Cumberland Mountain Fall Festival,* which is held annually in Middlesboro the first weekend of October as a celebration of the area's English heritage. Call the Tourism Office at (606) 248-2482, or visit bellcountytourism.com for information about any of these topics.

Follow North Twentieth Street to the top of the hill, turn left on Edgewood, right onto Arthur Heights, and left when the road comes to the edge of the cliff. The second house on the left at 208 Arthur Heights is *Cumberland Manor,* a 20-room grand Victorian home built in the early 1890s especially for John B. Cary, the secretary-treasurer of Middlesboro Town Company, the English company that developed the Cumberland Gap area. (In the early 1900s the U.S. Post Office Americanized the official spelling of the town's name from the English *-ough* to *-oro,* but you still see both spellings in use.) The street is named after Alexander Arthur, Middlesboro's founder. Cumberland Manor has six rooms available for between $109 and $159 per night. A tornado that narrowly missed the house in the late 1980s managed to clear the trees from the front hillside, leaving an open view of the town below. Call (606) 248-4299 for reservations or visit cumberland manorbedandbreakfast.com

Between Middlesboro and Pineville is the *Kentucky Ridge State Forest,* which includes *Pine Mountain State Resort Park.* Both have entrances off US 25E. Follow signs to the Herndon J. Evans Lodge at the top of the mountain, where you can get trail maps and park information. Call (606) 337-3066 or (800) 325-1712 or visit parks.ky.gov/parks/resort-parks/pine-mountain. At the park's

true*blue*

Middlesboro is home to the oldest municipal golf course in the nation.

nature center, notice what looks like a petrified tree trunk by the entrance. The trunk was found at a strip mine in northwest Bell County. The tree, which may be 300 million years old, grew in a swampy area and was buried in flood sediments, which caused it to rot. Over the course of a few million years, sand percolated through the cavity and hardened, making a fossilized sandstone cast of the tree.

One of the most special trails in the whole state park system is the *Hemlock Garden Trail,* which goes through a 782-acre area protected by the Nature Preserves system. The Hemlock Garden is a ravine featuring massive hemlocks, tulip poplars, beech trees, and a beautiful mountain brook. On the southwestern boundary of the park, it can be reached on the *Laurel Cove Trail* or the *Rock Hotel Trail.* Linger as long as you are able. After all, how often are you in the presence of living beings more than 200 years old?

During the last weekend in May, the *Mountain Laurel Festival* (606-337-6103; tmlf.org) is held to celebrate the blooming of the much-loved mountain flower. The whole event is held in the Laurel Cove Amphitheater, a beautiful natural stage that seats more than 3,000 people, and culminates in the crowning of a Mountain Laurel Queen. The *Great American Dulcimer Festival* (800-325-1712; americandulcimerconvention.com) is also held outdoors during the third or fourth weekend of September. This is a wonderful, small festival during which dulcimer makers sell, demonstrate, and teach in booths during the day. At night spectators wrap up in quilts under the stars and watch some of the best performers play on a stage behind a reflective pond. Styles range from traditional to classical, pop, big band, and country rock, all played on lap or hammered dulcimers.

There is a special place to eat any meal of the day or to get an afternoon pick-me-up in the form of an old-fashioned hot-fudge sundae in downtown Pineville. You just have to stop by the *Flocoe Restaurant* (606-337-2034) at 122 Kentucky Avenue at Walnut Street directly across from the Bell County Courthouse. The building was formerly an apothecary and soda fountain. The daughter of the pharmacist restored it to its glory and opened this comfortable restaurant. The Flocoe—named for a woman named Flo (daughter of the man who built the building) and her friend Coe—dates back to the 1920s. It's been a gathering place for generations. The fare is hearty "homestyle"—barbecue, potato salad, soup, beans, and lots of fruit cobbler. The Thursday special is the

trueblue

Among the country music stars from eastern Kentucky are Billy Ray Cyrus from Greenup County, the Judds from Ashland, Tom T. Hall from Carter County, Keith Whitley from Elliot County, Loretta Lynn and Crystal Gayle from Johnson County, and Dwight Yoakam from Floyd County.

best seller—chicken and dumplings with mixed greens. Friday features soup beans and cornbread. Meals are accompanied, of course, by strong black coffee. Flocoe is open Tuesday through Friday from 7:30 a.m. to 4 p.m.

Eighteen miles southwest of Pineville via Highway 190 in Frakes is the **Henderson Settlement,** a United Methodist ministry started in 1925 as a school and community outreach center. Now Henderson Settlement is a multipurpose community service facility and the only Methodist mission in the country with an agricultural development program—1,300 acres of land, livestock, orchards, gardens, and a big community greenhouse. The old high school houses a library, offices, and a weaving room where people can learn and pursue the craft. Visitors are welcome to tour the place or to come for an extended stay for a retreat or work camp. Call ahead for reservations at (606) 337-3613; hendersonsettlement.com.

The Red Bird Mission in Beverly is another similar United Methodist mission complex with a school, health clinic, community outreach program, work camps, and a craft shop. From Pineville follow Highway 66 north for 26 miles. From the Daniel Boone Parkway, take exit 34 and go south on Highway 66 into the mission at 80 Queendale Center. Directly across the street from the mission hospital is **Red Bird Mission Crafts,** in operation since 1921. The area craftspeople represented there are especially skilled at making hickory bark furniture, exquisite willow baskets, and handwoven rugs. Hours are 9 a.m. to 4 p.m. Monday through Friday. You can reach the craft shop at (606) 598-2709, (800) 898-2709, or rbmission.org.

Head northeast on US 119 to **Harlan,** a little mountain town populated primarily by people of Welsh descent. Natives say that because the Welsh have always been fantastic vocalists, it's no surprise that Harlan's fame is musical. The **Harlan Boys' Choir,** an all-male, award-winning choir, received national acclaim after performing at the inauguration of President George H. W. Bush in 1989. What most people don't know is that the choir was an offshoot of a 1945 girls' group called **The Harlan Musettes,** now under the direction of Marilyn Schraeder. Mary Beth Christman directs the boys, who range from third grade through high school. The repertoire is classical and the sound exquisite. Visit the website at harlanboyschoir.com for a performance schedule.

Another Harlan original is the **Poke Sallet Festival,** held during the first full weekend in June. The festival affords you plenty of opportunities to eat poke sallet, barbecued chicken, corn pone, and buttermilk—a mountain meal if ever there was one. Poke sallet is a cold salad of very young poke plant leaves (which are bitter and mildly poisonous when the plant is several months older); the leaves are cooked way down, like turnip greens, and have a flavor similar to asparagus. They're said to have healing powers. Call (606) 573-4495 or visit pokesalletfestival.com for more information on the festival.

Some people perpetually have fishing on the brain. If that describes you, try your luck at two wildlife management areas, *Cranks Creek Lake* and *Martins Fork Lake* (harlancountytrails.com), just south of Harlan. Both are beautiful spots for just relaxing, too.

If you like to explore on foot, another gorgeous place to spend time in any season is *Stone Mountain* (naturepreserves.ky.gov/nature preserves/pages/stonemtn.aspx), a 200-acre gorge that is part wilderness and part history lesson. From Harlan take US 421 south to Highway 1138 and park in the Herb Smith lot. The long, twisty hike up the hollow of Stone Mountain follows a historic, hundred-year-old wagon road that leads to an amazing tunnel, which was built for wagon-carried freight to be connected with a Virginia railroad. The tunnel was built by punching through the sandstone caprock with hand-operated drills, hammers, and not a little black powder. At the Virginia end of the tunnel, you can see the vast Powell Valley.

Head north of Harlan on US 421, straight up the mountain. At the summit of Pine Mountain, you'll see a sign for *The Little Shepherd Trail,* a 38-mile gravel trail that runs along the ridge of the 2,800-foot Black Mountain all the way to Whitesburg.

On the other side of Pine Mountain, make a hard right onto Highway 221, go east "a fur piece" (in this case, about 10 miles) and turn onto Highway 510, then immediately into the driveway of the *Pine Mountain Settlement School* (606-558-3571; pinemountainsettlementschool.com) at 36 Highway 510. Here you will find 800 acres of forest and farmland, native woods, and stone buildings. The history of the place begins with an early settler named William Creech, who recognized the need for a school based on what he knew of a settlement school in Hindman. That school was founded by Katherine Pettit, who, in turn, based her ideas on Jane Addams's work in urban settings. From 1913 until 1972 the Pine Mountain Settlement

Harry M. Caudill

Be sure to stop at one of the high lookout points along US 119, where you can get a more abstract sense of the texture and shape of the land. You'll also get a very nonabstract sense of the meaning of "mountaintop removal," a method of strip mining coal by taking off whatever is above it, usually the entire top of a mountain. With this panorama before you, pay mental tribute to one of Letcher County's great native sons, the late Harry M. Caudill: writer, teacher, lawyer, politician, and outspoken activist in Appalachian social and economic issues. His historical writings, including *Night Comes to the Cumberlands* and *Theirs Be the Power,* are disturbing and powerful books about the troubled power relations in these mountains. In his storyteller (preserver) mode, Caudill wrote a number of honest, intimate portraits of his people in books such as *The Mountain, the Miner and the Lord.*

School was a remarkably wholesome and successful school, community center, and medical facility.

After the regular school closed in 1972, the folks at Pine Mountain decided to flow with the real needs of the community, and it became an environmental education center. Good timing—eastern Kentucky was and is suffering massive environmental exploitation in a nation tending toward over consumption, waste of resources, overpopulation, and a general lack of concern for and understanding of the fragile, crucial cycles of the natural world. The school definitely takes an activist approach. In 2000 the school led a successful effort petitioning the state of Kentucky to declare 5,226 acres unsuitable for surface mining. The acreage includes the school, its view shed, and a water source area on the south face of Pine Mountain. To introduce the petition, school representatives used the words of founder William Creech Sr., just as he wrote them in 1915: "I don't look after wealth for them. I look after the prosperity of our nation. I want all young-uns taught to serve the livin' God. Of course, they won't do that, but they can have good and evil laid before them and they can choose which they will. I have heart and cravin' that our people may grow better. I have deeded my land to the Pine Mountain Settlement School to be used for school purposes as long as the Constitution of the United States stands. Hopin' it may make a bright and intelligent people after I'm dead and gone." For more information, write Pine Mountain Settlement School, 36 Highway 510, Bledsoe 40810. Visitors are welcome to tour the fascinating campus daily from 8 a.m. to 8 p.m.

The next major town to the east is *Cumberland.* It's small (population 2,172) but busy. In the beginning, though, it was really small; in 1870 six families settled this spot, and by 1911 Cumberland was incorporated with a population of 185 souls.

In town follow the signs to the campus of Cumberland's Southeast Community College, then to its Godbey *Appalachian Cultural and Fine Arts Center,* at 700 College Road, for more mountain history. Tours of the entire facility, including the three-story atrium space with rotating art exhibits and traditional crafts on display, are free. Most interesting for scholars or casual travelers is the center's amazing photo and oral history archives. Call (606) 589-2145, ext. 1313, for general information or to find out about special events.

Downtown on West Main Street, next to the Rebecca Caudill Public Library (named for the famous children's book author, who was born nearby), is the *Poor Fork Arts and Craft Guild,* a shop at 281 West Main Street that features the craft items made by the guild's 75 members. Hours are 10 a.m. to 5 p.m. Tuesday through Saturday. Call in the winter to be sure it is open. Call (606) 589-2545 or visit poorforkartsandcrafts.org.

Directly up the mountain from Cumberland off US 119 is the *Kingdom Come State Park* (606-589-2479; parks.ky.gov/parks/recreationparks/kingdom-come). Here is another access point to the Little Shepherd Trail. The trail and the park are named after John Fox Jr.'s famous novel about Appalachian life, *The Little Shepherd of Kingdom Come.* In 1903 Fox's book became the first American novel to sell over one million copies. This park is known for its incredible vistas and rich mountain woodlands. Two of the most spectacular sites are the Log Rock, a natural rock arch that looks like a log, and Raven Rock, a huge hunk of stone that thrusts some 290 feet into the air and has at its base a capacious sand cave, which is used as an amphitheater for concerts and other performances. Stop by the visitor center for trail maps.

Follow the valley (and the railroad) just 2 miles southeast from Cumberland along Highway 160 to a tiny little town called *Benham,* a place that instead of evolving was made, every bit constructed intentionally, in 1911 by International Harvester as a company town right "on" the seam of coal that the company was mining. In the preceding decade, company towns had gotten terrible reputations for the sordid conditions of such isolated, temporary communities. Benham, however, was among the company towns built after national attention had been drawn to the situation, and large, profitable companies chose to show off their benevolence by building exceptionally pleasant and civilized "encampments" for their workers. The rows of identical houses were often pre-made kit-type structures ordered from Sears or Montgomery Ward.

All this social history and more about the mining process is illustrated by excellent displays in the **Kentucky Coal Mining Museum,** at 231 Main Street, in the original commissary building. The scale-model coal tipple is wonderful! Admission is $5 for adults, $4 for seniors, and $2 for children. Hours are Monday through Saturday from 10 a.m. to 5 p.m. and Sunday from 1 to 4 p.m. Call (606) 848-1530 or visit kentucky.coal.museum. Next door is the **Coal Miner's Park,** which features a walking track, picnic and shelter area, an old L&N caboose, and the Coal Miner's Wall. You can't miss it. Just watch for the two-ton lump of coal and the 1940s electric locomotive engine that moved the miners inside the mine. Across the street and up the hill in the old community school building at 100 Central Avenue is **The Benham School House Inn** (606-848-3000 or 800-231-0627; kycoalmuseum-portal31. southeast.kctcs.edu), a restaurant and an active inn with 30 rooms.

Continue on Highway 160 for 2 more miles to another company town, **Lynch,** built in 1917 by U.S. Steel, Coal, and Coke Company. It's worth the trip to see the **Kentucky Coal Museum and Portal 31 Exhibition Mine Tour** of what was at one time the largest coal camp in the world, where 10,000 people of 38 nationalities lived and worked in more than 1,000 structures. Today you can see the original lamp house, rail depot, firehouse, bath facility, powerhouse, water supply plant, conveyor, coal tipple, and mine portal. For 40 years more than one million tons of coal per year came out of that very portal. Visitors don protective gear and view animated exhibits as they ride several hundred feet underground through a portion of the mine. Mine hours are 9:30 a.m. to 3 p.m. Tuesday through Saturday. Call the mine at (606) 848-1530 or visit portal31.org.

Go down another 4 miles to the south and up to 4,145 feet on **Big Black Mountain,** the highest point in Kentucky. There's an old fire tower at the

trueblue

Kentucky's highest point is Black Mountain, off Highway 160 near Benham: 4,145 feet.

peak. This is one of the few places in the state where it would not be unusual to find a rattlesnake or even a black bear. Bird-watchers should keep their binoculars handy—this mountain supports breeding populations of species that are not usually seen anywhere else in the state, including the solitary vireo, the Canada warbler, and the rose-breasted grosbeak.

If you go back to Cumberland, head east along the gap line, and US 119 will take you northeast into Letcher County.

As you continue to wind along the Cumberland River bottom on US 119 for 15 miles, watch for Highway 806. In just 2 miles, Highway 806 leads to a little community called Eolia. Nestled between Pine and Black Mountains, the two highest in Kentucky, Eolia is said to get its name from the Native American word meaning "valley of the winds." So you'll know what it means when you see the sign for the *Valley of the Winds Art Gallery* (606-633-8652), the studio and sales gallery of a family of artists, Jeff and Sharman Chapman-Crane. For sale are original works by the couple. Visitors are welcome but should call first; the gallery is open by chance on most weekdays and many weekends.

Get back on US 119 and head east 1 mile to Highway 932 on the right (east) side of the road. Turn and go 1.7 miles to the entrance of the *Bad Branch Nature Preserve* (606-633-0362; naturepreserves.ky.gov/nature preserves/pages/badbranch.aspx) on the left. This place is so special that I barely have the nerve to include it here, but if you visit, you must promise to treat it with great care, to soak it into your soul, and to support nature preserves here and everywhere in any way that you are able. This gorge, which is rimmed by 100-foot cliffs, is home to a unique ecosystem of rare plant species and breathtaking wildflowers. The trail leads you through a hemlock and rhododendron kingdom along some of the only clean, pure water you're going to see. At the end is a spectacular 60-foot waterfall arching over the edge of a sandstone cliff. Open sunrise to sunset daily.

Get back on US 119 again and head over Pine Mountain into *Whitesburg.* Downtown, next to the north fork of the Kentucky River, is the *Appalshop* building, which is open to visitors. Appalshop is a community-oriented, not-for-profit arts and education center working to preserve traditional culture and history and to encourage conscientious involvement in contemporary arts and social issues. Appalshop is best known for making powerful documentaries about folk-culture figures and about social activism in Appalachia. While visiting, you can ask to watch almost any of Appalshop's videos—for example, *On Our Own Land,* about the history and demise of the broad form deed in Kentucky, or *Chairmaker,* about the life and work of Dewey Thompson, a furniture maker from Sugarloaf Hollow. The Headwaters Television series is a weekly broadcast of these documentaries on public television.

June Appal Recordings, Appalshop's own record label, also has made a massive cultural contribution by recording Appalachian musicians and storytellers, famous and obscure, ranging from contemporary folk dulcimer artists, such as John McCutcheon, and traditional mountain banjo players, such as Morgan Sexton (who won a National Heritage Award from the National Endowment for the Arts in 1990), to mountain storytellers, including Ray Hicks. Appalshop's Roadside Theatre is a small theater and storytelling troupe that delights and instructs folks all over the region. Appalshop also runs a community radio station, WMMT 88.7 FM; you are hereby commanded to tune in while in the area. Like the river, Appalshop's efforts flow out into the whole Kentucky-Virginia area, giving us all an education and a renewed sense of pride and hope. For literature and catalogs write Appalshop, 91 Madison Street, Whitesburg 41858, or call (606) 633-0108. Also, ask about the schedule of live performances held in the theater year-round. The website is interesting: appalshop.org.

For work from regional artists and craftspeople, stop by *Cozy Corner Crafts* at 104 North Webb Avenue (606-633-9637). The store includes all sorts of folk art and woodcarving, but you'll immediately sense that the shop spotlights quilts. All the quilts in the store are pieced and quilted by hand. And the prices are reasonable enough that you will feel comfortable actually using them on your bed; as any quilter would tell you, the bed is the best place for a quilt. Hours are Monday through Friday from 10 a.m. until 8:30 p.m.

Other works by area craftspeople are featured in the *Pine Mountain/ Letcher County Crafts Co-op* in town at 331 Highway US 119 North. Stop by to see demonstrations of work. Admission is free. Hours are Monday through Saturday from 10 a.m. to 5 p.m. Closed Tuesday and Sunday. In the winter they close at 4 p.m. daily. Call (606) 633-0185.

On the west side of the county in a community called Blackey is an area museum disguised as a general store, the *C. B. Caudill Store and History Center;* appalshop.org/cbcaudill. From Whitesburg take Highway 15 north, then turn on Highway 7 south toward Isom. The store is just past Blackey on the right. There are usually a few fellows chatting on the big front porch. The store, which opened in 1933, was for many years owned by Joe Begley, an upbeat, dedicated activist who used his store to unite diverse groups over issues such as the 77th Strip Mining Bill and the area health clinic. "Everyone should be a politician," he said. "Even Christ was a protester, and a strong one at that." But the walls of the store tell some of their own stories. Joe intentionally collected mining artifacts, everything from hats, boots, lights, and tools to scrip, old mine company currency useful only within the mining camps. His unintentional collections are amusing—scan the shelves for things like 50-year-old tubes of hair restoration cream. Begley, who died in March 2000, was honored as a man of rare courage who never failed to take a stand on issues facing the people of the mountains. With assistance from Appalshop, the store has remained open as a museum.

Also ask at Appalshop about the *Carcassonne Dance* at the Carcassonne community center. Beginning at 7 p.m. on the second Saturday of each month, April through December, people get together for a big square dance, the traditional kind with a caller and usually a live "house" band. You don't need experience or even a partner—just comfortable shoes and lots of spirit. All ages are welcome. Call (606) 633-7958 for more information. From C. B. Caudill Store, stay on Highway 7 for a few hundred yards and turn right on the first road on the right, Elk Creek Road. Follow the pavement to the very top of the mountain.

Back on Highway 7, go west past Blackey and the Caudill Store, turn south on Highway 1103, and follow the signs to the *Lilley Cornett Woods.* Because this is one of the few old growth forests in the state, it is of great value to ecological researchers and to beauty addicts alike. The wise and eccentric Lilley Cornett purchased this land just after World War I and did not allow any live timber, except for blighted chestnuts, to be cut. His children continued the tradition, and finally in 1969 the state purchased the land and continues to preserve it. Time is the key. Old-growth forests are characterized by a large number of trees that are more than 200 years old, many of which are of great commercial value.

In order to protect the forest, visitors are not allowed to hike without a guide. The guides, however, are real treats, and they will take you out whenever you arrive. You'll learn more in an hour hiking with these folks than you could in a year reading dendrology books. The visitor center is open daily from 8:30 a.m. to 5 p.m., April 1 through October 31. From November 1 to March 31, it is open by appointment only. For more information, contact Superintendent, Lilley Cornett Woods, 91 Lilley Cornett Branch, Hallie 41821, or call (606) 633-5828 or visit naturalareas .eku.edu/lilley-cornett-woods-appalachian-ecological-research-station.

On the east end of Letcher County, very near the Virginia border on Highway 805, is a town called *Jenkins,* originally a mining camp built by Consolidation Coal Company—note the rows of identical houses.

During the last weekend of August you are welcome to join the local folks for a real hometown festival, *Jenkins Homecoming Days Festival.* It's just what you'd hope for—kids' carnival, craft booths, lots of silly festival food, music, and some pretty zany contests. For festival information, call the people at the railroad museum.

Jenkins, like Lynch and Benham, was built as a company town. You'll notice the telltale signs: rows of nearly identical frame houses clustered in a tight grid. This town was once part of the Rockefeller family holdings. To get a real sense of this history, stop by the former train depot that now houses the *David A. Zegeer Coal-Railroad Museum.* Myriad little objects pertaining to the everyday life and work of the miners (non-Rockefellers) in this town are on display, including *scrip,* the only legal, non-money form of currency you're likely to see in America outside of video arcades and subways. Open Tuesday through Saturday from 11 a.m. to 5 p.m. and Sunday from 1 to 5 p.m. Call (606) 832-4676 for information.

Leaving Jenkins to the east on US 119, you'll soon be entering Pike County, the largest county in the state. South of Pikeville, in the center of the county on Highway 1789, is *Fishtrap Lake,* a large lake known for its largemouth bass, bluegill, and crappie. Directly south of Fishtrap Lake on

Windows into Geologic History

The ostensible reasons for engineering the massive road cut-through near Pike-ville, which straightened the course of the Levisa Fork of the Big Sandy River, were to provide more direct road and rail transportation in the area; to reduce the frequency and severity of flooding in the town; and, after the former river channel was filled with rubble, to create over 400 acres of new flat land adjacent to town. An unintentional but spectacular fringe benefit of the road cut was an opportunity for geologists to see a whole series of "exposures," or windows into geologic his-tory, as opposed to the usual fragmentary view gained from smaller cut-throughs or from core samples. In the series of cuts near Pikeville, someone with a trained eye can see a frontal section view of an ancient river delta, the Pocahontas delta system, which ran off the Appalachians about 300 million years ago, during the Mississippian-Pennsylvanian era. A geologist would see a river with channels, levees, and splay deposits flowing into overbank deposits of shale and coal. She would see vertical layers of former channels of the ancient river as they migrated back and forth across the valley, like rococo layers of marzipan in an Italian wed-ding cake that has been cut into vertically stepping tiers.

the state border with Virginia is the *Breaks Interstate Park,* where the Russell Fork River, a tributary of the Big Sandy, has done its darndest to imitate the Grand Canyon. For more than 5 miles, the river canyon has high jagged walls, some exceeding 1,600 feet in height. It is the largest canyon east of the Mississippi River. It is believed to have been formed primarily during the late Paleozoic era, some 250 million years ago. Unlike the Grand Canyon, this gorge is lush and tree covered. There are more than 12 miles of hiking trails, and the park has four fantastic overlooks, one of which is at the Rhododendron Lodge and Restaurant. Contact Breaks Interstate Park, 627 Commission Circle, Breaks, Virginia 24607, or call (276) 865-4413; breakspark.com.

In October white-water rafting is possible on the mighty Russell Fork River. Since it drops in elevation 350 feet in a long series of minor waterfalls and rapids, with a few calm pools in between, it is rated among the best rafting rivers in the country. Some of the rapids are Class VI and require both skill and raw nerve to get through. Guided trips are available through *Sheltowee Trace Outfitters* at 2001 Kentucky 90. Call (800) 541-7238 or visit ky-rafting.com.

For better or for worse, Pike County is known nationally as the locale of the infamous Hatfield-McCoy feud, a violent interfamily vendetta that began during the Civil War and was sustained almost until the 20th century. Buried in **Pikeville** in the **Dils Cemetery** are several major figures in the feud from the McCoy side. This cemetery also was the first in eastern Kentucky to be racially integrated. In 1996 a Pikeville College professor began an inventory of the African-American graves; since then, markers have been placed on many that had no headstones. The city of Pikeville has leased the cemetery from Dils family descendants, and it is open year-round during daylight hours. Take Bypass Road to the east side of town; the cemetery is just north of Bypass's split with Highway 1460 on the east side of the road. For more information visit the Pike County Tourism, Convention and Visitors Bureau at 831 Hambley Boulevard between 9:30 a.m. and 4:30 p.m., Monday through Friday, or call (800) 844-7453.

The feud is over, but the families aren't quite finished with the whole business. Every year on Labor Day weekend Pikeville hosts the annual **Hatfield and McCoy Reunion.** It has become a festival of sorts, unifying the two families and celebrating their heritage and genealogy. Visitors are welcome to come learn the history and enjoy regional food, craft booths, dance troops, and all kinds of live entertainment and kids' events. For annual locations and more about it all, call (800) 844-7453.

Authentic Italian cuisine in Pikeville? Yes, indeed. At **Chirico's Ristorante,** at 235 Main Street, founder and chef Frank R. Chirico passed along to his three sons the classic Italian recipes from his grandmother Gracia Chirico. The menu includes an extensive collection of calzones as well as pizza and heavier dishes such as spaghetti, lasagna, and Manicotti Chirico. Hours are 10 a.m. to 10 p.m. Monday through Thursday, 10 a.m. to 11 p.m. Friday, and 3 to 11 p.m. on Saturday. Call (606) 432-7070 or visit chiricosristorante.com. You can walk off the calories by heading a couple of blocks over to Sycamore Street and climbing the 99 steep steps up to the Administration Building of **Pikeville College,** appropriately known as the "college on the hill." The college was established in 1889 as an outreach of the Presbyterian Church and now offers liberal arts education (plus a great physical workout getting up the hill) to about 1,200 students.

At the visitor center you can also find out about the **Pikeville Cut-Thru,** a massive rerouting of highways, railroads, and rivers on the west side of town. After 14 years of labor, millions of dollars, and a whole lot of blasted and hauled rock and dirt, the cut-through was completed in 1987. You have to see it to believe it. The overlook is at the top of Bob Amos Park. To get there take the Pikeville exit off US 23. You are on Highway 384 West (Cedar Creek Road). Very quickly turn left onto Bob Amos Drive and follow the road to the top. The park is a good place for a picnic but closes at dusk.

Asphalt roads may seem to dominate eastern Kentucky now, but there was a time when railroads were king. Head southeast from Pikeville on US 460, which becomes Highway 80, and you'll end up in Elkhorn City. The **Elkhorn City Railroad Museum** at 100 Pine Street offers exhibits of memorabilia from that time, including a caboose, everybody's favorite extinct railcar; switchstands; meters; and so forth. Know what a velocipede is? Find out. Admission is free. The museum is open Tuesday through Saturday from 10 a.m. to 4 p.m. and noon to 4 p.m. on Sunday. Closed December through February. For details, call (606) 754-8300 or the Elkhorn City Historic Society at (606) 754-5080 or visit elkhorncityrrm.tripod.com.

Big Sandy Country

A few miles west of **Paintsville** off Highway 40, you can visit **Mountain HomePlace** (606-297-1850; visitpaintsvilleky.com/mh-home) and get a sense of what farm life in the mountains was like in the mid-1800s. Set up as a living history farm, the complex includes a home, crib barns, horse-powered gristmill, chicken house, blacksmith shop, and small school, as well as costumed interpreters going about the activities of daily life—tending gardens, feeding stock, hewing logs, making shingles, processing sugar cane, and even preparing and eating their daily supper. Mountain Home-Place is open April through October from Monday through Saturday 9 a.m. to 5 p.m. and Sunday noon to 5 p.m. Admission is $6 for adults, $5 for seniors, $4 for children, and free for children age 4 and under. There's a wonderful gift shop with items made by local craftspeople.

In downtown Paintsville you can tour one result of coal mining, the **John C. C. Mayo Museum,** a large, ornate house built by the local baron between 1905 and 1912 for a "mere" $250,000. The house is currently home to Our Lady of the Mountains, a Catholic elementary school, so hours are by appointment only. Call (606) 789-3661. Next door to the museum/school is the *Mayo Methodist Church,* also built by Mayo. (Local legend has it that there was once an underground tunnel connecting the two buildings.) The church's prized Pilcher organ was a gift from Mayo's friend Andrew Carnegie.

Johnson County's history involves some outstanding women. Country music stars Crystal Gayle and Loretta Lynn are both Johnson County natives. Loretta Lynn was born and raised in a beautiful setting in *Butcher Hollow,* near Van Lear. From Paintsville take Highway 302 south and follow the signs to the board-and-batten cabin where she lived. The place was rebuilt for the filming of the 1980 movie *Coal Miner's Daughter*, a biography of the singer's difficult but triumphant life. Remnants of an orchard make the place feel authentic. Stop by Webb's Stop and Shop (606-789-3397), owned by Loretta Lynn's brother Herman Webb, if you want to take a tour. They're given as long as the weather is good and Herman or someone else is around to guide the tour. The store is usually open daily from 10 a.m. to 5 p.m. Larger groups should call ahead.

· Just west of Butcher Hollow on Highway 302, in Van Lear's tiny downtown in the former Consolidated Coal Company office building,

trueblue

A Johnson County native, country and pop singer Crystal Gayle's "real" name is Brenda Gail Webb. Her sister, country music star Loretta Lynn, gave Crystal her stage moniker after the name of a hamburger chain.

is the *Van Lear Historical Society Coal Miners' Museum.* If you haven't yet seen a real-life mining camp, check out the model of a typical company town in the museum. Hours are 1 to 5 p.m. Monday, 11 a.m. to 5 p.m. Tuesday through Friday, and 1 to 5 p.m. Saturday. Call (606) 789-8540; admission is $4. To get there, take US 23 south to Highway 302, then go east on Highway 78 or Miller's Creek Road. Inside there is a fully restored 1950s-era soda bar called Icky's where these days you can buy snacks and gifts.

During the first full weekend in August, the Coal Miners' Museum comes to life for the *Van Lear Town Celebration.* Soup bean and fried catfish dinners are served in the museum. All day Saturday there are sports tournaments in the park.

Another legendary area woman is Jenny Wiley, an early settler of the Big Sandy area who survived a remarkably tragic capture by Shawnee

The Best-Kept Dirty Little Secret in America

The lush temperate forests of the ancient Appalachian Mountains are some of the most biologically diverse on Earth. In the heart of this verdant region, Inez, Kentucky, in Martin County, was the site of one of the southeastern United States' worst environmental disasters in October 2000. A coal slurry impoundment located over an abandoned coal mine shaft with an illegally thin base (under 15 feet, although federal regulations require at least 150 feet) failed and released a viscous black sludge of more than 300 million gallons of water and toxic coal waste into the underground shaft and into local streams. About 75 miles of rivers and streams turned an iridescent black, causing a fish kill along the Tug Fork of the Big Sandy River and some of its tributaries. As the spill contained heavy metals, including arsenic, mercury, lead, copper, and chromium, towns along the waterways were forced to turn off their drinking water intakes. The pollution was evident as far away as Cincinnati along the Ohio River.

This tragedy is the result of a relatively new method of extracting coal in Appalachia, called mountaintop removal (MTR)—or "strip mining on steroids."

Recipe for Disaster

1. Purchase mountain

2. Clear-cut forest and scrape away topsoil

3. Set off explosives to blast apart rock

4. Bulldoze millions of tons of overburden (former top 800 feet of mountain) into valley

5. Remove thin vein of coal

6. "Wash" coal with toxic chemicals

7. Store toxic waste liquid in sludge lagoon on hillside

8. Sell coal to power plant

9. Repeat

Repeat the process long enough, and the entire Appalachian mountain range would be annihilated and transformed into a barren, toxic moonscape. There is a swelling movement to rein in and ultimately ban the heinous excesses of MTR. To see heart-stopping photos of the practice, check Ohio Valley Environmental Coalition's website at www.ohvec.org. As you travel this region, you will not be likely to see evidence of this or any other style of surface mining from the road—mining companies have made a concerted effort to avoid being visible.

Indians and, after nine months of captivity, during which time she gave birth, subsequently escaped. She died at 71 and is buried in a cemetery 5 miles south of Paintsville on Highway 321 near the site of **Harmon Station,** the first white settlement in eastern Kentucky. Mathias Harmon was one of the hunter–Indian fighters now known as Long Hunters because of the length of their sojourns in the wilderness. In 1750 he and his companions built a fortlike log hunting lodge on this site; in the late 1780s they built a more permanent blockhouse.

Jenny Wiley's captors took her north along the Big Sandy River to its confluence with the Ohio River. They went downstream, looking for a place to cross the river. Unable to cross into Ohio, they instead journeyed up the Little Sandy River Valley to Dry Fork and across a ridge to Cherokee and Hood Creeks. Though the landscape has obviously changed greatly since 1789, you can roughly follow their Kentucky route along the **Jenny Wiley Train Heritage Byway,** a 154-mile loop drive. You start at **Jenny Wiley State Resort Park** near Prestonsburg, travel north to Paintsville, and along US 23 through Ashland to Greenup. From Greenup take Highway 1 to Grayson and Highway 773 from Grayson to Hitchins. Then get back onto Highway 1 at Blaine, where you pick up US 23 to return to Paintsville to complete the loop.

Before or after this excursion, Jenny Wiley State Resort Park (606-886-2711 or 800-325-0142; http://parks.ky.gov/findparks/resortparks/jw) is a good place to relax. The park is located between Paintsville and Prestonsburg on Highway 3, just east of US 23/460. At the heart of the park is Dewey Lake, a clear lake famous for its white bass run in April. In the park you can tour one of the last one-room schoolhouses to close in Kentucky. January through March and September through December, the park offers Elk Sighting Tours to nearby areas in which elk have been introduced since 1997. A variety of tours are offered, costing from $5 to $10. If you want to go, make reservations well in advance because the tours have become quite popular. Call the park naturalist at (606) 886-2711, ext. 2269, for information.

The park has the usual array of overnight lodging in the park lodge, at cabins, or at campsites. It may sound a little cheesy, but it's also breathtaking to take the seasonal sky lift out over the wooded hollows.

The **Jenny Wiley Summer Music Theatre** presents one very colorful, musical version of the legendary Jenny Wiley story in addition to three

Broadway musicals, which have included *Hello, Dolly!* and *The Sound of Music.* You can take in a different performance every night for four nights in a row. The outdoor performances are at the Jenny Wiley State Resort Park in an amphitheater open from late May through late August, Wednesday through Sunday; the house opens at 7:30 p.m., with curtain at 8:15 p.m. There is also an indoor theater at 218 Second Street. Call (606) 886-9274 or (877) 225-5598 or visit jwtheatre.com for more information.

Prestonsburg is also home to the *Mountain Arts Center,* a beautiful 47,000-square-foot entertainment complex that opened in late 1996. This center, with recording studio, classrooms, and a 1,000-seat performance hall, began as the dream of a retired music teacher, Billie Jean Osborne. Osborne, who is from Betsy Layne (country singer Dwight Yoakam grew up a few houses away), envisioned a theater where eastern Kentucky audiences could enjoy top entertainment. Refusing to take no for an answer, she spurred a coalition of state and local officials to make her theater a reality. The center features top entertainers in all genres—from country and gospel to classical music—along with regular performances by the Kentucky Opry, Osborne's own country music showcase. Performance times vary; call (606) 889-9125 for ticket information. The website is macarts.com.

The Mountain Arts Center is on a section of US 23 that has been designated *Kentucky's Country Music Highway.* Along a stretch running from Ashland to Letcher County, through seven counties, signs honor a dozen

The Civil War in Prestonsburg

In addition to being the site of Daniel Boone's winter camp in 1767–68, Prestonsburg was also the site of two wintertime Civil War engagements. Each May a reenactment is held at the *National Historic Landmark.* (For more information call 606-886-1341.) The Battle of Ivy Mountain, which lasted less than an hour and a half, resulted in the Union's capture of Piketown (now Pikeville), where the Confederates had been stationed. The Battle of Middle Creek, in January 1862, occurred along the creek between Paintsville and Prestonsburg. The battle marked the beginning of Union domination of Kentucky and was a major accomplishment for the Union commander, James Abram Garfield, who became the 20th president of the United States and died months later from injuries sustained from an assassin's bullet.

country and bluegrass music stars who came from the region, from Billy Ray Cyrus (Greenup County) and the Judds (Boyd County) to Patty Loveless (Pike County).

The *East Kentucky Science Center* is drawing crowds from great distances in large part due to its state-of-the-art, 80-seat planetarium. The universe is yours when the star machine creates the night sky for any date, from any point on the planet. Planetarium show times are 2 p.m. on Tuesday through Friday and 12:30 and 2 p.m. on Saturday. The exhibit hall hosts changing science shows throughout the year and is open to the public on Saturday from noon to 5 p.m. Special science educational events, with an emphasis on hands-on activities, are scheduled throughout the year. There's also a snappy Emporium (gift shop). The science center is located at 7 Bert Combs Drive, on the Prestonsburg Campus of the Big Sandy Community and Technical College. There are plentiful signs in town. Call (606) 886-3863, or visit bigsandy.kctcs.edu/EKSC for more information.

Built in 1817 as the main residence on a 300-acre farm, *Samuel May House* in North Prestonsburg is now the oldest standing brick house in the whole Big Sandy Valley. The house was built in the classic Federal style. The address is 1035 North Lake Drive. Tours are by appointment only. Call the Prestonsburg Convention and Tourism Bureau at (606) 886-1341 or prestonsburgky.com.

The David community, which is about 6 miles southwest of Prestonsburg on Highway 404, is home to the *David School,* a nonsectarian, not-for-profit, wonderful school committed to educating local high school dropouts from low-income families. In 1972 Dan Greene founded the school in an old mining camp with hopes of helping kids who were functionally illiterate. Now, more than 95 percent of the David School students have finished their high school education, and there's always a waiting list. Other schools around the state and nation are looking to Greene's program as a model. If you are inspired, stop by.

Due south of the David School is a longer-lived educational institution built upon similar hopes, *Alice Lloyd College* (606-368-6000 or 888-280-4252; alc.edu). Take Highway 7 south, then Highway 899 southwest into Pippa Passes, in Knott County to 100 Purpose Road. The school's founder, Alice Lloyd, was a Radcliffe graduate who contracted spinal meningitis at the age of 40 and moved with her mother to the mountains of Kentucky to die in an abandoned missionary house. Despite her illness, she typed letters with her left hand to businesspeople and friends in Boston, asking for help in establishing a school. It was opened in 1917 on the hillsides of Caney Creek Valley, where it stands today.

Alice Lloyd, who lived until 1962, gave her students a free education, but there was one string attached—she requested that after graduation the students return to eastern Kentucky to work and live. Almost 4,000 graduates have become teachers in the region, and more than 1,000 have become mountain doctors and other professionals. Visitors are welcome to tour the beautiful campus all year.

Just a few miles away on Highway 550, slightly south of Highway 80, is Hindman and, strung along Troublesome Creek, the *Hindman Settlement School* (606-785-5475; hindmansettlement.org), yet another educational facility that long has been a social and cultural gold mine. The school was founded in 1902 on the folk school plan and operated successfully for many years, but like other settlement schools, it has changed functions and now serves as a special school for area children with dyslexic characteristics. Today it hosts some of the best workshops in the state on traditional dance and mountain crafts and culture, the most famous of which is the Writers' Workshop held at the end of July. Visitors can tour the campus free, Monday through Friday between 8 a.m. and 5 p.m. Stop by the school's *Marie Stewart Crafts Shop* to see a wide range of traditional regional crafts. The shop is a co-op, and all of its members are juried. You may be lucky and be there on a day when the craftspeople are giving demonstrations. The museum and crafts shop are located on the back of Uncle Sol's Cabin, next to the main office. Although the shop is not always staffed, the office members are happy to open the shop during the hours of 9 a.m. to 4 p.m. Monday through Friday. For more information call (606) 785-5475 or check the website at hindmansettlement.org.

You're in store for an architectural museum of sorts at the *Pioneer Village,* due south of Hindman. Take Highway 160 south to Carr Fork Lake, then take Highway 15 south just a little farther into Red Fox and watch the east side of the road for the long driveway to the village. This group of cabins was moved to this location in Rainbow Hollow when the Carr Fork Dam was built. Some of the log structures date as far back as the 1780s. Presently the cabins are standing, but the logs are not chinked (filled in between with mud, rock, straw, etc.).

Water-based relaxation, camping, picnicking, swimming, and all sorts of fishing are available April through December at **Carr Creek State Park** and the 750-acre lake, **Carr Folk Lake,** created by the dam that caused the cabins at Pioneer Village to be moved. The lake has been well stocked with crappie and largemouth bass. Water from this lake eventually ends up in the Kentucky River. Call (606) 642-4050 or visit parks.ky.gov/parks/recreation parks/Carr-Creek/default.aspx.

Nearby **Hazard** is a booming little riverside town at the end of the Daniel Boone Parkway. Because it sits on and near some of the widest, richest seams of coal in the area, coal is at the heart of almost everything here, a fact made loud and clear during the third weekend of September when Hazard hosts the **Black Gold Festival** (606-436-0161; blackgoldfestival.com). In town, spend a little time at the **Bobby Davis Museum** (234 Walnut Street; 606-439-4325) next door to the visitor information center (606-439-2659). This free museum is a visual history book of the area from the 19th century through World War II. Hours are 8 a.m. to 4 p.m. Monday through Friday. The town has an interesting website with lots of historic images and fascinating stories; hazardkentucky.com.

The **Mother Goose House** (downtown Hazard on Route 476) is a local landmark in Perry County and a piece of wacky architecture that has been noted nationally by folk art enthusiasts (including *The New York Times*, PBS, and Oprah Winfrey). The goose house took six years to build and was finished in 1940 by George Stacy, an L&N railroad employee who modeled the building after a goose he had shot. He actually had his wife cook the goose and carefully clean the skeleton so that he could use it as a kind of blueprint for establishing proportions. The exterior walls are built from area sandstone. The space inside has three bedrooms, a living room, kitchen, bath, dining room, and large family room. Later, Stacy added a grocery store and gas station below the house. The windows are egg-shaped and the roof forms the goose head and upper body—obviously a mother because she is sitting on her oval-shaped nest. Her eyes are automobile lights that used to blink in the night. Stacy lived in his house until his death. The building is now a private residence, so you may enjoy it as a drive-by attraction only.

An architectural treat is in store just north of Hazard in Buckhorn on Highway 28, which is off Highway 15 North. The Log Cathedral, now functioning as the **Buckhorn Lake Presbyterian Church,** is an unusually large and beautiful log structure built in 1907 as part of the Witherspoon College campus. Harvey S. Murdoch of the Society of Soul Winners helped found a Christian elementary and high school and called it a college in order to give the students extra status. The massive logs are white oak, cut from the surrounding woods. Inside, the space is lovely and impressive. The gem in the crown of the cathedral is a Hook and Hasting pipe organ, which has been restored and sounds great. Sun streaming through the old amber-glass windows bathes the oak sanctuary (and you) in a warm and beautiful golden glow. To experience it, stop by the parsonage next door. You're also invited to come for services.

trueblue

Kentucky has 15,000 square miles of water surface and more miles of running water than any state, except Alaska.

If you'd like to make an appointment to tour the church, call (606) 398-7382. For more history, check the website, buckhorn.org.

To see the region on foot, try some hiking trails in the **Buckhorn Lake State Resort Park** (606-398-7510 or 800-325-0058; parks.ky.gov/parks/resortparks/buckhorn-lake/) 20 miles northwest of Hazard. Take Highway 15 North, then Highway 28 to the west and watch for signs to 4441 Kentucky 1833. There's a lodge with a dining room overlooking the lake, campgrounds, and a marina where you can slip your canoe into the 1,250-acre **Buckhorn Lake.**

Like the mountain schools in the area, **Frontier Nursing Service,** in Hyden off US 421 (southwest of Hazard in Leslie County), is an institution committed to promoting health and growth, but in this case its main concern is with the physical body. Mary Breckinridge started Frontier Nursing as a school in 1925. Her original students and the generations of nurses to follow have made strong impressions on the minds of everyone who has encountered them riding on horseback to remote hollows and mountain towns to deliver babies and administer health care. Folks at Frontier Nursing have revised their charter and are also involved in child care, general education, and regional economics. The grounds are lovely, and the history of the service is inspirational. Make sure to go in the tiny chapel, which has a 15th-century Flemish stained-glass window, and to see the Wendover Big House, a log home built in 1925 for the founder. Eight rooms for rent in the house and barn are the only lodging in the county. The rate ranges from $50 to $85, including breakfast. For information call (606) 672-2317 or visit frontiernursing.org.

The Gorgeous Gorge

The *Red River Gorge* in the Daniel Boone National Forest is one of the most beautiful and best-loved wilderness areas in Kentucky. Actually, the area was quite obscure until its existence was threatened in the late 1960s by a proposed 5,000-acre impoundment on the Red River's north fork. Intense controversy raged until 1975, when the plan was nixed. All the publicity caused the park to be badly overused by visitors who weren't ecologically sensitive. Today the park has been reorganized; large areas are strictly protected, and visitor education is an important part of forest management.

. **true**blue

Kentucky's Red River Gorge area has the largest concentration of rock shelters and arches east of the Rockies.

The gorge was formed by erosion and weathering, in much the same way that the Grand Canyon was carved out by the Colorado River. The north fork of the Red River cut through the area more than 340 million years ago and left behind some fantastic geologic phenomena in limestone, conglomerate sandstone, and siltstone, all of which are tucked under a layer of shale. The most outstanding of these phenomena are the 80 natural rock arches, a number surpassed in the United States only by Arches National Park in Utah.

The Daniel Boone National Forest is 60 miles east of Lexington on the Bert T. Combs Mountain Parkway. A good place to begin exploring the Red River Gorge, at the northern end of the forest, is *Natural Bridge State Resort Park* at 2135 Natural Bridge Road (800-325-1710 or 606-663-2214; parks.ky.gov/parks/resortparks/Natural-Bridge/default.aspx), a full-fledged state park with a big lodge, cottages, camping, a pool, recreation areas,

There's a Morel to This Story

Eastern Kentucky communities have festivals celebrating all kinds of foods, from Gingerbread Days in Hindman in September to the Kentucky Apple Festival in Paintsville in early October. There's even a Poke Sallet Festival, honoring a local green, in Harlan in June. But the most exotic eastern Kentucky food festival has to be the *Mountain Mushroom Festival* in Irvine in late April. Up to 20,000 people show up in this town of 2,800 with mushrooms on the mind—grilled, fried, baked, and en casserole. For many years folks in Estill County have gone to the woods to hunt for the morels, or wild mushrooms, that pop up in poplar thickets and apple orchards in the spring. Locally, these delicacies are called landfish for their somewhat fishy taste. The annual festival includes a hunt to see who can find the biggest morel, a mushroom cook-off, and even a Fungus Run. Call the Estill County Chamber of Commerce at (606) 723-2450 or visit estillcountyky.net for the current year's festival dates or visit the festival website at mountainmush-roomfestival.org. If you're planning to do any mushroom gathering on your own, make sure you know what the edible variety looks like. (Check out the poster hanging in the Irvine City Council chambers.) You don't want to take home a poisonous variety.

and a variety of hiking trails leading to a spectacular natural stone bridge. This park is not very isolated, but it can serve as a point of reference for outings to more remote places. From I-64 take the Bert T. Combs Mountain Parkway southeast, get off at the Slade Interchange onto Highway 11, and follow signs to the park.

On the way in or out, you should have a meal at *Miguel's Pizza* (606-663-1975; miguelspizza.com), a little building with a beautifully carved wooden front door on the left near the park entrance at 1890 Natural Bridge Road. Order a veggie pizza, and you'll likely find it laced with whatever's in season—heavenly. Their expanded menu offerings include salads, pasta, sandwiches, fancy ice cream, and a new smoothie bar. If you're a climber, take note that this is the only store in the area that sells a good variety of climbing supplies. Miguel's is open seven days a week, from 7 a.m. to 9:45 p.m. Closed December 1 through March 1.

The *Kentucky Reptile Zoo* (606-663-9160; kyreptilezoo.org) is a very well-run and educational reptile center at 200 L & E Railroad Place. And its founder, Jim Harrison, is well respected in venom research circles. He is a leading supplier of snake venom for medical research and also is helping a university in Brazil breed rattlesnakes whose venom may be used to help hold human skin together after surgery. In addition to seeing more than 100 species of snakes (including pythons and black mambas) and three alligators, your visit can include an informational demonstration by Harrison or a staff member and possibly a demonstration of venom extraction. Open 11 a.m. to 6 p.m. Memorial Day through Labor Day. Open March through Memorial Day and from Labor Day through October on Friday through Sunday from 11 a.m. to 6 p.m. Open in November on weekends as weather allows. Call before visiting. Closed December through February. Admission is $7 for adults, $5 for children ages 3 to 15, and free for children under 3. To get there take exit 33 off the Mountain Parkway, turn into the rest area, then turn left at L&E Railroad Place. You'll see the sign.

There is a designated driving loop through the area beginning in Nada, 1½ miles west of the Slade Interchange on Highway 15. Take Highway 77 north through the *Nada Tunnel*, a 10-foot-wide, 13-foot-tall, 800-foot-long tunnel cut by hand in 1877 to give small-gauge trains access to the big timber in the area. Stay on Highway 77 and it will run into Highway 715, which runs parallel to the river. At Pine Ridge, Highway 715 connects with Highway 15 again, which leads back to Natural Bridge. Ask for a map in the lodge at Natural Bridge.

Big timber is the subject of a small museum in the recently restored *Gladie Creek Cabin*, which you'll pass on this loop drive. This was the 1884 cabin of John Ledford, who bought and logged more than 4,000 acres here. The USDA Forest Service recently rebuilt the cabin and filled it with historic objects that refer to the early years of the logging industry in eastern Kentucky, including log branding irons, tools, models of old equipment, and photographs.

Gladie Creek Historic Site/Environmental Learning Center also serves as the visitor center for the north end of the Daniel Boone National Forest. This is another good place to get trail maps, weather reports, and general advice about hiking or anything else concerning the National Forest. Hours are 8 a.m. to 4:30 p.m. Monday through Friday and vary on weekends. Call the Stanton Ranger District (606-663-8100; fs.usda.gov/recarea/dbnf/recreation/recarea/?recid=39566) for information. The center is open daily from 9 a.m. to 5:30 p.m. from mid March to mid November. From mid-November to mid-March the center is open Monday through Friday from 8:30 a.m. to 4:30 p.m. Aside from the driving loop, another way to reach Gladie Creek is from the north. Take Highway 77 south to Highway 715; go east for about 11 miles and watch the right side of the road.

The absolute best way to be in the Red River Gorge is to be hiking, crawling, if you must, for driving does not do the woods justice. You must sweat, propel yourself by your own energy, drink when you're thirsty, eat when you're hungry (or can't wait any longer for the granola bar), feel the leaves brush against your legs, feel the sunshine on your shoulders when you come to an opening in the forest canopy, hear and see the animals, and so taste the life of the mountains. More than 165 miles of foot trails in the Daniel Boone Forest offer ample opportunity to be here the right way. Get maps from the Hemlock Lodge at Natural Bridge, at Gladie, or anywhere you see a ranger. Hike as many trails as you're able.

Ask at the lodge, or anywhere you see a ranger, about the *Clifty Wilderness* area, a 13,300-acre area that adjoins the Red River Gorge. Hiking, camping, canoeing, horseback riding, and fishing—these are all great ways to spend time here, where there are some 170 species of trees and more than 750 flowering plants, several of which are rare or endangered. Call (606) 663-2852 for maps and information (wilderness.net/NWPS/wildview/?WID=127).

true*blue*

There are about 175 species of native and introduced tree varieties that grow wild in Kentucky, including 17 species of oak.

The *Sheltowee Trace* (Trail #100) is the only backpacking trail that traverses the entire length of the Daniel Boone National Forest. It goes 257 miles through nine counties, beginning in Rowan County in the north and ending in Tennessee, where it connects with the John Muir Trail (named for the father of the Sierra Club), which connects to the great Appalachian Trail. If you're planning a backpacking trip, check with a ranger. The Sheltowee Trace is marked with a white diamond or turtle-shaped blaze. The word *sheltowee* is Shawnee for "big turtle," Daniel Boone's Native American name when he was captured and adopted by Shawnee chief Blackfish.

For a taste of the area's social and cultural history, stop by the *Wolfe County Historical Museum* on Main Street in downtown Campton. From the Mountain Parkway take exit 43, go downtown, and watch for the signs. It's only open on Sunday from 2 to 4 p.m.

The *Pioneer Weapons Hunting Area* is a 7,480-acre area in the National Forest, north of the gorge, which is designated for hunting deer, turkey, grouse, and squirrel, but you must use only primitive weapons—black-powder muzzle loaders, bows and arrows, blow guns, spears, rubber bands, whatever. Before you hunt, be sure to call the forest supervisor (606-784-6428; fs.usda.gov/recarea/dbnf/recreation/recarea/?recid=39554) so that you understand the regulations.

If you turn toward the north from the Corner Restaurant on Highway 36, take the first street to the right, follow it to the end, and you'll see a trail going up the hillside. This trail leads to *Donathan Rock,* a great huge rock teetering near the edge of a cliff from which you get a perfect aerial view of Frenchburg below. Park in town and walk over. Traveling a mile farther north on Highway 36 brings you to the *Roe Wells School.* Watch carefully for it on the left—the sign is small. The schoolhouse is a typical, quaint, one-room country school. Look in the windows; the old desks and books, chalkboard, and even a few messages from the teacher remain. It would make a perfect movie set. Visitors are welcome to walk around and look in the windows. Right now there is no one available to give tours.

Leaving Frenchburg in the southeasterly direction, there are several surprises in store for you. Watch for the old *Botts School.* Although it's now

Strange as It Sounds

Eastern Kentuckians have their own way of saying things, and as you travel this part of the state you'll not only notice a distinctive accent, but you'll also encounter some fascinating local expressions. For example, man or woman, don't be surprised if you're called "honey" by total strangers of both sexes. A ghost is a "haint"; "loaded for bear" means angry or looking for a fight; and a "passel" is one way to indicate a large quantity. If someone tells you to "quit lollygaggin' around," it means to stop delaying or taking so long; and there are a passel of other local expressions. One day a friend from Hazard and I were having lunch at a local restaurant when an acquaintance of hers came in. In the course of conversation, I mentioned that I wasn't from the area. "Oh, honey, I knew that," he said. "You talk way too plain to be from around here."

a community building, you can still feel its age; it was a one-room school-house since before the time Menifee County was a county. If it catches your fancy and you want to see inside, stop by the Botts General Store that's directly across the street. Either way, you'll get some stories.

One of the most special surprises in this immediate area is *Furnace Mountain Inc.,* a spiritual community founded in 1986 by Zen master Seung Sahn. The community owns 500 acres of beautiful woodland near Clay City in Powell County, where visitors are welcome to hike or join in daily medi-tation practices. The main function of Furnace Mountain is to host a variety of retreats, primarily traditional three- to ninety-day Zen Buddhist retreats. Retreats are also conducted in other disciplines such as 12-step programs, Christian meditation, and clinical pas-toral education.

what'sinaname?

If I were giving an award for the best town name in the state, the prize would have to go to Leslie County's Hell Fer Certain, a little, not-even-on-the-map community north of Hyden just off Highway 257. Runners-up in the area would include Devil's Jump Branch, Con-fluence, Cutshin, Thousandsticks, Yeaddis, Smilax, Yerkes, and Krypton (watch out, Superman!).

Kwan Se Um San Ji Sah, which means "Perceive World Sound High Ground Temple," is indeed a place that sits beautifully on high ground and affects the way one perceives the world, due to its exquisite blend of eastern Kentucky craftsmanship with Far Eastern aesthetics. This timber-frame temple has the classic tapering vertical lines and uplifting roofline of Oriental architecture and the materi-als of the mountains—recycled Doug-las fir siding, a cherry wood floor, and deep sky-blue ceramic roof tiles. For more information, write Furnace Mountain Zen Retreat, P.O. Box 545, Clay City 40312, leave a message at (606) 723-4329, office@furnacemountain.org, or visit zenmind.org.

A nice area for hiking and birdwatching is *Pilot Knob State Nature Preserve,* located off Highway 15 near Cave City. The preserve includes one of the tallest "knobs," or large hills, in the area—a 730-footer from which Daniel Boone supposedly looked out over the bluegrass region for the first time. There are so many Daniel Boone exaggerations made in Ken-tucky that one is always a little suspect of such claims, but it is nonetheless a good spot for modern explorers to gaze upon a lovely vista. Open most days. Also see naturepreserves/Pages/pilotknob.aspx. In downtown Clay City on Main Street, there is a free museum devoted to the area's work history. Artifacts at the **Red River Historical Museum** at 4541 Main Street include lots of tools from the railroad and the area's iron and logging industries. Also, there's a huge rock with supposedly ancient carvings. Hours May through October are Saturday and Sunday from noon to 5 p.m. Call (606) 663-0696 or visit theredrivermuseum.org.

You can get your bluegrass music inside and out at **Meadowgreen Park Bluegrass Music Hall** at 465 Forge Mill Road. This hundred-acre park with music hall is home base for the Kentucky Friends of Bluegrass Mountain Club, an organization whose goal is to preserve the musical heritage of the Appalachian Mountains. There are indoor shows October through April and large outdoor festivals in spring and fall. For more information write Kentucky Friends of Bluegrass Music, 303 Bluegrass Lane, Clay City 40312, call (606) 663-9008 or visit kyfriends.com.

You are still in beautiful country when you travel to the south side of the Red River Gorge. From Natural Bridge head south on Highway 11 through Zachariah and Zoe to **Beattyville,** a friendly little mountain town. The last full weekend in October, Beattyville is host to the world's only **Woolly Worm Festival,** devoted to the humblest of all meteorologists. Call (606) 464-0494 for festival information or visit beattyville.org/tourism/festivals-and-events.

From Beattyville take Highway 11 south and turn east on Highway 30 to Booneville. Continue on Highway 30 east and you'll come to **Jackson.** This town was originally known as Breathitt, but in 1845 it was renamed to honor President Andrew Jackson, who died that year. The **Breathitt County Museum** (329 Broadway; 606-666-4159; breathittmuseum.com) has exhibits on logging and coal mining along with Civil War artifacts. The photo collection of life in the area during the 1940s is especially impressive. Hours are Monday, Wednesday, and Friday, 9 a.m. to 3:30 p.m. From Highway 15 south veer off to the southeast on Highway 476 to 711 Clemons Fork Road to Robinson Forest, a large research and educational forest owned and managed by the University of Kentucky. Visitors can take a self-guided hike along a nature trail and see a wide variety of flora and fauna typical of this area. The forest is a unique example of an old-growth forest ecosystem on the Cumberland Plateau. A climb up the Camp Robinson Lookout Tower is worth the effort. To get to the tower, take Highway 426 way into the forest and turn left on Clemons Road to the tower trail. The forest is open daily, year-round. Call (606) 666-5034 for more information or check 2.ca.uky.edu/ forestry/robfor.php.

Iron Country

If these United States can be called a body, Kentucky can be called its heart.

These words are from the first stanza of "Kentucky Is My Land," a poem by the late poet laureate of Kentucky, Jesse Stuart, a wholesome, hopeful writer whose work was deeply rooted in his eastern Kentucky homeland. Because W-Hollow was Stuart's home and source of inspiration, more than 700 acres have been made into a pastoral museum and maintained as Stuart knew it—cattle graze in some pastures and young forests are being allowed to grow to maturity. The *Jesse Stuart State Nature Preserve* lies between Highways 1 and 2 just west of Greenup, off US 23. Visitors can walk the hills and fields Stuart walked and visit Op's Cabin, the old white clapboard house where he did some of his writing. For those who know his work, the fictional Laurel Ridge is Seaton Ridge. His home borders the preserve but is private property. The Kentucky State Nature Preserves Commission (502-573-2886; naturepreserves.ky.gov/naturepreserves/Pages/jessestuart.aspx) maintains the nature preserve and the Jesse Stuart Foundation, a nonprofit organization devoted to preserving and sharing Stuart's work. To order books, write the foundation at 1645 Winchester Avenue, Ashland 41101, call (606) 236-1667, or visit jsfbooks.com.

Continue south on Highway 1 to *Greenbo Lake State Resort Park,* where the lodge is named after Jesse Stuart and even includes a reading room where you can enjoy his novels, short stories, and poems. The last weekend in September the park hosts a Jesse Stuart Weekend, during which speakers lecture on the life and works of Stuart, a guided tour of W-Hollow is given, and exhibits are open. Otherwise, the lake is marvelous for fishing, the dining room is popular, and camping is available. The 24-mile-long Michael Tygart Trail connects the park with the Jenny Wiley National Recreation Trail. Call (606) 473-7324, or check parks.ky.gov/resort parks/Greenbo-Lake/default.aspx for more information about the park or the festival.

Poetry in Motion—Relocated to Eastern Kentucky

It has been 150 years since large numbers of elk ranged freely in these mountains. In fact, every elk was entirely extirpated from Kentucky until now. Every year for the next decade, 200 elk will be released into the wild with the hope that in two decades their population will increase to more than 8,300. This program may be the largest relocation of game animals in modern times. Initially the elk will be released in Perry, Knott, and Breathitt Counties in wildlife refuge lands inside the Robinson Forest and in the Cyprus Amax Wildlife Management Area. It all makes perfect sense. You just have to know the code.

Nine miles south of the park, at the intersection of Highways 1 and 3111, is the **Oldtown Covered Bridge,** spanning the Little Sandy River near the site of a Shawnee village. The 194-foot-long, two-span, Burr-type bridge was built in 1880 and has not been restored. Bennett's Mill Bridge is 1 foot longer and 25 years older, has one less span than the Oldtown Bridge, and is functional. It was built in 1855 for access to **Bennett's Grist Mill** on Tygart Creek. What is amazing is that the original frame and footings are intact. This bridge is on Highway 7, just west of the Greenup County Locks and Dam. (**Warning:** Grays Branch Road, the direct route from the dam, is a rough dirt logging road.)

The county seat, **Greenup,** is a very interesting little river town at the confluence of the Little Sandy and Ohio Rivers. Though it's suffered through some terrible floods (the 1937 flood destroyed its hundred-year-old courthouse), there are still some old places worth seeing. Stop by the Greenup Library at 508 Main Street (606-473-6514) and get a free map of **Greenup's walking tour.**

Follow the Ohio River south on US 23 into **Ashland,** the largest city in Kentucky east of Lexington and headquarters for Ashland Oil and AK Steel (not to mention that it's the hometown of country music stars Naomi and Wynonna Judd and Wynonna's movie-star sis, Ashley). Downtown you'll notice a surprising number of large, ornate houses built by early industrialists during the last half of the 19th century. My favorite is at 1600 Central Avenue. The highest peaks of the roof sport two cast-iron dragons, reminiscent of French *fatiagés* or the figures on ancient Macedonian

Lower Shawneetown

Though no one knows the exact spot, somewhere in Greenup County is the site of Kentucky's very first white settlement before Fort Harrod. Sometime prior to 1753 French fur traders and Shawnee Indians settled across the Scioto River at a place referred to in records as Lower Shawneetown. However, all traces of the settlement disappeared before 1800. So, there's some work here for archaeologists in need of a project.

tombs, meant to ward off evil spirits. It was originally built at the corner of Winchester Avenue and Seventeenth Street but was hauled intact to the present site some 20 years later by a team of mules. The dragons did their job.

Downtown in Ashland, at 1620 Winchester Avenue, is the **Kentucky Highlands Museum and Discovery Center.** The museum is organized by subject and period, and exhibits range from Adena, Fort Ancient, and Hopewell Indian cultures to rail, steam, and industrial histories, the evolution of radio, a World War II room, and an impressive antique clothing collection. Hours are 10 a.m. to 4 p.m. Wednesday, 10 a.m. to 7 p.m. Thursday, 10 a.m. to 4 p.m. Friday, and 10 a.m. to 6 p.m. Saturday. Admission is $6.50 for adults, $5 for seniors and children ages 3 to 16, and free for children 2 and under. Call (606) 329-8888 or check highlandsmuseum.com for special programs and more information.

Not far from the museum in downtown Ashland is **Central Park,** a 47-acre area set aside when Ashland was laid out in the 1850s. It contains a number of ancient Native American mounds that have been restored to their original proportions. They were found to contain human bones and pottery and other artifacts that correspond with the Adena period (800 BC to AD 800). The mounds and historic houses are part of a 2-mile walking tour of downtown Ashland. Stop by the visitor center at 1509 Winchester Avenue, for a free map between 9 a.m. and 5 p.m. Monday through Friday. Call (800) 377-6249 or (606) 324-1007, or check visitashlandky.com.

Architecture buffs, brace yourselves. The **Paramount Arts Center** (1300 Winchester Avenue; 606-324-3175; paramountartscenter.com) is out of this world. Art deco has never been better, and the people of Ashland cared enough to give this place an enormous face-lift (but what a face!). If you're in town on a night when a cultural event is scheduled, go, no matter what's playing. It has booked acts from Marcel Marceau to the Sistine Chapel Choir to Ray Charles and continues the excellence. Or you can just tour the building between 9 a.m. and 4 p.m. Monday through Friday. Whether you've been to Ashland before or not, you may have already seen the Paramount Center in Billy Ray Cyrus's "Achy Breaky Heart" video. Billy Ray was born in nearby Flatwoods, Kentucky.

In the early 1920s Paramount Famous Lasky Corporation planned to build a chain of "talking picture" theaters like the Paramount across the nation to showcase Paramount Studios films. After a few theaters were built, the Depression hit and truncated the plan. In 1931 this joint was built for $400,000. The ceiling is painted with the famous art deco pseudo-Moravian sunburst surrounded by leaping gazelles. On the red walls are murals of 16th-century theatrical figures. The seats are done in plush red velvet. Ornamental pewter and brass are everywhere, even in the bathrooms. Opulent is the word.

About 10 miles from Ashland on US 23N is *Russell,* home to numerous antiques shops and restaurants. Downtown Russell has an antiques district with a number of stores. The largest is *White Eagle Antiques* (515 Bellefonte Street; 606-836-2830; whiteeagleantiques.com). There's a plethora of things, new and old, from primitive furniture to glassware, and an unusual assortment of railroad- and boating-related items. In the midst of garden statuary and fountains is a courtyard where you can catch your breath. Also try the *Antique Junction* (440 Bellefonte Street; 606-836-3238).

Just north of Russell on US 23 you will pass *AK Steel Mill* (formerly Armco; 606-329-7111), an enormous operation perched on the banks of the Ohio. It was the world's first continuous sheet-rolling mill when it was opened in 1923. By the 1950s a process called hot strip milling replaced the old system. Now many of the trains rolling in and out of Russell's train yard are hauling materials to and from the steel mill and its massive coke ovens on the other side of Ashland, near Catlettsburg.

In this area, US 23 runs alongside the Big Sandy River, which forms the boundary with West Virginia. It is a route that allows travelers access to the rich culture and history of the entire region. Where the Big Sandy meets the Ohio River sits the town of Catlettsburg, a former timber center where loggers rode rafts of logs down the Big Sandy only to blow their money in the town's saloons. These days more than half a million tons of freight traverse the river annually. Many boats transport petroleum products to and from the massive Catlettsburg Refinery where more than 2 percent of the gasoline made in the United States is produced. The town's Kentucky Harbor is the largest inland port in the United States.

Because Catlettsburg's economy is half nautical, it's no surprise that one of the area grocery and supply stores operates half on land and half on water. *The Boat Store* (1907 Center Street; 606-739-5166; catlettsburgboat store.com) primarily serves tugboats and tows. The boats can stop by for fuel and almost any imaginable supply or they can send in their order ahead of time and the Boat Store crew can meet them midstream—the boats are lashed together with the trip in progress and supplies are unloaded. Those of us not traveling by boat can't shop from the grocery supply store, but they do welcome us to their gift shop called Towboat Treasures (same phone; towboattreasures.com), open from 9 a.m. to 5 p.m., Monday through Friday. A landlubber can buy nautical clocks, brass compasses, clothing, jewelry, model tugboats, license plates that say "Tugboat Power," and the like.

The river is the lifeblood of this town, but it has also wrought repeated devastation with each flood. Although any floodwall is a monument to hard times, the one in Catlettsburg also serves as a monument to achievement and pride. One portrait painted on the wall is of native son *Billy C. Clark,* a nationally acclaimed author whose fiction makes use of his hometown's history. As early as his teen years, Clark wrote stories of life on the river and its colorful characters. One of his best-known novels, *A Long Row to Hoe,* is often used in university courses as a study in Appalachian culture. The book's beginning tells an auspicious story of the author's birth in 1928. Although she was going into labor, Clark's mother took a streetcar across the Big Sandy Bridge from Huntington, West Virginia, as terrible floodwaters were rising and lapping at the bridge. She was determined to give birth in Kentucky so that Billy would not be "a foreigner." When that very bridge was replaced in 1999, the town named it for Clark.

The town of *Louisa,* south of Ashland on US 23, is at the confluence of the Big Sandy and its two main forks, the Levisa and the Tug. These rivers are characterized by narrow crooked channels and radically variable depths caused by floods and draughts, and they can be blamed (or praised) for keeping the region relatively isolated, since navigation was so difficult until the mid-20th century. Human beings tend to try to tame rivers and usually lose, either immediately or eventually. An interesting example is the *Louisa Needle Dam,* a unique moveable dam and lock built in 1897 just downstream from the town. You can visit the site. To cross between Louisa and Fort Gay, West Virginia, you'll drive on a bridge that made the pages of *Ripley's Believe It or Not* as the only bridge to cross two rivers (the Tug and Levisa), to connect two cities and two states, and to have a right-hand turn in the middle—a ponderous combination.

Want a brief respite from culture but not from water? One good anti-dote is going fishing. The *Yatesville Lake State Park,* southwest of Louisa on Highway 3, is regionally famous for its largemouth bass. There's a full marina. For landlubbers there's an interpretive center with a comprehensive exhibit of all sorts of engineering battles with the Big Sandy River. There's also an interesting reconstructed wetlands area on a high bluff near the entrance to the Yatesville Lake Wildlife Management Area. Camping is available in the park. Call (606) 673-1490 or visit parks.ky.gov/parks/recreation parks/Yatesville-Lake/default.aspx.

Must be something in the water, as they say. The very small town of *Blaine,* located on Highway 32 on the western end of Yatesville Lake (about 20 miles from Louisa) is the hometown of two shining stars in country music, Ricky Skaggs and Larry Cordell. Skaggs is known worldwide as a chart-topping ambassador for bluegrass and roots music. His childhood musical roots are in Blaine-area church music. He became famous at the age of 6 when he performed on stage with the father of bluegrass music, Bill Monroe. Some of Ricky Skaggs' No. 1 hits were written by his boyhood friend and Blaine son, Larry Cordell. A singer/songwriter in his own right, Cordell is well known in country music as the songwriting genius behind hits for the likes of Alison Krauss, Garth Brooks, Kathy Mattea, and Diamond Rio. His own band is called Lonesome Standard Time.

Two pig-iron furnace ruins near Ashland are accessible to the public. One is the *Clinton Furnace,* built by the Poage brothers in 1833. Take US 60 south, turn left (east) on Highway 538, and left again on Shopes Creek Road to the furnace ruins. The other, *Princess Furnace,* was put into operation in 1864. From town take US 60 south, then Highway 5 north; watch for a rough stone structure near the road.

A Pig-Iron Primer

The furnace ruins in the Ashland area were all once part of a much larger community of pig-iron operations. Because the sites are usually in bad condition and none of them are part of guided tours, let me explain how they worked. It was a clumsy process, but these furnaces produced tons and tons of rough pig iron that were refined into steel, wrought iron, and ingot iron. The Civil War was fought with bullets and cannonballs from these humble industries. The earliest furnaces of the late 18th century produced approximately three tons of iron from nine tons of ore—today's steel furnaces need only about half an hour to produce the same amount of steel the old furnaces could produce in a year.

Enormous stones were quarried from the nearby mountains and used to build the furnaces by the sides of hills. A bridge was built to the top of the chimney, where they dumped the "charge," which consisted of iron ore, also mined locally; limestone, which acts as a fluxing agent; and charcoal, for heat. The charcoal, in turn, was made by burning prime hardwood down to lumps of black, porous carbon. When all this was dumped into the top of the furnace, pig iron and slag came out the bottom and cooled in ditches. When you visit these old furnaces, climb inside, if possible, and look up the stacks; often they taper beautifully to a small round opening at the top. The quality of this stonemasonry is superb. It's important to know what's possible.

The furnace tour continues west of Ashland in Carter County. Just 2 miles north of Grayson is a little community called *Pactolus,* which also has a rundown furnace right by the road. This one was a blast furnace that used hydropower from the Little Sandy River. If your interest is piqued, continue north on Highway 7 to the ruins of the *Iron Hill Furnace,* once the largest charcoal-powered blast furnace in the region. Stay on Highway 7 until it merges with Highway 2, then continue to Highway 1773, turn left (west), and go 4 miles to Boone Furnace on Grassy Creek. The blast furnace, built by Sebastian Eifort, started producing iron in 1857.

South of Grayson is the *Mount Savage Furnace,* one of the best preserved and most beautifully made furnaces in the state. If you want to see only one furnace, this is the judge's choice. Take Highway 7 south of Grayson and turn east on Highway 773. The furnace is on the left, about 1½ miles east of Hitchins. The gorgeous stonework was done in 1848 by a Prussian mason named John Fauson.

Carter County is home to ***Carter Caves State Resort Park,*** one of the most magnificent small parks in this region of the United States. From Grayson take I-64 or US 60 west, then go north on Highway 182 to 344 Caveland Drive. In addition to a lodge, camping facilities, a pool, canoe trips, and hiking trails, there are 20 navigated caves, three of which are lighted for tours. Many of the caves are wild and can be seen only if you're excited by the idea of real spelunking. For more information, call (606) 286-4411 or visit parks.ky.gov/parks/resortparks/Carter-Caves/default.aspx. Two of the park's most significant parts are ***Bat Cave*** and ***Cascade Caverns,*** both of which are state nature preserves. Bat Cave is part-time home to one of the nation's largest wintering populations of the Indiana bat, a federally endangered species. The bats hang in tight clusters in cracks and on the ceiling. There are no winter tours of this cave because it is important not to disturb these creatures during the winter; they have stored just enough fat to keep them alive during hibernation, and flying would use up their reserves. Cascade Caverns is not contiguous with the rest of the park. Take Highway 182 south, turn west onto Highway 209, and follow signs. Aboveground, on the north slopes by the caverns, are some rare plants that are usually found much farther north, and there are a number of mountain maple trees, shrublike trees found here along the stream that flows out of the cave toward Tygarts Creek, where the hemlock forest and old yews will take your breath away. During the summer the park offers guided canoe trips. Better yet, when the water is high enough—from late winter through early spring—you can take your own trip beginning anywhere upstream and ending in the park. East of Olive Hill, where Highway 1025 goes under I-64, you can launch a canoe and take a gorgeous 12-mile paddle to the park. Though generally innocuous, there may be Class II rapids and dangerous deadfalls along this part of Tygarts Creek, so be careful. For information about any facet of Carter Caves State Resort Park, call (606) 286-4411 or, for lodge reservations (800) 325-0059.

Another look at the Civil War and its effect on Carter County is offered in the form of a summertime outdoor musical called *Someday*. It's a love story with Class II rapids and deadfalls, just like the creek. From mid-June to mid-July, show time is Friday and Saturday at 8:30 p.m. Call (606) 286-4522 for information and tickets. The drama takes place inside ***Grayson Lake State Park*** (606-474-9727; parks.ky.gov/parks/recreationparks/Grayson-Lake/

default.aspx) just south of I-64 if you take exit 172 to 314 Grayson Lake State Park Road. There's a large man-made lake surrounded by sandstone, a campground, a marina, and lots of fish. The adjacent Grayson Lake Wildlife Management Area is said to be home to bald eagles, among other wildlife, especially birds. Bring your binoculars.

Morehead is a typical university town except that it's plopped right down in the hills of eastern Kentucky. A friend of mine chose to go to Morehead State because he loves to rock climb and sail, two sports one can't pursue in one's free time at most Kentucky colleges. Sailing and all other forms of boating and water play are available at *Cave Run Lake*, an 8,270-acre lake fed by the Licking River. If you're interested in learning about how such massive bodies of water are formed and maintained, arrange a tour of the Corps of Engineers dam and towers. If you want a less technical view, just dive in. Fishing may be the most popular thing to do at Cave Run. In fact, it's becoming known as the "muskie capital of the world." For information on fishing, camping, or anything concerning the lake, call the USDA Forest Service at (606) 784-6428 or visit caverun.org.

How about seeing Cave Run Lake from an eagle's point of view? Take the Lakeview Ridge Hiking Trail, beginning at the Forest Service's visitor center (606-784-5624) on Highway 801, where you can also get maps and more information, Monday through Friday, 8 a.m. to 4:30 p.m. For about a mile the trail is merged with the Sheltowee Trace, then it goes high above the lake for another 4 miles and ends at Shallow Flats, where there is a wetland interpretive area.

Glamour Fish

Muskellunge, musky, *Esox masquinongy,* briartooth, water wolf . . . whatever you call a muskie, you'd better be ready for it when it hits your line. Maybe it's considered a "glamour" fish because it puts up such a fantastic fight. Maybe it's because a muskie can measure up to 50 inches and weigh more than 40 pounds. If it's because they taste so great, you may not be able to find out if you hire a fishing guide, who may insist on catch-and-release. Maybe you don't care about eating fish, but you do want to get up close and personal with a long, silver dude with a severe underbite. Call *Cave Run Muskie Guide Service* for a good time, (606) 776-6567 or visit kymuskie.com, any time of year.

And if you were wondering where all those muskies and other fish come from, tour the *Minor E. Clark Fish Hatchery,* also off Highway 801 between the lake and US 60 (you'll see signs). With 111 rearing and brood ponds on more than 300 acres, this is one of the largest state-owned, warm-water hatcheries in the United States. Admission is free, and visitors are welcome Monday through Friday from 7 a.m. to 3 p.m. Call (606) 784-6872 for more information.

At *The Kentucky Folk Art Center* (606-783-2204; moreheadst.edu/kfac) in Morehead at 102 West First Street, you'll find a surprising, thought-provoking, and ultimately impressive collection of carvings, paintings, assemblages, walking sticks, painted furniture, gourd creatures, and other works by folk artists from across Kentucky. The collection began in one room of the Morehead State University art department and was later moved to a small house on campus. Now an independent, fully accredited, nationally recognized museum, it is housed in a renovated historic building at 102 West First Street, near the US 60 bypass. By some definitions, folk art comprises objects that are part of everyday life and that somehow reflect the beliefs, social structure, and experiences of the people in a given region; formal training is usually not received outside the culture from which it springs. You'll understand better when you see the collection. You'll also find yourself thinking deeply and laughing your head off—great responses to art of any kind. There's also a museum store, a rare, fun place to buy birthday presents. The Kentucky Folk Art Center is open Monday through Saturday. Admission is free.

At the Folk Art Center, also ask about scheduling a tour of the *Cora Wilson Stewart Moonlight School.* This humble one-room schoolhouse was where this dedicated teacher started the nation's first adult education night school in 1911 to combat illiteracy. She went on to receive important state and national positions in education. The building is owned by Morehead University and was moved from its original location to First Street, next to the early 1900s train depot that houses the Morehead Tourism offices.

Morehead's biggest celebration is the *Appalachian Celebration,* a weeklong festival held in July. Events, which take place on the university campus, include storytelling, displays by local folk artists and craftspeople, and all kinds of wonderful traditional bluegrass, country, and mountain music. Most events are free. Call (606) 783-2204 for a schedule or more information.

Down at the bottom tip of Cave Run Lake, where the Licking River begins to look like a river again, is the town of West Liberty, the Morgan County seat. Come to town the last weekend in September for the *Morgan County Sorghum Festival.* In the evenings people around here put on their dancing shoes. During the day someone always sets up a mule-drawn sugar cane mill at the Old Mill Park on the banks of the Licking River, so you can see how sorghum molasses is made the old-fashioned way. Call (606) 743-3300 or visit morgancountysorghumfestival.com for more information.

More Good Lodging in Eastern Kentucky

ASHLAND

Ashland Plaza Hotel
Fifteenth and Winchester Streets
(606) 329-0055
ashlandplaza.net

BEATTYVILLE

Travelwise Motor Inn
Highway 11
(606) 464-2225

BENHAM

School House Inn
100 Central Avenue
(606) 848-3000
Country inn in restored school building.

BUCKHORN

Buckhorn Lake State Resort Park
Highway 1833
(606) 398-7510
parks.ky.gov/parks/resort parks/buckhorn-lake/

HAZARD

America's Best Value Inn
359 Morton Boulevard
(606) 436-4777 or
(877) 209-3242
abvihazard-ky.com

Hampton Inn
70 Morton Boulevard
(606) 439-0902 or
(800) 426-7866

Super 8 Motel
125 Village Lane
(606) 436-8888
Your basic motel. Clean. Near the business district.

IRVINE

Snug Hollow Farm Bed & Breakfast
790 McSwain Branch
(located on Highway 594)
(606) 723-4786
snughollow.com
300-acre organic farm with cabin or rooms in farmhouse.

JACKSON

Jackson Inn
Highway 15
(606) 666-7551
jacksoninnky.com

MCKEE

Lakes Creek Bed & Breakfast
350 Lakes Creek Road
(606) 287-7953
bbonline.com/ky/lakescreek
A large restored 1894 log cabin. Horse boarding and trails.

MIDDLESBORO

Days Inn
1623 East Cumberland
(606) 248-5630

MOREHEAD

**Brownwood Bed &
Breakfast & Cabins at
Cave Run Lake**
46 Carey Cemetery Road
(606) 784-8799
caveruncabins.com
Four cabins near Cave
Run Lake.

Holiday Inn Express
110 Toms Drive
(606) 784-5796

PIKEVILLE

Landmark Inn
190 South Mayo Trail
(606) 432-2545
landmarkpikeville.com
Pool, restaurant

PRESTONSBURG

**Jenny Wiley State
Resort Park**
75 Theatre Court
(606) 889-1790
(800) 325-0142
parks.ky.gov/parks/
resortparks/Jenny-Wiley/
default.aspx
Camping, cabins, or state
park lodge.

Super 8 Motel
U.S. Highway 23
(606) 886-3355

SAND GAP

Mountain Springs Inn
1244 State Highway 2004
(606) 965-2789
mountainspringsinn.com
Twelve guest rooms and
family reunion–sized dining
in a house in the woods.
Horse boarding and/or
trail rides on their horses.
Includes a hearty country-
style breakfast.

More Fun Places
to Eat in Eastern
Kentucky

ASHLAND

Chimney Corner Cafe
1624 Carter Avenue
(606) 324-7500
chimneycornercafe.tripod
.com/main.htm
Elegant and unpretentious.
Homemade breads,
fabulous dishes like
crab-stuffed orange
roughy, great salads and
desserts. Live local music.
Reasonable prices. Dinner
only, Monday through
Saturday.

Crisp's Dairy Treat
1200 Kentucky 716
(606) 928-8193
Great hot dogs and fried
apple pies. Summertime
brings tangerine swirl, a
local favorite. Open until
late evening, later in the
summer.

Lamp Post Café
1450 Greenup Avenue
(606) 325-5283
Locally famous for
inexpensive, great country
breakfasts.

BUCKHORN

**Buckhorn Lake State
Resort Park**
4441 Kentucky 1833
(606) 398-7510
parks.ky.gov/parks/resort
parks/buckhorn-lake

CLAY CITY

Kathy's Country Kitchen
20 Black Creek Road
(606) 663-4179
Home cooking with daily
specials.

GRAYSON

Melini Cucina Italian Ristorante
209 South Carol Malone Boulevard
(606) 475-1521
melinicucina.com
Owned by a fabulous cook, born and raised in Italy. Ham calzone, spinach and veggie calzones, Melini stromboli, and baked lasagna. Open daily for lunch and dinner.

GREENUP

Greenbo Lake State Resort Park
955 Lodge Road
(606) 473-7324
parks.ky.gov/parks/ resortparks/Greenbo -Lake/default.aspx
Variety of sandwiches, entrees, and regional specialties such as country ham and fried catfish.

HAZARD

Frances' Diner
1315 Combs Road
(606) 436-0090
Twenty-four-hour home-style country cooking "forever and ever amen."

Peking Chinese Restaurant
454 Main Street
(606) 439-5001
Downtown. Basic Chinese-style menu.

MOREHEAD

Melini Cucina Italian Ristorante
(see Grayson above for other location)
608 East Main Street
(606) 780-8865
melinicucina.com
Owned by a fabulous cook, born and raised in Italy. Ham calzone, spinach and veggie calzones, Melini stromboli, and baked lasagna. Select Italian wines. Open daily for lunch and dinner.

PINEVILLE

Pine Mountain State Resort Park
1050 State Park Road
(606) 337-3066
parks.ky.gov/parks/ resortparks/pine-mountain
Varied menu including traditional Kentucky dishes.

PRESTONSBURG

Billy Ray's Playhouse-Restaurant
101 North Front Avenue
(606) 886-1744
Down-home cooking with daily specials. Home of the Pool Room Burger and Billy Ray's Prime Roast.

Jenny Wiley State Resort Park
39 Jenny Wiley Road
(606) 886-2711
parks.ky.gov/parks/resort parks/Jenny-Wiley/default/ aspx

SLADE

Natural Bridge State Resort Park
Highway 11 near Slade
(606) 663-2214
parks.ky.gov/parks/ resortparks/Natural -Bridge/default.aspx

Northern Kentucky

Like some of its most fascinating inhabitants, northern Kentucky is a bit eccentric. Places to explore range from exquisite Gothic cathedrals and puppet theaters in dense urban areas to anachronistic service stations and prehistoric museums in sparsely populated rural regions. Mark Twain once said that when the world came to an end, he wanted to be in Kentucky because it's always a good 20 years behind. Such misconceptions!

Innovation has always been at the heart of this area's delightful idiosyncrasies. Northern Kentucky boasts architecturally significant bridges, downhill snow skiing, and refreshingly creative farms that specialize in everything from irises and turkeys to maple syrup. Historic buildings and fine craftspeople round out the picture, making this relatively small area one of the most diverse in the state.

Heart of the North

Cynthiana, a small town on US 27 about 30 miles north of Lexington, offers interesting history.

NORTHERN KENTUCKY

Major events such as foundings, wars, and weather catastrophes shape the history of a community, but so do lots of smaller happenings—the first phone call, a new wing on the school, or the passing of a local "character." At the *Cynthiana/Harrison County Museum* on South Walnut Street, you can learn about both kinds of events and how they affected life in this community. You'll discover that Cynthiana was chartered as a town on December 10, 1793, and learn about the two Civil War battles, but you also can learn that the first train pulled into town on May 18, 1854; that the first dial telephone call was made at 2:01 a.m. on November 18, 1962; and that the first convenience store opened in 1967. There are all kinds of artifacts, from

AUTHOR'S FAVORITE PLACES IN
NORTHERN KENTUCKY

Big Bone Lick State Park
Big Bone
(859) 384-3522
parks.ky.gov/parks/historicsites/
big-bone-lick

Blue Licks Battlefield State Park
Blue Licks
(859) 289-5507
parks.ky.gov/parks/resortparks/
blue_licks

Cathedral Basilica of the Assumption
Covington
(859) 431-2060

Curtis Gates Lloyd Wildlife Management Area
Crittenden
(859) 428-2262

Dinsmore Homestead
Burlington
(859) 586-6117
dinsmorefarm.org

Mutter Gottes Kirch
(Mother of God Church)
Covington
(859) 291-2288
mother-of-god.org

Newport Aquarium
Newport
(859) 261-7444
newportaquarium.com

Pendleton County's Wool Festival
first weekend of October
kywoolfest.org

Kincaid Lake State Park
(859) 654-3378
parks.ky.gov/parks/recreationparks/
Kincaid-Lake/default.aspx

Vent Haven Museum
(of ventriloquistic figures)
Fort Mitchell
(859) 341-0461
venthavenmuseum.com

old photos and Civil War uniforms to bonnets and hula hoops, all donated by local citizens—and nothing is refused. The museum is open Friday and Saturday from 10 a.m. to 5 p.m. Admission is free. For more information check the website at cynthianaky .com/cynthianamuseum.

trueblue

Main Street in Cynthiana has more cast-iron-front buildings than Chicago.

In **Williamstown** there are several antiques shops to explore. If you really want to get away from it all, spend the night at **Mullins Log Cabin** at 1435 Denny Road in Cordova, south of Williamstown via Highway 36. There's no phone, no television, no electricity, not even running water (the old-fashioned privy is out back, about 150 feet from the house). In a nod to modern civilization, the cabin now has city water from a spigot outside the cabin. The cabin has become popular for "pioneer weddings," in which some couples even don period clothing and arrive in horse-drawn carriages. Contact owner Judy Mullins at (859) 322-3082 or mullinslogcabin .net for information about visiting or staying overnight.

Thaxton's Licking River Canoe Rental and Paddlers' Inn near Butler offers canoeing and tubing excursions on the Licking River. Seeing the countryside by its natural roadways can connect one to the land in a way that driving a car cannot; no road noise, no cursing at your fellow human beings for passing on a hill; nothing between your skin and the living world. In recent years customer demand to not have to drive far for overnight lodging led the Thaxtons to add cozy waterside cabins to the mix. "Our customers pretty much aggravated us into it," explained Jim Thaxton. Thus was born Paddlers' Inn, a collection of seven cabins, five at the main outpost and two at nearby Kincaid Lake. Complimentary paddling privileges are included, so you can paddle in and out, but some people come just for the getaway. Some of the cabins have kitchens and hot tubs. Thaxton's has also added tubing to its offerings. Call (877) 643-8762 toll-free or (859) 472-2000 for more information and the schedule of excursions. Cabins rent for $59.95 to $99.95 a night. Cabins are "pet friendly" with a one-time pet cleaning fee of $25. The outpost is located in Butler, about 9 miles north of Falmouth, near a bridge on US 27 at 33 Kornbeck Road, a few hundred yards south of its intersection with Route 177. The website gives plenty of details at gopaddling.com.

Falmouth, located about halfway between Covington and Lexington, was founded in 1793. One of the most notable historic buildings is a handsome two-story log cabin built around 1790 called the **Alvin Mountjoy House.** It's one of the few existing 18th-century cabins with a basement. The house is not open for tours anymore, but drive by at 203 Chapel Street, which runs parallel to Main Street.

The **Kincaid Regional Theatre** is a small, professional summer theater that features new shows every season. From mid-June through the end of July, you can see Broadway musicals in Falmouth Auditorium. In downtown Falmouth go east on Shelby Street, south on Chapel Street, and look for signs. Curtain time is 8 p.m. Thursday through Saturday and 2:30 p.m. Sunday. Dinner packages are available, as are lunch packages for afternoon shows. For reservations or a performance schedule, write KRT, 400 Main Street, No. 3, Falmouth 41040, call (859) 654-2636, or visit krtshow.com.

Every quilter I know harbors a special kind of gratitude for **The Quilt Box,** one of the largest and most comprehensive quilt shops in the state. When I first laid eyes on Charlotte Willis's marvelous quilt, *Kentucky Pride,* my initial question was, "Where did she find such gorgeous materials?" This shop has them: Natalie Lahner has made it her mission to carry every

A Right Smart Piece

When asking directions in Kentucky, you need to understand how far "a piece" is. Unfortunately, I can't give you an absolute definition. "Just a little piece" can mean a couple of miles or a few hundred yards, depending on the look in a person's eyes and the tone of the voice. If you don't imply, by your demeanor, that you will believe the directions, the direction-giver may as well lie . . . and might. A body can travel "a little piece" without completely running dry on patience. Private polling tells me "a little piece" is equivalent to "two whoops and a holler." "A far piece" is as far as language permits us to discuss distance and is, in fact, unattainable. "A right smart piece" is pretty far, but you can get there. And, finally, you must be warned about "no piece at all" or it will fool you all your life, because it sounds like you're already there, but it's farther than that. Newspaperman Allen M. Trout defined it this way: "Say you take a chew of tobacco when you start. When you have walked far enough to have chewed and spit all the flavor out, you have come no piece at all." Those who abstain from tobacco use will surely be lost.

quilt-related item imaginable, including more than 5,000 bolts of 100 percent cotton fabric in colors and patterns that will make you drool, along with patterns, notions, books, and finished quilts. They also make custom quilts based on wallpaper, upholstery samples, or unusual designs.

The store is in a restored 150-year-old log structure, which is tastefully married to the Lahners' residence, a reproduction 17th-century house. (An addition was completed in 1997.) Kids love seeing the chickens on the loose. Husbands enjoy sitting on the deck while their wives shop for fabrics. The shop hours are from 9:30 a.m. to 4:30 p.m. Monday through Friday, 9:30 a.m. to 4 p.m. Saturday. From I-75 take the Dry Ridge/Owenton exit (159) and go west on Highway 22. Turn right on Highway 467 or Warsaw Road, go exactly 2.4 miles, and look for the Walnut Springs Farm mailbox and the sign for The Quilt Box. Follow the gravel road 0.4 mile to the second house on the road at 490 East Flynn Road. Call (859) 824-4007.

At the intersection of Highways 227 and 330 in Owenton sits a great vineyard offering a wealth of reasons to visit. **Elk Creek Vineyard** has tasty wines and food, along with lovely accommodations and activities. Many folks may not know it but in 1798 Kentucky was the site of America's first commercial vineyard planted by the winemaker for the Marquis de Lafayette. By the late 1800s, Kentucky was the third largest grape and wine producer in the United States. But Prohibition dealt a severe blow to the Kentucky wine industry. Many vineyards were neglected and fell into ruin. Nestled among the rolling hills, Elk Creek Vineyards was established in 2003 and is already producing award-winning wines. The vineyard also features a deli, art gallery, cooking classes, bed-and-breakfast lodging, massage therapist, live entertainment, gift shop, and outdoor entertainment at the amphitheater during the spring and summer. Stop by for a tasting and tour. The friendly folks will make you glad you did. Summer hours are Monday through Thursday 10 a.m. to 7 p.m., Friday and Saturday, 10 a.m. to 9 p.m. Closed Sunday. Winter and spring hours close about an hour earlier on Monday through Thursday. For more information, call (502) 484-0005; elkcreekvine yards.com.

If sporting clays are your hobby, the **Elk Creek Hunt Club** is just down the road from the winery. The new club is popular with pros and amateurs alike. It takes about two hours to shoot a round of sporting clays. Lessons are available. A world-class facility, Elk Creek offers three separate courses—one over water—and 45 newly remodeled and paved sporting clays stations on 35 shooting fields which can be shot as 50 or 100 target rounds. Elk Creek's sporting clays courses are spread over a 2,500-acre hunting preserve. Golf carts are available for rent. Located at 1860 Georgetown Road, the club is open from 9 a.m. to dusk. Closed Monday. Call (502) 484-4569; elkcreekhuntclub.com.

Sanity Land

A few miles south of **Owenton** on US 127 sits a pink frame house in a yard full of angular alligators and stylized, wide-eyed beasts hidden in a massive bamboo forest. This is not a cubist zoo, but **Seigel Pottery,** 2545 Highway 127 South. Although Greg Seigel has a reputation for producing clay reptiles and collectible marbles, he also makes a variety of functional pots, but not without some humor. For example, a big, sturdy dinner plate glazed with a long pink spiral surrounded by blue comma-shaped dots is called *Boys and Girl.* Many of the sculptural pieces are decorated with local clays and fired in a wood-burning kiln, which produces a rich, earthy effect. The Seigels work at home, so hours are by chance. Rebekka Seigel is nationally known for her exquisite modern quilts. If you have a serious love for this art, ask to see a few of her favorites, or whatever is in progress. She also teaches seminars in quilt technique and design. You can reach the Seigels at (502) 484-2970 or potbaker.com.

Also in Monterey is **Larkspur Press,** sponsor of many of the aforementioned literary readings and a fine, fine little press that is Gray Zeitz's pride and joy. Larkspur books, primarily small chapbooks or broadsides by Kentucky writers, are of high quality in form and in content. All productions are done in letterpress from type set by hand and printed on paper that makes you want to touch and linger. Visitors are welcome, but call ahead, because Zeitz keeps odd hours. Write to Larkspur Press at 340 Sawdridge Creek West, Monterey 40359, call (502) 484-5390 or visit larkspurpress.com.

To get to Port Royal from Monterey, take Highway 355 north. From the Frankfort area go north on US 421 a little way, then veer onto Highway 193 and go "a right smart piece." There is nothing to see in **Port Royal** but the land and the people who live by the land. That's all there is to see in many other areas of the state, but I'd like for those who are familiar with writer, teacher, and farmer **Wendell Berry** to take a good look at northern Henry County, where he makes his home. The Kentucky River forms the eastern border of the county. Here the river basin is wide, the flat bottomland soil rich, the steep hills wooded and deserted. This varied terrain insists that it be farmed in various ways. Except in the wide river bottomland, the arable areas are limited to small, odd-shaped patches, which Wendell Berry chooses to farm with a team of draft horses.

One of the truths Berry repeats is that finicky areas like these are not unique to Henry County. The idiosyncrasies of all lands must be intimately and humbly understood before we can live on them as responsible stewards, he contends. We talk of preserving the wilderness, but we don't preserve the farmland from which we feed ourselves. Farmers are, after all, people who use nature directly, not only for themselves but also for consumers, by proxy. Wherever you live and travel, look at the land and think about the mystery of your dependency on nature and about how you can respond responsibly. Don't try this alone—talk to people and read Wendell Berry's work.

trueblue

People from across the nation send or bring their Christmas cards to the little town of Bethlehem, in Henry County, for a special Christmas postmark.

From Port Royal follow Highway 389 north into Carroll County, through the town of English, where there are ramps onto I-71, and into **Carrollton.** For such a small town, it has a tremendous amount of visible remnants of its history. This National Historic District encompasses 25 blocks and includes 350 buildings, many of which are more than 200 years old. It's perched right above the confluence of the Kentucky and Ohio Rivers. A self-guided walking tour is about the best way to see the 19th-century and Victorian architecture. Start with the museum in the 1880 **Old Stone Jail** on the Courthouse Square. Some of the cells have been restored, and during the restoration work, hidden contraband was found and is now on display. The jail was used to detain prisoners as recently as 1969.

Afterwards, visit the Carrollton/Carroll County Tourism and Convention Commission at 515 Highland Avenue (502-732-7036; visitcarrolltonky .com) for maps and more historic information. There is an excellent historic driving-tour booklet available. Hours are 9 a.m. to 5:30 p.m. Monday through Friday, noon to 5 p.m. Saturday.

Another historic tour in the area is of the **Butler Turpin House,** a very ornate Greek Revival home built in 1859 and appointed inside with period furnishings and heirlooms of the family. The stone kitchen is especially interesting. The house is located in the **General Butler State Resort Park,** just off I-71 at exit 44 to Highway 227 (signs are prevalent) at 1608 State Highway 227. Guided tours of the Butler Turpin House are given.

General Butler State Resort Park has become regionally famous for hosting mountain-bike competitions. Call "Bike Butler" at (502) 484-2998 for a seasonal schedule. There are four major competitions each year—the Sun-Fest in June; Mud, Sweat, and Tears in July; an Off-Road Triathlon in August; and the Kentucky Open in September. It's a sport that is almost scarier to watch than to participate in. The park also has a lodge with a restaurant, cottages, and a campground. For information about either the Butler Turpin House or the General Butler State Resort Park, call (502) 732-4384 or check parks.ky.gov/parks/resortparks/general-butler/default.aspx.

If you visit Carrollton in late winter or early spring, take a drive out US 42 East to **Interstate Greenhouse & Nursery,** home of fresh winter strawberries. It's all part of Kentucky's effort to diversify its agricultural efforts from tobacco. At Interstate, owners Tommy Williams and Bruce Wash converted two former tobacco greenhouses into hydroponic gardens. They plant the strawberries in November and usually begin to pick in February. Planted both horizontally and vertically so they can be constantly nourished by liquids, not soil, the plants are an interesting sight, and the harvest is a delicious winter treat. The greenhouses usually yield thousands of quarts over a period of weeks, but ripening time can vary, so call ahead to see how things are progressing. The address is 3708 Highway 227; the phone number is (502) 732-8710.

East of Carrollton on US 42 is another historic house that is open for tours, the **Masterson House.** Built in 1790, it may be one of the oldest existing brick houses in this region along the banks of the Ohio River anywhere between Pittsburgh, Pennsylvania, and Cairo, Illinois. The bricks were made and fired on-site during construction. The restorers have even planted historic trees started from seedlings gathered from other pioneer homes. Admission is $2, and it is open only on weekend afternoons from

1:30 to 4:30 p.m. between Memorial Day and Labor Day. For more information call Sam Burgess at (502) 732-5713. Ask about Heritage Days in May and September.

Just upriver a few miles is *Warsaw,* a peaceful one-traffic-light river town in the smallest county in Kentucky. There the *Gallatin County Historical Society* has restored and furnished an 1843 Gothic Revival–style home. Follow 1-75 to I-71 west and take the Warsaw exit. Stop by *Maines Hardware* (201 West Market Street; 859-567-5311). Buy some home and garden supplies. In town turn right by the courthouse (the second-oldest continuously operating courthouse in the state, circa 1837) at the only stoplight and look behind the funeral home for the *Hawkins-Kirby House* at 105 East Market Street. To arrange a tour, call (859) 567-4591.

You don't have to call anyone to get a fabulous view of Ohio River traffic from an observation tower at the *Markland Locks and Dam,* on US 42 in Warsaw. It's a great place for a picnic, too. Any questions? Call (859) 567-7661.

Odd Bones

Eccentricity saves lives. (How's that for a bumper sticker?) The little-known *Curtis Gates Lloyd Wildlife Management Area* (800-858-1549) would not exist if the eccentric Mr. Lloyd had not written a 24-page will that thoroughly outlined the future management plan for his 365-acre farm down to every detail. The farm is now part of a 1,179-acre wild area. Before he died in 1923, Lloyd erected an enormous granite monument to himself in the woods. One side reads: "Curtis G. Lloyd born 1859—died 60 or more years afterwards. The exact number of years, months and days that he lived nobody knows and nobody cares." The other side says: "Curtis G. Lloyd monument erected in 1922 by himself for himself during his life to gratify his own vanity. What fools these mortals be!" A fool? Not quite. His preserve boasts one of the shamefully few stands of virgin timber in Kentucky. A forest teeming with wildlife and wilderness left to its own beautiful accord—a black walnut, 36 inches in diameter, towers over acres and acres of huge red oaks and poplars. (Please be careful during deer hunting season!) To think that I-75 is within earshot. From Crittenden follow US 25 south a few miles to 230 Gardnersville Road and look for the sign.

Big Bone Lick State Park is probably the only prehistoric graveyard you'll ever lay eyes on. From Florence take US 127 south (through Sugartit) and turn west on Highway 338 (Beaver Road) at Beaverlick to the town of Big Bone, then follow signs to the park at 3380 Beaver Road. Probably during the end of the Ice Age (more than 10,000 years ago), many of the largest mammals on the continent that came to this area to lick the rich veins of salt and sulfur died, leaving their bones scattered around the massive mineral deposit. Some of the bones have been identified as belonging to the huge ground sloths, tapirs, musk oxen, giant bison, and deerlike animals called cervalces, all now extinct. No one knows exactly the cause of the worldwide destruction of these species. Some say that glacier expansion drove animals south and created an overly dense population that eventually starved. Others blame an epidemic, unscrupulous primitive hunters, or the hand of a god.

The salt lick also was used by Native Americans and, after 1729, by pioneers who boiled down the brines to make highly valued salt. Legend has it that early Virginian settlers, who were fascinated with the massive bones, used mastodon ribs for tent poles and vertebrae for stools. Even Thomas Jefferson was intrigued. He reportedly had more than 300 specimens kept in the White House for research, but a servant pounded them into fertilizer. Not all the bones are lost, however; Big Bone Lick State Park's museum houses an incredible collection of vertebrate fossils from the area. Hours vary throughout the year. Call (859) 384-3522 or go to parks.ky.gov/parks/historicsites/big-bone-lick for information.

Are you ready for a lesson in botany? Directly across the road from the state park is ***Big Bone Gardens,*** a six-acre pleasure garden and sales nursery owned by Mark Lawhorn and Mary Ellen Pesek. There are two big "twin" ponds, a bog area, two little ponds full of decorative aquatic plants that are for sale, and a super-duper campy concrete garden sculpture collection (baby deer and hoboes). Plant prices range from $2 to $50, and the varieties range from common native waterside grasses to Asian lotus plants. The gardens are open on weekends from mid-April through mid-July from noon to 5 p.m. and by appointment otherwise. Park at the Methodist church across the street (but not during Sunday services, please). For an appointment call (859) 869-1314 or visit big-bone-gardens.com.

The tiny town of *Rabbit Hash* sits high on the banks of the Ohio River on Highway 20. It's not much of a town now, but it has an amazingly inveterate business, appropriately called the *Rabbit Hash General Store,* that has not boarded up its windows since 1831. That's more than 180 years of the screen door slamming on the funny little wooden-frame store. In addition to the usual "convenient store" items, there are locally contributed antiques and crafts. Stop by any day and have a soda. Hours are 10 a.m. to 7 p.m. daily, year-round. Located at 10021 Lower River Road, the store also has some mighty talented folks making music there on Saturday nights at 7 p.m. and Sunday afternoons at 2:30 p.m. For more information, call (859) 586-7744 or visit rabbithash.com.

Kentucky has hundreds of bed-and-breakfast establishments, but this one, *Burlington's Willis Graves B&B Inn,* is one of the classiest, inside and out. The 1830s Federal-style brick home was built for Willis Graves, Burlington's county clerk for the first two decades of the 19th century. The home has been exquisitely renovated—Flemish bond brickwork and Federal mantels are all original. Unlike many bed-and-breakfasts, the furnishings are appropriate. Two rooms are available in an 1850s log cabin, now spiffed up to include fancy bathrooms and fireplaces. The inn is only a 12-minute drive from the Cincinnati/Northern Kentucky International Airport, so it's a good option for business travelers. There's even high-speed Internet access in all the rooms. Rates range from $110 to $235 per night. Call (888) 226-5096, or check out the bed-and-breakfast's website at burligrave.com.

Located in a historic house at 5963 North Jefferson Street, the *Tousey House Tavern* is redefining the meaning of Southern cooking. Built in 1822 by Erastus Tousey, the Tousey House has been many things over the years: a home, tavern, livery, hotel, boarding house, gift shop, consignment shop, and restaurant. Former Judge Bruce Ferguson and his wife Elizabeth restored the historic property to its former beauty in 1987. Now owned by the Wainscott family, the Tousey House Tavern has a mouth-watering menu with favorites such as the Tousey Hot Brown—oven roasted turkey, Proscuitto ham, melted cheese, and housemade light mornay sauce over toast points with applewood cured bacon and tomato. Or try a dish of "Southern Comfort," also known as chicken and dumplings, featuring pan seared breast of chicken served with dumplings, carrots, and cream gravy. Reservations recommended. Call 859-586-9900; touseyhouse.com.

Make a weekend of it and spend Sunday at the *Burlington Antique Show.* On the third Sunday of each month from April through October, a high quality antiques show fills the grounds (even some of the horse stalls!) of the Boone County Fairgrounds at 5819 Idlewild Road. People come from great distances to buy and to sell. Admission at 8 a.m. is $3. Early bird admission at 6 a.m. is $5. Children 12 and under free. Free parking. Call (513) 922-6847; burlingtonantiqueshow. And stop by the *Cabin Arts and Quilt Shop* (859-586-8021; cabinarts.com). They stay open on antiques show Sundays, just for you. They have everything a quilter could need (1,500 bolts of cotton fabric!) and handmade gifts and toys for the rest of us. Turn right off Highway 18 at the flashing light at the Old Courthouse corner onto Jefferson-Idlewild Road; the cabin is ¼ mile on the right at 5878 North Jefferson Street.

Have a different, more adventurous notion of a vacation Sunday? Try a trail ride at the *Little Britain Farm* at 5307 Idlewild Road. They also give riding lessons. Total greenhorns are welcome. Call (859) 586-7990; littlebritainfarm.com.

Just 6.5 miles west of the hectic interstate on Highway 18 at 5656 Burlington Pike is a place that recaptures life in a quieter, slower-paced time. *The Dinsmore Homestead* is a living-history site designed to show modern folks what daily life was like in the 1840s. The homestead includes a house, furnished with furniture and belongings of the family that owned it

Speaking Figuratively

You know that polite-but-blank stare your children sometimes give you when you're trying to tell them something? Imagine a whole room of it, and you have an idea of what awaits you at *Vent Haven Museum* in Fort Mitchell (33 West Maple Avenue; 859-341-0461; venthavenmuseum.com). Vent Haven is home to more than 500 ventriloquistic figures (the world's largest known collection), left as a legacy by one William Shakespeare Berger, a Cincinnati businessman and amateur ventriloquist. Assembled between the 1930s and Berger's death in 1972 at age 94, his collection includes figures of all shapes, sizes, and heritages, some predating the Civil War; others are able to walk, move their noses, spit, and smoke cigarettes. It's a little disconcerting but fascinating, and a tour (by appointment only, May through September) will sure be something to talk about. Donation is $10 for adults, $5 for seniors and children age 12 and under.

Gobble Gobble

Although thousands of people on I-75 see the sign on the side of the barn daily, **Tewes Poultry Farm** is off the beaten path in spirit. The Tewes family (pronounced TOO-wis) raises and processes more than 3,000 turkeys annually, and processes more than 600 chickens every two weeks, in addition to keeping some Leghorn hens for eggs. Dan Tewes, patriarch of the 100-acre operation, and his late wife, Mary, had 18 children. There are 78 grandchildren and a growing number of great-grandchildren. Several generations of the Tewes work together to sort and wash eggs, tend to customers, and take care of the hundreds of daily tasks necessary on a "small" farm.

Way before the interstate existed, the Teweses made final payments on their land by selling Easter chicks dipped in pastel-colored food dyes. Today I-75 cuts through the front pasture, a lumberyard sits adjacent to the house, and planes rush overhead to the Greater Cincinnati International Airport. Easter chicks would barely pay the feed bills and aren't considered ethical anymore. Despite the changes, the Teweses carry on a diverse, wholesome operation. Stop to get fresh fryers, big-breasted roasters, turkeys, bacon, eggs, and a vitamin-like dose of friendliness. The birds are dressed on Thursday or Friday, so the birds are fresh for the weekend. Tewes Poultry Farm is just north of Florence. From I-75 take the Buttermilk Pike exit and go into Crescent Springs. Turn left on Anderson Road and look for the farm about a mile on the left at 2801 Crescent Springs Road. They're always home and you're always welcome, but call ahead anyway at (859) 341-8844 (tewesfarm.com).

for five generations, beginning in 1839. There are numerous special events and workshops throughout the year, from basket making to an heirloom plant sale. There are also hiking trails. The homestead is open for tours from April through mid-December on Wednesday, Saturday, and Sunday from 1 to 5 p.m. Admission of $5 is charged. Call (859) 586-6117 for information or take a virtual tour online at dinsmorefarm.org.

From The Dinsmore Homestead, drive east on Highway 18 and turn left on North Bend Road (Highway 237). After a few miles turn right onto Petersburg Road (Highway 20) and take it to Highway 8. Turn right onto Highway 8, follow it to Constance, and look for the **Anderson Ferry** (859-586-5007; andersonferryofficial.com), a two-boat operation in business since 1817. Today this is the quickest crossing from Cincinnati, via Ohio's Highway 50, to the airport on I-275, especially when the bridges nearer town are choked by rush-hour traffic. The two ferries, *Boone 7* and *Boone 8,* or *Little Boone,* haul passengers on demand year-round. From November through April hours are 6 a.m. to 9:30 p.m., and from May through October 6 a.m. to 9:45 p.m. On Saturday the ferry starts running at 7 a.m., and on Sunday the start time is 9 a.m. The ferry runs about every 15 minutes. Cars are charged $5.

Metro Area

If *Covington*'s century-old *Cathedral Basilica of the Assumption* at the corner of Twelfth and Madison Streets at 1140 Madison Street (859-431-2060; covcathedral.com) were in a major coastal city or in Europe, people would rave about it. As it is, this remarkable work of French Gothic architecture is little known to the world. The building is closely modeled after Paris's Notre Dame and the Abbey Church of Saint Denis, complete with flying buttresses and fantastic gargoyles perched high on the facade. Glass is everywhere. Eighty-two windows, including two enormous rose windows, glow endlessly with the changing sun. Measuring 24 feet by 67 feet, the hand-blown, stained-glass window in the transept is said to be the largest in the world. The rich color, variety of shapes, and expressive details can leave you staggering and dizzy in the huge chamber. In one chapel are several paintings by Frank Duveneck, a Covington native who became an internationally known portrait and genre painter and sculptor. My favorite is the austere center panel of the Eucharist triptych of Mary Magdalene at the foot of the cross. To the visual strength of the space, add the music of three massive pipe organs, and you will be transported. (The basic building was constructed, beginning in 1894, for the price of $150,000, the cost of many of today's middle-American homes.)

The altar in the Blessed Sacrament Chapel reads "Behold the Bread of Angels Becomes the Food of Wayfarers," so the faith-inspired beauty of this temple of worship is available to us worldly wanderers. The basilica is open from 9:30 a.m. to 4 p.m. Monday through Friday. Call in advance to arrange a guided tour at (859) 431-2060, ext. 17.

Adjacent to the basilica is the former chancery and the *Cathedral Museum,* where the cathedral treasures are on display. Gold and silver vessels for worship are decorated with cloisonné enamel and semiprecious stones. The chalice of the first Catholic missionary to Kentucky, Father Badin, is included in the collection. Museum and gift shop are open when the cathedral is, except on Monday.

Mutter Gottes Kirch (859-291-2288; mother-of-god.org) at 119 West Sixth Street is another of Covington's fabulous churches that is open to visitors. Call in advance for a guided tour. Started in 1870, Mutter Gottes Kirch (translated, Mother of God Church) was built in Italian (rather than French) Renaissance basilica design. Clock-bearing twin spires over the front facade seem to be held in place by the large apse dome. Inside, the lower panels of the magnificent stained-glass windows depict Old Testament promises while the upper panels depict the corresponding fulfillments. Other inspirational art includes sculpture, some by Covington artist Ferdinand Muer; Stations of the Cross; an 1876 Koehnken and Grimm pipe organ; beautiful floor tile; and large frescoes and murals by Johann Schmitt, who was once Frank Duveneck's teacher and whose work is in the Vatican.

Four galleries with new exhibitions presented nearly every month make the *Carnegie Visual and Performing Arts Center,* at 1028 Scott Boulevard, a bustling art district in itself. There's also a 750-seat theater. Call the galleries at (859) 491-2030 or the theater at (859) 655-8112 when you're in town to find out what's scheduled (thecarnegie.com).

Go through Covington's Riverside Drive-Licking River Historic District on the east side of town by the "Point" where the Licking River empties into the mighty Ohio. Follow Second Street east until it becomes Shelby Street and wraps around to become Riverside Drive. On the strip of land between the street and the river is the *George Rogers Clark Park,* so named because Clark supposedly stopped at the site to gather forces on his way to Ohio to fight Shawnees. In the park are a few new pieces of sculpture by George Danhires. The most fun is a bronze likeness of James Bradley, an African-born slave who worked his way to freedom, crossed the Ohio River, attended seminary in Cincinnati in 1834, and went down in history as the only former slave to participate in the famous, fiery Lane Seminary debates on abolition. Bradley is depicted as reading thoughtfully

true*blue*

The only replica of the tomb of Jesus in the United States is in the Garden of Hope in Covington.

on a park bench facing the river. The piece is so realistic that passersby stop talking so as not to disturb the man.

The bright blue Covington/Cincinnati Suspension Bridge, just a few blocks west of the Licking Riverside Neighborhood, has been renamed the *John A. Roebling Suspension Bridge* in honor of the engineer who designed it. When it opened in 1867, after 22 years of construction, the bridge was the longest of its kind in the world (1,057 feet) and served Roebling as a prototype for his later Brooklyn Bridge in New York City.

Although *Main Strasse* has been billed as a miniature German village in downtown Covington, historically the area is ethnically heterogeneous. German, Irish, and African Americans have lived in this architecturally fascinating neighborhood, which has been developed into a shopping district for tourists. You can find everything from antiques and doll boutiques to restaurants and bakeries. At the edges of the developed area are local pubs with Irish names.

true**blue**

Some scenes from the film *Rain Man,* starring Dustin Hoffman and Tom Cruise, were filmed in the northern Kentucky/Cincinnati area.

One of the best restaurants in town is not German, but Cajun and Creole. *Dee Felice Cafe,* at 529 Main Street, next to the Goose Girl Fountain, is hot. The food is spicy, and the jazz is cool. From a bowl of gumbo to spicy blackened seafood and chicken, the flavor tugs at the Southern palate. It's hard to believe that the ornate building was originally a pharmacy. No Super-X can hold a candle to these pressed tin ceilings and miniature Corinthian columns, details of which are preserved in the restaurant and painted audacious colors. Every night a live band plays Dixieland, blues, and lots of jazz on a stage behind the long bar. The founder, the late Dee Felice, was a jazz drummer in his own right; he used to play with James Brown, Mel Tormé, Sergio Mendez, and others. Lunch hours are Sunday only, from 10 a.m. to 3 p.m. Dinner begins at 5 p.m. nightly. The phone number is (859) 261-2365 and the website is deefelicecafe.com. Reservations are suggested for dinner.

Iron horse history buffs, take note of the *Railway Museum of Greater Cincinnati* at 315 West Southern Avenue. This museum has a number of immaculately preserved items, such as a 1906 Southern Railroad open platform business car, a diner built for the Golden Rocket, several locomotives, sleeping cars, post office cars, cabooses, and more. The grounds are open year-round, Saturday from 10 a.m. to 4 p.m. You can watch as volunteers restore antique engines and equipment. Admission is $4 for adults and $2 for children 10 and under. For more information, check cincirail museum.org.

Unique knickknack nautical decor and more await you any hour of the day or night at *Covington's Anchor Grill* (438 Pike Street; 859-431-9498). Eating with neighborhood locals becomes a dining experience when you put a quarter in the jukebox. The mechanized C. C. doll band display comes to life in the corner of the grill while overhead a rotating ballroom star light sets the mood. Open 24 hours a day, seven days a week!

Perched high on a bluff above Covington, the Interstate, and the Ohio River is the *Behringer-Crawford Museum* (859-491-4003; bcmuseum.org) in Devou Park, a 700-acre recreational green space at 1600 Montague Road, on the west side of I-75. This unique museum houses a really impressive collection of fossils and prehistoric artifacts from the immediate region in addition to exhibits featuring Civil War relics and other artifacts from more recent history. Some of the Ice Age animal specimens were collected by archaeologist Ellis Crawford from the prehistoric site at Big Bone Lick. Hours are Tuesday through Friday from 10 a.m. to 5 p.m., 1 to 5 p.m. on weekends. Admission is $7 for adults, $6 seniors, $4 for children 3 to 17.

Now that you've been high above the Ohio River and looked down at its serpentine, sparkling surface, wouldn't you like to go below it to see inside the river? The *Newport Aquarium* (859-261-7444; newportaquarium.com) has a 53-foot-long wall of clear acrylic that brings you eye level with native species of the Ohio River—big bottom-feeding catfish, nightmare-inducing gar, soft-shell turtles, shovel-nosed sturgeon, and more than you ever imagined. The aquarium is a state-of-the-art facility with exhibits focused on the rivers of the world, a shoreline museum (with an area designed for visitors to touch creatures like starfish and sand dollars), a collection of dangerous and deadly aquatic life (including electric eels and red-bellied piranha), and more. One exhibit allows you to walk through a clear tunnel through shark-filled waters. Titillating and educational, the aquarium is located in a super-modern building with nautical imagery of masts and sails. Go toward the Ohio River on Third Street until you see the Newport on the Levee complex.

Wilder Spirits

Some of the wildest ghosts in Kentucky have been spotted at **Bobby Mackey's** (44 Licking Pike; 859-431-5588), a country-and-western club in Wilder, not far from Newport. Over the years, more than 30 people, employees and patrons alike, have reported seeing ghosts. And these aren't your friendly ghosts—one man claimed to have been attacked by a ghost in a club restroom. Local legend has it that the hauntings are the result of the building's use for satanic worship in the 19th century and its speakeasy days during the 1920s. The owner has tried exorcism and has even posted warning signs so patrons know that not all the spirits at this nightclub come in bottles.

The aquarium is located at 1 Aquarium Way. Open daily from 10 a.m. to 6 p.m. Admission is $23 for adults, $15 for children ages 3 through 12.

Northern Kentucky ushered in the new millennium with a very visible and permanent monument. Not far from the aquarium, at Fourth and York Streets in **Newport,** is the **World Peace Bell,** billed as "the world's largest free-swinging bell." The bell weighs 66,000 pounds and is 12 feet in diameter and 12 feet high. (By comparison, the Liberty Bell in Philadelphia is a mere 2,080 pounds.) The bell was the result of a community effort led by local businessman Wayne Carlisle, who envisioned marking the millennium with a symbol of freedom and peace. Designed by a family-owned company based just across the Ohio River in Cincinnati, the Verdin Bell Company, the bell was actually cast in France. (The foundry in Nantes was one of the few in the world with a furnace that could melt the 100,000 pounds of bronze.) After the casting—on December 11, 1998, the 50th anniversary of the Universal Declaration of Human Rights in Paris—the bell was shipped to the United States, arriving in New Orleans in July 1999. As it traveled up the Mississippi and Ohio Rivers, the bell made stops at cities along the way to great fanfare. In October 1999 it was installed in the glass and steel pavilion that was to be its permanent home. The first northern Kentucky swinging of the bell was at midnight on December 31, 1999, to welcome the year 2000. Pictures on the bell represent significant achievements of mankind, from the Gutenberg press to the first step on the moon. If you want to see it swing and hear its deep, resonant ring, come at noon. The bell also chimes on the hour.

In the heart of Newport is the perennial favorite, ***Pompilios*** restaurant (600 Washington Avenue; 859-581-3065; pompiliosrestaurant.com). Established in 1933, Pompilios is a family-run restaurant and bar that has continued to provide authentic Italian food for 60 years. Even on weeknights the place is packed—people stand amicably on the sidewalk waiting to get in. Pompilios gained national notoriety when it was appeared in the film *Rain Man* with Dustin Hoffman and Tom Cruise. Remember the scene when the autistic Raymond counts at a glance the number of toothpicks in a box that the waitress has dropped? Oh, and people also talk about the time when the cast and crew of *Airborne*—a forgettable 1993 flick featuring then-unknown Jack Black (*Tenacious D, School of Rock*)—wined, dined, and filmed a scene at Pompilios. Open 11 a.m. to 11 p.m. Sunday through Thursday, and 11 a.m. to 10 p.m. Friday and Saturday.

Across the Licking River and northeast of Newport is the ***Weller Haus Bed and Breakfast,*** in Bellevue's Taylor Daughters' Historic District at 319 Poplar Street (2 blocks south of Highway 8). For $109 to $219 you can eat a classy breakfast and sleep peacefully amid 18th-century antiques or relax on the patio overlooking an English-style garden. Call (800) 431-4287 for reservations (wellerhaus.com).

Since 1939 ***Schneider's Sweet Shop,*** at 420 Fairfield Avenue (Route 8), has been ***Bellevue***'s most exquisite temple of the sweet tooth. Using old-fashioned equipment and timeless craftsmanship, Jack Schneider creates truly fantastic homemade ice creams and candies. The place is famous, especially during the winter holiday season, for its opera creams, unusual little chocolate candies with rich, creamy centers, available in the tristate area only. Schneider's other famous originals include the summer top-seller, Ice Ball with Ice Cream, a scoop of vanilla ice cream with shaved ice packed around it and a healthy dose of specially concocted syrup poured over the top. They have won the award for best caramel apple in the Cincinnati area and have the popular vote for Jack's own favorite, cookies 'n' cream ice cream. This heaven is open Monday through Saturday from 10 a.m. to 9 p.m. and Sunday from noon to 9 p.m. Closing time is 10 p.m. in summer. Call (859) 431-3545; schneiderscandies.com.

The patron saint of travelers is ready to welcome you in Bellevue. One of the most interesting and unusual bed-and-breakfasts in the area, ***Christopher's Bed & Breakfast,*** 604 Poplar Street, is housed in a former church. Built in the late 1800s, the 8,100-square-foot structure originally housed Bellevue Christian Church. In 1996 Steve and Brenda Guidugli purchased the century-old building and converted it into a residence. They retained all of the original stained-glass windows. Two guest rooms and one suite are available, each with private baths with whirlpools. The suite has a two-person Jacuzzi. Rates are $115 to $210 per night. Call (888) 585-7085 or (859) 491-9354 for reservations. Or be high-tech and reserve online at christophersbb.com.

Said to be the world's smallest house of worship, the **Monte Casino Chapel** (859-344-3309; thomasmore.edu/chapel/monte_casino.cfm) measures just 6 by 9 feet—no better place for an intimate conversation with God. Just close the door and let fly. The chapel was built in 1910 in a vineyard on a hill just outside of Covington by Benedictine monks. In the late 1960s the chapel was moved to its present site on the campus of Thomas More College, a small liberal arts college in Crestview Hills. From I-75 take I-275 east and exit onto Turkeyfoot Road. Monte Casino Chapel is next to a large pond on the left side of the road.

Not said to be the world's smallest house of drama, the **Village Players of Fort Thomas** do, nonetheless, use a very small, intimate, three-quarter stage where plays are performed year-round except in June. The theater is located at 8 North Fort Thomas Avenue. The mailing address is P.O. Box 75082, Fort Thomas 41075. Fort Thomas is southeast of Bellevue. For a schedule and other information, call (859) 781-3583 or check the-village-players.com.

Buffalo Trace Area

The river towns strung along the mighty Ohio and the areas that spread away from them are usually historically significant and, for that reason, often a touch schizophrenic, caught between the stillness of the past and the fluid present. **Augusta,** in Bracken County, is one of the few such towns that has struck a happy balance while remaining scenic. From Covington or Newport, either hug the banks of the Ohio River by following Highway 8 east, or buzz along the newer "AA" Highway 546, which connects Alexandria and Ashland. If you take the AA, watch for its intersection with Highway 1159. Turn left (north) and meander around for a moment at the

Walcott Covered Bridge, a 75-foot-long wooden bridge spanning Locust Creek, which was active from 1824 until 1954. Walk onto the bridge and read the descriptions of bridge types, definitions of terms, and explanations for methods of construction.

At the ferry landing on Riverside Drive, the *Augusta Ferry* (606-756-3291; augustaky.com/ferry-cam-2/), one of the very few functional ferries on the Ohio River. It's operational year-round 8 a.m. to 8 p.m. The ride costs $5 per car. Pedestrians on foot may ride the ferry free. Imagine yourself crossing the water when the town was new and the ferry was powered by mules.

Just a block down from the river and next to Augusta Park, at 103 West Second Street, is *The Parkview Country Inn,* a charming bed-and-breakfast decorated with art and antiques. The building dates to the 1830s and has served as a tavern and boardinghouse, hotel, and even a factory—in the 1960s and 1970s it housed a sewing operation that made mattresses for the U.S. Army. There are ten guest rooms, including one that is wheelchair accessible. There's a full-service restaurant. Call (606) 756-2603 for information and reservations (parkviewcountryinn.com).

For snacks, stop by the *Augusta General Store* at 109 Main Street, a great place to stop for sundries and much more; the store includes a soda fountain, bakery, deli, and grill. The phone number is (606) 756-2525.

A popular event in the area is *"The Old Reliable" Germantown Fair,* held the last week in July at the Germantown fairgrounds on Highway 10. No one seems to be able to explain the "Old Reliable" aspect beyond the fact that it happens every year. For more information, visit germantownfair

Lights, Camera, Action!

You may have already seen Augusta if you watched the television miniseries *Centennial,* because the town was used to film scenes taking place in St. Louis, Missouri, in the 1880s. Because Augusta has no flood wall, Water Street (or Riverside Drive) was a ready-made set, except for a few details—the film crew put down 4 inches of dirt on the street to cover the pavement and pulled down power lines and business signs. The houses along the river were, as they always are, picture-perfect. Since then, several Public Broadcasting System (PBS) productions have been filmed in Augusta, including the classic *Huckleberry Finn.*

.com. Follow Highway 8 along the river to Maysville. If you arrive from the west, there is a functional **covered bridge at Dover.** Highway 1235 crosses Lee's Creek by means of this 61-foot-long Queensport truss bridge, which had a tollbooth at one end when the oldest part was built in 1835.

Maysville is the next town upriver, the site of the closest bridge to the north and the hub of activity for the whole area. To steep yourself in area history, go to the **Kentucky Gateway Museum Center** (606-564-5865; kygmc.org), at 215 Sutton Street, in an 1878 structure originally built to be the town's first library. Because of the historic significance of the area as an early point of access to the west, the little museum tells the bigger story of the expansion of America. Hours are 10 a.m. to 5 p.m. Tuesday through Friday, 10 a.m. to 4 p.m. Saturday, and 1 p.m. to 4 p.m. Sunday. Admission is charged.

The downtown flood wall in Maysville is becoming an art gallery on a grand scale, with the creation of huge murals depicting scenes from the area's history. The larger than life **Maysville Flood Wall Murals** are privately funded and are created by Louisiana artist Robert Dafford, who has painted more than 20 murals for the city of Paducah in western Kentucky. The first three murals showed the town's pioneer landing spot, Limestone Landing, as it might have looked in the 1700s, 1800s, and 1900s, but now all have been completed. Maysville has many historic buildings and sites, from a pioneer graveyard, to the 1850s New Orleans–style homes of Mechanics Row, to the childhood home of singer Rosemary Clooney. Pick up a free walking tour brochure at the visitors bureau.

Follow Second Street past Sutton and park anywhere. On the north corner of Sutton and Wall Streets is the shop of a fine furniture maker. **Joseph Byrd Brannen & Co., Antique Furniture Reproductions** is an inspirational one-person operation. Joe Brannen is asked to make all manner of hardwood furniture, but his true love is for traditional 18th- and 19th-century American furniture in cherry, walnut, mahogany, and curly maple, a wood with delicious figuring and a mean grain from which many woodworkers keep a respectful distance. Joe does use power tools, but he finishes all of his work by hand, using planes or scrapers that are fueled by pure elbow grease. The difference is noticeable and worth the extra cost. He always has a few finished pieces of furniture on hand and welcomes visitors Monday through Friday from 9 a.m. to 5 p.m., and on Saturday from 9 a.m. to noon.

The Tables Do Turn

The Maysville-Washington area was settled by Simon Kenton, who first claimed the land. Kenton later sold it for 50 cents an acre to Arthur Fox and William Wood, who laid out the town of Washington. Like a good imperialist, Kenton had come to the area in search of sugar cane so that he could get rich making Jamaican-style rum. The hills were indeed covered with cane, but it was wild Kentucky cane, a tall, woody native grass, the only bamboo species native to North America. Nothing sweet about it. Like a good capitalist, Kenton realized his error and went on to exploit some other aspect of the land. He eventually opened a small store in a cabin in Washington; that cabin now stands next to the visitor center. Legend has it that Kenton couldn't pay his bills and was thrown into debtor's prison in Washington, the very town he founded. The tables do turn.

For a brochure and price list, write 145 West Second Street, Maysville 41056, or call (606) 564-3642.

Drive west another 2 blocks to Rosemary Clooney Street, so named when the singer's first motion picture premiered in Maysville, her hometown. Go toward the river and you'll find the only active Amtrak station in Kentucky and a great place to eat called *Caproni's on the River* (320 Rosemary Clooney Street; 606-564-4321). Its national fame began in the 1930s, when it was just a cafe at which eastbound soldiers stopped during train layovers. Today, two long balconies look out over a wide, slow-moving part of the Ohio River. The other selling points are super food, high-quality local and foreign wines, and imported beers. The menu is diverse, with steaks, prime rib, country ham, and lots of pasta and seafood dishes. Reservations are recommended on the weekends.

Another of Kentucky's few remaining covered bridges is east of Maysville in Lewis County. From Maysville take Highway 10 through Plumville and turn left (east) onto Spring Creek Road. Just as you cross the county line at the intersection with Cabin Road you'll see the *Cabin Creek Bridge* on the south side. The 114-foot-long bridge was built in 1897 and closed to traffic in 1983.

Driving the 4 miles straight uphill on US 68 between Maysville and Washington will take you a matter of minutes. In the 18th century, however, the climb consumed a whole day. Heavily loaded wagons and carts that had just come across the Ohio River at Maysville (then called Limestone) were worn out by the time they reached the ridge, so they stopped at Washington for a rest. I wouldn't call these pioneers tourists, but their patronage caused the town to grow from a few humble cabins into a bunch of humble cabins.

When Kentucky joined the Union in 1792, people west of the Alleghenies thought that **Washington,** population 462, might become the capital of the United States. (Obviously, the other Washington got the vote.) If time could have frozen at that moment, you probably would have seen a town much like the historic restoration that stands today. You can get a more complete story of the town and its characters from one of the tour guides at the visitor center, which is located in one of the original 119 cabins from 1790. Guided tours of the town are offered. Call (606) 759-7411 for more information about tours and prices (washingtonky.com).

One of the most popular tours focuses on the area's role in the Underground Railroad. The first stop is the **Harriet Beecher Stowe Slavery to Freedom Museum,** where exhibits include slave manacles and collars, original slavery documents, and many items relating to Stowe and her famous 1852 book, *Uncle Tom's Cabin.* Stowe is thought to have first witnessed a slave auction during a visit to this house in 1833. Its owners at the time were the Sellmans, whose daughter Elizabeth was a student of Stowe's at the Western Female Institute in Cincinnati. The tour also includes a tour of **Paxton Inn,** a station on the Underground Railroad. According to local legend, slaves hid on a narrow hidden staircase until they could be moved across the Ohio River. Quilts hung on clotheslines or fences served as signs or warnings. The log cabin pattern, for example, indicated a "safe house."

Washington is full of small antiques and specialty shops selling everything from rare books to homemade candies to clocks, yarns, dried herbs, and copper lamps. To view a collection of horse-drawn carriages in the **Carriage Museum,** call (606) 759-7305 or visit washingtonky.com/carriage_museum.htm.

Just a few miles from Washington off US 68 is the community of **Mays Lick.** Founded in the late 1700s, this tiny community has numerous historic buildings and churches and a couple of small shops.

US 68 follows a north-south path made by buffalo traveling to and from the salt deposit at Blue Licks. From Maysville go south on the buffalo trace to the **Blue Licks Battlefield State Resort Park** (10299 Maysville Road;

859-289-5507 or 800-443-7008; parks.ky.gov/parks/resortparks/blue_licks). The place had always been one of importance to the native people as well as to the settlers who mined salt there. Its connotation darkened when in August 1792 more than 60 Kentucky pioneers were killed in a bloody Revolutionary battle against Native Americans and Canadian soldiers ten months after the British surrendered at Yorktown. All this in a 15-minute battle! A large granite obelisk at the park marks the area where the fighters, including Daniel Boone's son Israel, were buried in a common grave.

Take a hike along the buffalo trace beginning in the parking area. This 15-acre area is set aside as a state nature preserve in order to protect one of the last and largest stands of Short's goldenrod, a federally designated endangered species. Notice how the goldenrod grows thickest in the open areas. It is speculated that grazing and trampling by buffalo, now nonexistent in Kentucky, helped the plant survive; the buffalo also may have carried the seeds in their thick fur and thus spread the graceful yellow plant. (Goldenrod, by the way, is not responsible for your hay fever. Blame ragweed.) Goldenrod blooms in September, but as tempting as it is, please don't pick any.

The displays in the park museum are concerned with the cultural and geographic history of the area. Several original pieces of Daniel Boone's salt-making equipment are in the museum, donated by descendants of Simon Kenton. In 1778 Boone and a few others made a salt expedition and were taken prisoner by the Shawnees, who adopted many of the white men into their families. Boone was adopted by the chief, Blackfish. Later Simon Kenton retrieved the equipment. Today the park has fishing facilities and all the usual recreational trappings. Cottages and lodge rooms are available. The lodge dining room serves breakfast, lunch, and dinner daily. Call (859) 289-5507 for information. In mid-August the park sponsors a historic reenactment of the battle during a festival that features period demonstrators and other related entertainment.

This is definitely the region of covered bridges. ***Johnson Creek Covered Bridge*** crosses the creek on the original buffalo trace just north of Blue Licks Battlefield State Park. Built in 1874, the dilapidated structure is 114 feet long and 16 feet wide, with Smith-type trusses. Take US 68 east from the park, then take Highway 165 north to Highway 1029 and watch for the bridge, which is closed to traffic.

In Fleming County, south of Maysville, there are three covered bridges. The first is the 60-foot-long **Goddard (White) Covered Bridge,** the only surviving example of Ithiel Town truss design in the state, a latticelike design that uses rigid, triangularly placed beams as supports. Photographers love this spot because a picturesque country church can be seen through the bridge. From Maysville go to the county seat, Flemingsburg, by way of Highway 11 south. Then follow Highway 32 east almost 6 miles to Goddard. This time, you can drive over the bridge. For more information call (606) 845-5951.

trueblue

The Franklin Sousley Monument in Flemingsburg honors one of the World War II veterans who raised the American flag at Iwo Jima.

Follow Highway 32 down the road a piece and turn right (west) on Rawlings Road, or north on Highway 1895 (Maxey Flats Road). At **Ringos Mills** you'll find an 86-foot-long bridge built in 1867 that was part of a large 19th-century gristmill.

A more utilitarian-style covered bridge is a few miles away near Grange City. The 86-foot-long **Hillsboro Bridge** is roofed and sided with corrugated tin, and the abutments are made of "red stone." The construction is of the burr truss design with multiple king posts. It's a sight! It's also a shame that it's too run-down to use. To get there from Flemingsburg, drive south on Highway 111, pass Hillsboro, and watch the right side of the road.

Seven miles south of Blue Licks is a rural community called **Carlisle,** which boasts some 350 buildings that are on the National Register of Historic Places. One of them is said to be made of the only Daniel Boone cabin logs in Old Kentuck' that haven't turned into humus—actually, the cabin is still standing. To go, take US 68 northwest of town for 3 miles and watch for the state historic marker. Tours are offered by appointment. In downtown Carlisle the **Old Nicholas County Jail** and jailer's home have been refurbished down to the dungeonlike cells. Tours are offered by appointment, and on the second Thursday of every month, a delicious four-course lunch is served. Reservations are required and fill up fast despite the ability to serve 85 at a time! For information about the Boone cabin tours or the jail, call Carlisle/Nicholas County Tourism at (859) 289-5174 (carlisle-nicholas county.org) or the jail at (859) 749-7986.

More Good Lodging in Northern Kentucky

AUGUSTA

Asbury Meadow Bed and Breakfast
3737 Asbury Road
(606) 756-2100
asburymeadow.com
Historic home with comfortable guest rooms featuring modern amenities.

BURLINGTON

First Farm Inn
2510 Stevens Road
(859) 586-0199
firstfarminn.com
Bed-and-breakfast in an 1870s home on a working horse farm.

CARROLLTON

General Butler State Resort Park
1608 State Highway 227
(502) 732-4384
parks.ky.gov/parks/resortparks/general-butler/

DRY RIDGE

Value Stay
I-75, exit 159
(859) 824-3700

FLORENCE

Best Western
7821 Commerce Drive
(859) 525-0090

MAYSVILLE

French Quarter Inn
25 East McDonald Parkway
(606) 564-8000
frenchquarterinn.com

NEWPORT

Gateway Bed and Breakfast
326 East Sixth Street
(859) 581-6447
gatewaybb.com
Spacious rooms in an Italianate-style townhouse.

Grace Manor Bed and Breakfast
828 Linden Avenue
(859) 491-4213
gracemanorbb.com
1906 brick home located in Newport's East Row Historic District. Very near many attractions, including Newport on the Levee.

WILLIAMSTOWN

Days Inn
I-75, exit 154
(859) 824-5025

Red Carpet Inn
I-75, exit 154
(859) 824-4305

More Fun Places to Eat in Northern Kentucky

ALEXANDRIA

Sun Valley Pizza
11500 Alexandria Pike
(859) 635-0010
Just moderately priced carryout pizza and the like, but the steak hoagies are reputedly addictive.

BROOKSVILLE

Donna's Place
113 Locust Street
(across from the county courthouse on Highway 19)
(606) 735-2091
Down home–style breakfast, lunch, and dinner.

CARLISLE

Tracks Restaurant
Highway 36, southeast of town
(859) 289-5464
Model electric train runs on tracks near ceiling while you eat.

CARROLLTON

Cooper's Restaurant
1420 Gillock Road
(502) 732-4990
Catfish, barbecue, steaks,
and sandwiches.

**General Butler State
Resort Park**
1608 State Highway 227
(502) 732-4384
parks.ky.gov/parks/
resortparks/general-butler
Varied menu with buffet.

Point Park
Downtown Carrollton
Naturally attractive site
where the Kentucky and
Ohio Rivers meet. Bring a
picnic.

**Welch's Riverside
Restaurant**
505 Main Street
(502) 732-9118
For breakfast, lunch, and
dinner.

COVINGTON

Wertheim's
514 West Sixth Street
(859) 261-1233
Traditional German fare
plus pasta and chicken
dishes.

CYNTHIANA

Biancke's Restaurant
102 South Main Street
(859) 234-3443
bianckes.net
Always a big local crowd.
Good Italian and American
cooking for reasonable
prices.

FORT MITCHELL

Greyhound Tavern
2500 Dixie Highway
(859) 331-3767
greyhoundtavern.com
Landmark restaurant with
good country cooking.

FORT THOMAS

El Midway Cafe
1017 South Fort Thomas
Avenue
(859) 781-7666
Great fajitas and other
mesquite fare in a
restored 1890s saloon.

MAYSVILLE

Tippedore's
(in French Quarter Inn)
25 East McDonald
Parkway
(606) 564-8000
frenchquarterinn.com
Serving breakfast only.

NEWPORT

Hofbräuhaus
200 East Third Street
(859) 491-7200
hofbrauhausnewport.com
Authentic Bavarian fare
(like sauerbraten and
weisswurste, a white
sausage) and beer, of
course. A German beer
hall *mit der gusto!*

WASHINGTON

Marshall Key's Tavern
2100 Old Main Street
(606) 759-1173
Homemade soups,
sandwiches, daily
specials, and pies.

South-Central Kentucky

Kids aren't the only people who need to play and learn. This region's parks and large dammed lakes are like big playgrounds for adults. There are two of the world's natural wonders, Mammoth Cave, which highlights the most spectacular manifestations of Kentucky's unique karst geography, and the breathtaking Cumberland Falls, the second-largest cataract in the Western hemisphere and one of two in the world with a moonbow. South-central Kentucky is also associated with history. The north is Lincoln country and home to the state's only African-American history gallery, and the south boasts the beautiful Big South Fork National Park. *Bowling Green,* the largest city, is known, in part, for having the world's only Corvette plant. The whole region is spiced up with amusing town names, quirky craftspeople, and zany festivals.

From Caves to Culture

Being in the heart of Western Kentucky University's campus at 1444 Kentucky Street in Bowling Green, *The Kentucky Museum* is not off the beaten path, but its contents are

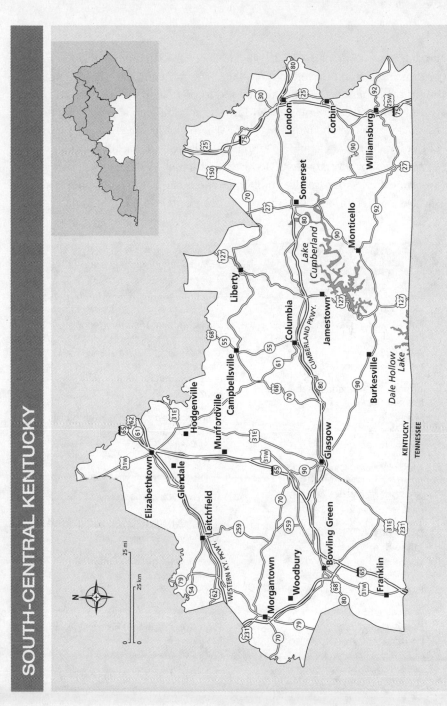

SOUTH-CENTRAL KENTUCKY

unique. This is one of the best collections of objects pertaining to Kentucky history and culture housed in one place. The museum also makes a special effort to exhibit fine traveling shows and to put together displays using borrowed objects that otherwise would never be in the public view. Traditional Kentucky quilts are the museum's forte. There's a Christmas crazy quilt made of silk hat liners, for example. During the holidays, a passel of relatives were snowbound for several weeks, so instead of flipping on the tube and watching game shows, they made a quilt together. Some of the quilts are political, such as the 1850 Henry Clay quilt with his portrait in the middle in crewel

AUTHOR'S FAVORITE PLACES IN
SOUTH-CENTRAL KENTUCKY

The American Cave Museum
Horse Cave
(270) 786-1466
hiddenrivercave.com

Appalachia—Science in the Public Interest (ASPI)
Mount Vernon
(606) 256-0077
appalachia-spi.org

Barthell Mining Camp
Stearns
(888) 550-5748
barthellcoalcamp.com

Battle of Tebbs Bend Civil War Battle Site
Campbellsville
(270) 789-3025
tebbsbend.com

Cumberland Falls
(especially the moonbow)
Corbin
(606) 528-4121
parks.ky.gov/parks/resortparks/
Cumberland-Falls/default.aspx

Elizabethtown Historic Walking Tours
Thursday night in the summertime
Elizabethtown
(270) 982-2209
touretown.com

Highland Games and Gathering of Scottish Clans
late May, Glasgow
(270) 651-3141
glasgowhighlandgames.com

The Kentucky Museum
Bowling Green
(270) 745-6080
wku.edu/kentuckymuseum

Riverview at Hobson Grove
Bowling Green
(270) 843-5565
bgky.org/riverview

Wolf Creek National Fish Hatchery
Rowena
(270) 343-3797
fws.gov/wolfcreek

Feather Crowns

You can't help liking Curiosity Hall, a narrow hall on one side of Bowling Green's Kentucky Museum filled with unusual relics with unusual ties to Kentucky. The oddities include things such as doll heads supposedly used during World War I to transport spy messages and an item known as a "death crown" or "feather crown," a ring of feathers found inside the pillow of a deceased person. Some say that the crown means that the person has gone to heaven. Others say that the feathers form a ring slowly during one's life, and when the ring is complete, the time has come to die. A friend told me that this belief was so deeply instilled in her during childhood that, despite her logical nature (she's an accountant), she still beats her pillows every morning to fight fate and destroy the feather ring. After a year of marriage, her husband got irritated enough with the habit to ask why in tarnation she did it. When she explained, he answered, "That's pathetic, honey. These are foam pillows."

work, which was a presentation piece from Mrs. Henry Clay to the wife of Senator John Jordan Crittenden. And some quilts are downright fascinating; for example, the dizzying 66,000-piece Spectrum Quilt, which is rare in that it was made in the 1930s by a man, a jeweler who had heard that the work would keep his fingers nimble. The list goes on. Museum hours are 9 a.m. to 4 p.m. Monday through Saturday, 1 to 4 p.m. Sunday. Admission is $10 for adults, $5 for seniors and children ages 6 to 16, free for children under age 6. Call (270) 745-6080 for further information (wku.edu/library/museum).

Another downtown museum in Bowling Green is *Riverview at Hobson Grove,* which grandly overlooks the Barren River. In the late 19th century the river was bustling with commerce, so that homes facing the river had to be worthy of the attention they received. The Hobsons built a magnificent, three-story, brick Italianate mansion, which has been restored and filled with period antiques. Excellent guided tours are given for $7 for adults and $2.50 for students, from 10 a.m. until 4 p.m. Tuesday through Saturday, 1 to 4 p.m. Sunday. Riverview is closed in January. The house's many outstanding features include elaborate hand-painted ceilings in the downstairs parlors, an odd-size "thief's step" on the second floor staircase landing (designed to trip up anyone not familiar with the house), and an unusual "ocular" window beneath the cupola, which was actually part of the ventilation system. In the tour you'll also learn a little about the Hobson family history, a story full of interesting twists and turns, from how the house was saved from destruction during the Civil War to the trapeze that one young Hobson suspended from the ocular window. The house is located at the center of a city park and golf course. To get to Hobson Grove, follow Main Avenue north to the outside of the Victoria Street bypass (Hobson Lane), pass the Delafield School, and watch for the sign to 1100 West Main Street. Call (270) 843-5565 for more information (bgky.org/riverview).

Corvette devotees are already aware that General Motors's only Corvette assembly plant in the world is in Bowling Green. The fascinating, hourlong tour of the plant itself is offered at 8:30 a.m., 11:30 a.m., and 1 p.m. Monday through Friday, except during model changes and on holidays. It's best to call and confirm at (270) 745-8019. Plant tours cost $7 per person. Across the street at 350 Corvette Drive, the *National Corvette Museum* at exit 28 off I-65 gives fans a good look at the history and glory of the racy, powerful, best sports car made in America. There are nostalgic displays and lots of souvenirs. One thing sure to spark your curiosity is the building itself, an unusually ugly, asymmetrical, yellow, almost conical structure with a huge red spire. A query about the design to a museum employee elicited the following explanation: "Well, when the museum opened, the newspaper said that some Corvettes of the '50s and '60s had a red cone coming out of the back light. Later, someone told us that from the air, the building looked like part of the dashboard. Finally, we called the architect, who said that neither was the case; he had simply wanted to create a building that was completely different." Which it is. Admission is $10 for adults, $8 for seniors, $5 for ages 6 to 16, and free for children under age 6. There's also a one-price family admission of $25. Hours are 8 a.m. to 5 p.m. daily. For museum information, call (270) 781-7973 or (800) 538-3883 or visit corvettemuseum.org.

trueblue

Although Kentucky never left the Union during the Civil War, a Confederate capital was established at Bowling Green.

There are several downtown sites worth exploring. The *Capitol Arts Center,* 416 East Main Street, is a classic over-the-top art deco movie theater. It's been renovated and now houses the Houchen Art Gallery and is used for all sorts of cultural events throughout the year. Call (270) 904-1880 to ask what's playing or stop by the gallery, Monday through Friday from 9 a.m. to 4 p.m. (theskypac.com/capitol-arts-center).

A local thespian group called the Public Theater of Kentucky performs everything from drama to comedy to musical shows nearby at the *Phoenix Theatre,* 545 Morris Alley. Call (270) 781-6233 or check ptkbg .org for more information about shows, which are scheduled from September through June. The Sunburst Youth Theatre does children's plays with child actors and offers a popular Shakespeare summer camp for ages 8 to 18.

Weekdays from 9 a.m. to 3 p.m. you're free to tour the beautiful, Gothic *St. Joseph Catholic Church* at 434 Church Street in Bowling Green. Call (270) 842-2525 or visit stjosephbg.org for details.

At 401 Kentucky Street, you'll find an unusual combination of interests. The *Depot Branch* of the Bowling Green Public Library shares quarters with what is in the process of becoming a full-fledged railroad museum. The actual depot houses the library branch, the offices of Operation Pride, a downtown revitalization group, and the offices of the Friends of the L&N Depot Inc., the nonprofit organization that owns and renovates the depot and the four railcars next to it. The library has a large early childhood center with lots of educational books and toys that circulate and a computer lab just for kids. There's also a large high-speed-Internet lab for public use. They're open daily. And if you happen to need new tires at the tire store next door, you can come read while you wait. You'll immediately notice the four beautiful L&N railcars outside the depot. One is a Chessie caboose, circa 1968. One is a circa 1953 sleeper car called The Towering Pine. One is a gorgeous 48-seat diner car built in 1949 and rebuilt in 1976, called the Duncan Hines. And one is the 1911 Presidential Car, the personal car for the president of the L&N Railroad. Currently the cars can only be toured by appointment (by groups of 10 or more with at least a week's advance notice) or during one of two festivals held on site—the Duncan Hines Festival in mid-August or Rail Fest in mid-December when Santa Claus pays a visit. A full museum and gift shop are in the works. Another interesting Bowling Green attraction is *Lost River Cave and Valley,* where the cave is said to have the shortest, deepest river in the world and the largest cave opening east of the Mississippi River. The cave's fascinating history includes use by Native Americans as long ago as 7,500 BC, operation as the nation's only "cave mill" in the late 1700s, and use

Adventures in Good Eating

Duncan Hines is truly a household name, even today, 50 years after the food label was established. Today, however, the name brings to mind processed foods and, the truth be told, culinary mediocrity. Originally, however, the power of the name Duncan Hines was comparable to the power of the current star-rating system used to classify restaurants and hotels. Mr. Duncan Hines, who was born in Bowling Green in 1880, had a celebrated reputation for recommending eateries. As a young man he'd been a traveling salesman and had to eat out often. Unsanitary conditions at roadside food stands, which were ubiquitous at the turn of the 20th century, caused deadly food poisoning. As he traveled, Hines made careful notes about places that met his standards of quality.

In the early 1930s Hines and his wife traveled extensively in the United States and made a list of "superior eating places," which they mailed to friends as a Christmas present in 1935. The list was wildly popular and resulted in a book the next year titled *Adventures in Good Eating*. In 1938 they published a companion book of recommended inns called *Lodging for a Night*. A sign in front of any such establishment stating "recommended by Duncan Hines" almost guaranteed the business success with travelers.

Bowling Green hosts an annual Duncan Hines Festival (duncanhinesfestival.com) in honor of this native gourmet every July. You can also drive the **Duncan Hines Scenic Byway,** beginning with a site on US 31 marking the Hines's former home and office. (Ask for a map at the visitor center, 352 Three Springs Road, off I-65 at exit 22, or call 270-782-0800.)

as an underground night club from the 1930s through the 1960s. Bank robber Jesse James is rumored to have hidden in the cave after robbing a bank in Russellville in 1868. A citizens' group, the Friends of Lost River, led the cave's revival as a tourist attraction. The group is exploring the possibility of restoring the waterwheel. In the meantime you can take a cave tour that begins with a short historical walk to the cave opening and concludes with a 25-minute boat tour into the cave. Before or after your tour you can explore 2 miles of hiking trails and a butterfly garden. Lost River Cave and Valley is open year-round, with tours daily, though the hours may vary seasonally. Admission to the cave tour is between $15 and $20. Call (866) 274-2283 or (270) 393-0077 or visit lostrivercave.com. The cave is located in Bowling Green at the intersection of US 31W (Nashville Road) and Cave Mill Road at 2818 Nashville Road.

If you drive the Duncan Hines Scenic Byway, you'll go through a little town called *Smith's Grove,* 14 miles north of Bowling Green, where a short walking tour of the 19th Century District includes a stop at the Smith's Grove cemetery, where Patrick Henry's sister is buried. (Get a tour map at almost any local business.) In its heyday, Woodbury was a busy little town on the Green River at the site of Lock and Dam Number 4. After the 1841 log structure washed away in 1965, the local historical society developed Woodbury into a museum complex. What was formerly the lockkeeper's home has been transformed into the *Green River Museum* (106 Park Street; 270-526-5342), a visual history lesson about the Woodbury area with an emphasis on the riverboat era (1840–1930). The museum includes artifacts from the prehistoric era as well. Hours are Saturday from noon to 4 p.m. from May through September. I'd suggest making a trip out even if the museum is closed because the site itself is beautiful and interesting. In addition to all the buildings, there is a very early cemetery and a dramatic overlook of the Green River and the remains of the dam and 1839 lock. To get there from Bowling Green, take the Natcher Parkway north to the first Morgantown exit; turn right off the ramp and go into town; turn right on Highway 403 and go 4.5 miles until you see signs for the park.

North of Woodbury on Highway 403, high on a bluff over the Green River, is *Morgantown,* a river-dependent port town in the 19th Century District. Every Fourth of July the town celebrates with the Green River Catfish Festival, downtown in the municipal park. River commerce brought wealth to the town late in the 19th century, evidenced by some of the remaining architecture. *Note:* Keep an eye on the Earth's undulations along the Green River near Morgantown, because there are supposed to be numerous ancient Native American burial mounds there.

If you travel northeast of Bowling Green, you will be in some of the most spectacular cave country in the world. Second to the Kentucky Derby, *Mammoth Cave National Park* at 1 Mammoth Cave Parkway is the best nationally known tourist attraction in the state, and for that reason, travelers can get information about cave history and trips anywhere within a hundred-mile radius. While definitely a well-beaten path (about 2.1 million people visit every year, and during the summer months it can be incredibly crowded), Mammoth Cave does have lesser-known aspects. Explore the cave in an old-fashioned way on a Gothic Lantern Tour. Or take a Wild

Kilroy's Ancestors

The **Old Simpson County Jailer's Residence** in Franklin was being renovated, and since it was expected that little if any original plaster could be repaired, workers weren't being terribly careful as they ripped out old paneling and wallpaper. Until they found, in a second-story room of the building, something that made everyone stop and stare in astonishment: drawings, possibly in charcoal, some almost life size, portraying Civil War soldiers, both Union and Confederate, including a portrait of the famous Confederate raider Gen. John Hunt Morgan. Though it may never be known exactly who created these sketches, it is known that the building was occupied by Union troops and used to house Confederate prisoners of war, and it is thought that what is left on the walls is authentic and rare Civil War graffiti. The building, now home to the **Simpson County Archives and Museum,** is at 206 North College Street, about 21 miles south of Bowling Green. Hours are Monday from 9 a.m. to 7 p.m., Tuesday through Friday from 9 a.m. to 4 p.m., and Saturday from 10 a.m. to 2 p.m. Admission is free. This is an excellent resource for researching family and local history. Call (270) 586-4228 or visit rootsweb.ancestry.com~kyschs/ for more information.

Cave Tour and crawl through tight passages. Whatever tour you decide to take, if you're coming in the summer, especially on weekends, it's a good idea to reserve your cave tour well in advance. Call (270) 758-2180 or visit nps.gov/maca.

Aboveground there are more than 70 miles of wonderful hiking trails. Visit the **Old Guides Cemetery,** near the Heritage Trail near the Cave's Historic Entrance. Among those buried here is Stephen Bishop, the cave's preeminent explorer in the 1800s. Bishop, like many of the people who helped map underground passages and served as tour guides in antebellum days, was a slave. His owner purchased Mammoth Cave around 1838. Bishop's many discoveries led to national renown and resulted in his freedom in 1856. He hoped to purchase the freedom of his wife and son and emigrate to Liberia but was unable to do so before his death in 1857. Mammoth Cave is open every day but Christmas.

The **American Cave Museum and Hidden River Cave** at 110 East Main Street in **Horse Cave** is an environmental education museum developed by the American Cave Conservation Association Inc. The association's worthy mission is to educate people, especially those who live on karst lands, about how the land works and about how our actions affect the health of the system. Venial sins like dumping trash in sinkholes become mortal sins in karst areas, where the whole groundwater system can easily be contaminated. Just the entrance to Hidden River Cave is accessible through the museum (for the first time since 1943). Previously, no one wanted to go near the cave and its underground stream because it carried the unpleasant stench of raw sewage.

Other exhibits in the museum include a whole wall display devoted to bats, a large cross section of a karst region, and stories and artifacts from mines, bootlegging operations, early tourist endeavors, prehistoric shelters, and ceremonial sites. For more information contact ACCA, 119 East Main Street, Horse Cave 42749, or call (270) 786-1466. Hours are 9 a.m. to 5 p.m. daily, with extended hours in summer (hiddenrivercave.com).

After spelunking, you'll probably be irresistibly tempted to retire to your own personal concrete wigwam motel room, complete with rustic hickory furniture, color television, and fake smoke hole and tent flaps at **Wigwam Village.** Take exit 53 off I-65 and turn left; at the second stoplight, head north on US 31W and go 1 mile until you see a semicircle of 15 white wigwams with a red zigzag design on the side at 601 North Dixie Highway. In the center is the 52-foot-high office wigwam, all built in 1937, long before

Funky Cave Projects and Artifacts

To date, the navigable cave system in the Mammoth Cave area is more than 300 miles long. The cave has provoked some odd projects, such as an underground hospital for tuberculosis victims. The cool, clean cave air would have been good for any victim of lung disease, but smoke from the cooking fires accumulated in the chamber where they lived and killed them quickly. What the doctors needed was more basic than holistic thinking—they needed common sense. Other cave project artifacts include leaching vats, which remain from the time when saltpeter (sodium nitrate or potassium nitrate) was extracted for making gunpowder during the War of 1812. Also make sure you hear the whole story of explorer Floyd Collins. For many years his casket was on display in the Crystal Onyx Cave; he had been searching for a new entrance when he died. In 1929, when local cave owners were competing fiercely for tourists, someone stole Collins's body and dumped it in the Green River because it was a popular attraction. His remains have since been reinterred in a less public place.

the interstate existed and before concrete construction was very sophisticated. Before Americans got their kicks on the now-legendary Route 66, these maverick lodgings rose boldly from the flat plains of south-central Kentucky. In 1935 an entrepreneur named Frank A. Redford built the first Wigwam Village in nearby Horse Cave and patented his design. The Cave City village was built in 1937, and later five more villages went up from Alabama to California. Only three remain. The other two are in Holbrook, Arizona, and Rialto, California. At the Cave City village, however, from March through November you can still sleep in a concrete tepee with original hickory and cane furnishings. Each has a private bath. Rates are very reasonable but if you want to lodge in one of these little gems (now Historic Landmarks), especially on a weekend, reserve it well in advance. The main building, which houses a gift shop, stands 52 feet high and is made of 38 tons of concrete and 13 tons of steel. Call (270) 773-3381 or check the website, wigwamvillage.com.

At the Hart of a Tradition

If you like handmade baskets, be sure to visit Munfordville in Hart County, not far from Mammoth Cave. Basket making has long been a tradition in this part of the state. By the mid-1800s numerous families in the western Hart County community of Cub Run were producing baskets and using them to barter for groceries and other goods. Shopkeepers in turn sold the baskets to customers or to traveling peddlers, and so the area's reputation grew. In the 20th century, when US 31W brought automobiles in force through the area, the basket makers set up stands along the road.

Although basket making in the area declined after the advent of the Interstate, in recent years the Mammoth Cave area basket industry has been revitalized. Many contemporary basket makers in the local Basket Guild create baskets in the traditional south-central Kentucky style, using white oak and making the bottommost ribs of the basket wide and flat with smaller, more rounded top ribs. Other novelty styles have also evolved; for example, basket maker Lestel Childress sometimes makes whimsical flower stand baskets, a style designed by his grandmother, Let Thompson.

In the late 1990s a family practitioner in Munfordville, Dr. James Middleton, started a basket-making contest at the Hart County Fair, usually held in late June or early July.

Lost and Found

Unless I'm in a big hurry, I rarely worry about getting lost, because I know that almost any Kentucky road is going to end up somewhere interesting. And if it doesn't, well, you just turn around. So I wasn't too concerned that my directions to the Amish store near Munfordville that April Saturday were somewhat vague. "It's outside of town a little piece," said the quilter who told me about the store.

"I'm not sure which store you mean, but if you turn left at the yellow flashing light and head out of town, then turn left again after a ways, you'll come to an area where a lot of Amish people live," offered a gas station attendant. Now, that was something to go on. When I saw the sign at Logsdon Valley Road for Yoder's Harness Shop, I figured that had to be the turn.

"Look! Something's going on over there," my travel companion exclaimed. Indeed, there was. Dozens of vans, trucks—and even more horse-drawn carriages—were parked in a field, and hundreds of people, Amish and "English" of all ages, were gathered under a tent. It turned out to be a consignment auction to benefit the Amish community school, with everything from handmade bookshelves to goats going on the block. In between bidding you could fill up on just-grilled hamburgers and homemade baked goods. Best bad directions I ever had.

Just a little south of the National Park, in Park City, on Highway 255 off I-65 at exit 48, are some of the most beautiful caves in the system that are open to the public. The **Diamond Caverns** are particularly known for their spectacular colors. Admission is $17 adults, $8 children ages 4 to 12, and it's open daily from 9 a.m. until 5 p.m. in the summer and until 4 p.m. in the winter. Call (270) 749-2233 for information (diamondcaverns.com).

Kentucky was a state deeply divided during the Civil War, and exhibits at the **Hart County Historic Society and Museum** (109 Main Street; 270-524-0101; hartcountymuseum.org) in Munfordville, 3 miles north of Horse Cave, demonstrate this point well. Among the Civil War artifacts at the museum are items belonging to two Hart County residents who fought in the conflict. Confederate general Simon Bolivar Buckner and Union major general Thomas Wood were childhood friends and West Point classmates who later found themselves fighting on opposite sides of the conflict. The Munfordville battleground site is being preserved by the county historical society at the Battle for the Bridge Preserve. Civil War reenactors perform the battle in meticulously designed costumes in mid-September, after Labor Day; the

168

168

168

168

168

168

168

168

168

168

168

168

168

168

168

historic battle occurred on September 16, 1862. A museum staff member can guide you there. Museum hours are 9 a.m. to 4 p.m. Monday through Friday and 8 a.m. to 4 p.m. Saturday. Several Amish communities are located in Hart County, and in summer months, you can buy fresh produce and other items on the courthouse lawn. Year-round, it's worth a drive out to 1985 Logdson Valley Road to Anna's Kitchen. Anna Miller makes delicious jellies and relishes; stop by any day except Sunday. There's a sign by the road—just knock on the door. Call (270) 524-0820 for information.

trueblue

Munfordville is locally referred to as Concrete Alley because it is the source of 10 percent of all commercially fabricated concrete yard-art statues made in the eastern United States.

East of Bowling Green, the next sizable town is **Glasgow,** host of the **Highland Games and Gathering of Scottish Clans,** held near the end of May or in early June at Barren River Lake State Resort Park, east of Glasgow on US 31. The games begin with a musical extravaganza called the Tattoo, then clan and society members get together for a Tartan Ball and Scottish Country Dancing. Last but not least exciting are the athletic and battle-ax competitions, which originated as martial exercises under King Malcolm Canmore in Scotland around 1060. It's amazing to watch these manliest of manly men wearing skirts (ahem, kilts) while "tossing" logs the size of telephone poles. The best known aspect of the gathering, however, is the Ceilidh, another set of musical performances by American and international musicians—praised by Fiona Ritchie of National Public Radio's *Thistle and Shamrock* show. For more information, contact Glasgow Highland Games Inc. 119 East Main Street, Glasgow 42141, or call (270) 651-3141 or visit glasgowhighlandgames.com.

The **Hall Place Bed and Breakfast** is a handsome place to spend the night and have a big country-ham breakfast. From downtown Glasgow take US 31E south (South Green Street) for 1½ blocks and look for the sign on the right. Although the house was built in 1852, the three bed-and-breakfast rooms have modern, private baths, wireless Internet, and full breakfast. Call (270) 651-3176 for more information.

From Glasgow take Highway 63 south to **Tompkinsville,** the Monroe County seat. Take Highway 90 to Highway 163 south of town for about

3 miles to the *Old Mulkey Meeting House.* Built in 1804 during a religious revival that swept through the region, it is not only the oldest log meeting house in the state but also a rare example of highly symbolic log architecture. The building's twelve corners represent the twelve apostles, and the three doors are meant to be reminders of the Trinity. Daniel Boone's oldest sister, Hannah, is buried in the cemetery alongside other early settlers.

Living-History Country

You'll likely find an antique or collectible car on display at the Elizabethtown tourism bureau as advertising for a local attraction, *Swope's Cars of Yesteryear Museum.* Bill Swope, a retired longtime auto dealer in town, has a collection of about 30 vehicles from the 1920s to the 1960s. You'll find the rest of them on display at 1100 North Dixie Highway. It's next door to the Swope dealership now run by Bill's son. The free museum is open from 10 a.m. to 5 p.m. Monday through Saturday. Call (270) 765-2181 for more information (swopemuseum.com).

Polarities can be wonderful teachers. Leave the Coke memorabilia and old cars and please, please, please take time to get an education at the *Emma Reno Connor Black History Gallery.* Go southeast of the courthouse on East Dixie Avenue, veer left onto Hawkins Drive, and look immediately for a white stucco house on the right with a sign that says "Black History Gallery." This was the childhood home of the late Emma Reno Connor, a teacher who recognized a disgraceful dearth of information about the lives and accomplishments of African Americans. She supplemented her lesson plans with pictures, articles, and stories of African Americans and later organized these teaching materials into museum displays.

An amateur museum that is composed of well-organized cutouts from magazines, original pen-and-ink portraits of great people, poems by Ms. Connor, and newspaper articles, this is also a powerful place full of love, knowledge, and opportunities to learn about the African-American experience. You'll enjoy learning about the lives and accomplishments of Satchmo (Louis Armstrong), Josephine Baker, Langston Hughes, Sojourner Truth, Gwendolyn Brooks, Frederick Douglass, and Martin Luther King Jr., to name a few outstanding people. Hours are noon to 5 p.m. Saturday and Sunday

And on That Farm She Had a . . .

I live on a farm, and people always ask, "How many animals do you raise there?" I often answer, "Several thousand" because, in addition to raising vegetable gardens, fruit and nut orchards, milk goats, chickens, ducks, a few cattle, a horse, and a passel of dogs, we're beekeepers. The bees are the only livestock that don't need fences or daily feeding. They're not pets in that I don't have an emotional relationship with them, but they are producers of the very best sweetener in the world, and they pollinate many of the plants we raise for food. We are at least the third generation in my family to buy our bees and beekeeping supplies from the **Walter T. Kelley Co. Inc.,** in **Clarkson,** about 40 miles southwest of Elizabethtown, or 4 miles east of Leitchfield on US 62. (The bees come through the U.S. Mail as buzzing masses in screen-and-wood boxes, and the post office calls at 5 a.m. for us to "come and get these durn things.") This company was started some 75 years ago and has a huge national customer base. It continues at its original location, where wooden beehives, supers, and frames are manufactured; beeswax is processed into comb foundation; and all sorts of other supplies are made, from stainless-steel tanks and centrifugal honey extractors to protective coveralls. Kelley's can also coordinate the sale and shipping of the gentle and hard-working three-banded Italian bees in swarms (sold by the pound) and their queens, all of which come from its bee yards deeper in the South. Visitors are welcome to stop by the office and see live bees in a glass-sided observation hive and to purchase honey and supplies. Beekeepers and educational groups can schedule full tours of the plant (by appointment only). Call or stop by Monday through Friday between 7:30 a.m. and 5 p.m. (except for lunch hour at noon), or on Saturday from 7:30 a.m. to noon. Call (270) 242-2012 or toll-free (800) 233-2899 for more information (kelleybees.com).

or as posted. Call (270) 268-9534 or (800) 437-0092 or visit touretown.com/visitors/See/Black-History-Gallery.aspx.

Many towns of historic significance offer walking tours of their downtowns, but few resurrect the characters in living color. In the summer try the *Elizabethtown Historic Walking Tours,* during which you meet and see a brief "performance" by Sarah Bush Johnston Lincoln (Abe's stepmother), P. T. Barnum, Jenny Lind, Carry Nation, and eight other historical figures portrayed by local people dressed in period costumes who are well versed in their figure's history. Carry Nation, for example, runs down the street with a Bible in one hand and her famous hatchet in the other to shut down Jim Neighbor's bar. (In real life she was prevented from destroying the joint when someone knocked her out with a bar stool.) The tour covers 25 buildings and takes about an hour. Free tours are scheduled for Thursday at 7 p.m. and start in the public town square. Call (270) 982-2209 or visit touretown.com.

The *Brown-Pusey House* (270-765-2515; brownpuseyhouse.org) was Elizabethtown's first public lodging house for travelers at 128 North Main Street. You can't stay overnight now, but you can take a free guided tour of the very stately Georgian colonial building. Gen. George Custer and his wife stayed here sometime in the 1870s. A genealogy library is also housed here. Hours are 10 a.m. to 4 p.m. Tuesday through Saturday.

Elizabethtown has another unusual seasonal event worth the trip to town. From the Wednesday before Thanksgiving until January 2 every year, Freeman Lake Park (directly behind the Coca-Cola plant on US 31W North) is transformed into a glittering wonderland during *Christmas in the Park.* Cut your headlights and take the luminaria-lined drive around the lake past more than 70 lighted Christmas displays built and donated by local businesses, including a huge swan floating in the water and Santa in a boat. The show is on from 6 p.m. until 11 p.m. nightly.

For mountain-bike enthusiasts, the Kentucky Mountain Bike Association and the Kentucky Wheelmen have developed a nice 6-mile trail system near a town called *Youngers Creek* (www.kymba.org/trails). Additional trails and a BMX-style course are planned for the field beside the pavilion and parking area so that younger kids and families can have a place to ride without having to climb the big hill. To get there take exit 10 off Bluegrass Parkway and turn north onto Highway 52. Next take a left on Highway 62 and another left onto Old Youngers Creek Road (Highway 583). Look for Miller Road and turn right. Watch for the parking area for the trail.

From June through September in the Freeman Lake Park you can visit the *Lincoln Heritage House,* which Thomas Lincoln, Abe's father, a carpenter by trade, helped to construct, and the *Sarah Bush Johnston Lincoln Memorial,* an early-19th-century cabin that re-creates the home of the woman who married Thomas Lincoln

trueblue

The Squire Pates House on Highway 334 near Lewisport was the site of Abraham Lincoln's first trial. He defended himself against charges of operating a ferry across the Ohio River without a license.

and became Abe's stepmother when the president-to-be was only 10 years old. Nearby there is also a renovated 1892 one-room schoolhouse. Hours are 10 a.m. to 5 p.m. daily from June 1 through October 1. Call (800) 437-0092 or visit touretown.com/Visitors/See/Lincoln-Heritage-House.aspx for more information.

Take Highway 220 northeast of Rineyville and get on US 31W to reach Fort Knox Military Reservation, with a couple of attractions worth seeing. To America's World War II generation there was perhaps no greater hero than Gen. George S. Patton. The *Patton Museum of Cavalry and Armor* (502-624-3812; generalpatton.org) at Fort Knox was dedicated in the general's honor on Memorial Day 1949, four years after Patton's death. In addition to a section dedicated to Patton's life, the museum includes a display of tanks and a variety of other military items—even a section of the Berlin Wall. The museum is on Fayette Avenue near the Chaffee Avenue entrance to the base at 4554 Fayette Avenue. It's open weekdays year-round from 10 a.m. to 4:30 p.m. and from 10 a.m. to 5:30 p.m. on Saturday. Admission is free.

true blue

The state bird of Kentucky is the cardinal.

Not far from the Patton Museum is the *United States Treasury Department Gold Depository,* America's "Gold Vault." Although no visitors are allowed inside, you can view the building from the outside and imagine the inside, where the nation's cache of pure gold bars is stored in a two-level vault protected by a 20-ton door and armed guards.

Right at the northern edge of the Fort Knox Military Reservation in a deep bend of the Ohio River is the little town of *West Point.* Ask any local shop owner for a map showing the path of a walking tour that directs you to more than 20 buildings on the National Register of Historic Places. On the south side of town at 16706 Abbotts Beach Road is *Fort Duffield* (502-922-4574; fortduffield.com), a park site where Union soldiers were stationed and built earthworks in 1861. On Wilson Road, south of US 31, are two hiking trails. The Bridges of the Past trail is a 1-mile walk along the old Louisville and Nashville turnpike that takes you by three pre–Civil War stone bridges. On request you can be guided through the area by an interpreter. The walk takes about an hour. Call (800) 334-7540. Originating nearby, the Tioga Falls

Hiking Trail is a 2-mile circuit that crosses into areas sometimes used for military training. (The trail is closed in that event.)

Excessive exposure to military equipment is bound to make a soul world weary. To restore some sense of faith in the world's good things, try a hike in the 730-acre **Vernon-Douglas State Nature Preserve,** located 15 miles east of Elizabethtown just off Highway 583. In the early spring the woods here are full of delicate, breathtaking wildflowers (naturepreserves .ky.gov/naturepreserves/Pages/vernondouglas.aspx).

A great place for lunch or dinner is south of Elizabethtown in a historic little railroad community called **Glendale.** Go south of town on US 31W for about 5 miles, then take Highway 222 west to Glendale. In the early 1970s, the old Glendale hardware store, which is smack-dab next to the railroad tracks at 216 East Main Street, was transformed into the **Whistle Stop Restaurant** (270-369-8586; whistlestoprestaurant.net), where they now serve really, really good Southern food for reasonable prices in a cozy depot atmosphere. Famous for its open-faced hot brown sandwich—a mountain of roast beef on bread, smothered with a rich cheese sauce—the restaurant's menu ranges from homemade soups to ham and asparagus rolls to fried chicken and taco salad. Desserts clarify the meaning of sin. Hours are 11 a.m. to 9 p.m. Tuesday through Saturday.

All of Glendale seems to be in a time warp. Though the village is small, it has a functional general store and several antiques and gift shops. During the first weekend in December, every building is decked out for a **Christmas in the Country** event, open to the public. Or come to Glendale on the

The Heck with Straight Lines

Notice on your map how the Kentucky border bulges just a bit to the south in this area? Legend has it that when the border was surveyed and this land was to be relegated to Tennessee, the owner of this land, a farmer named Sanford Duncan, invited the surveying team to a party at the Duncan Tavern (about 6 miles south of Franklin), a popular spot for travelers on the Louisville-to-Nashville trek because of the fine food and Kentucky liquor served there. The surveyors were so appreciative (and drunk) that they agreed to survey all of Duncan's land into Kentucky. The heck with straight lines.

third Saturday in October for the *Glendale Crossing Festival,* when the spirit of the old-time trading days pervades the town.

Another place that works to generate Glendale's nostalgic charm is *Tony York's on Main,* owned and operated by chef Tony York, which serves gourmet food in a supper-club setting. The current building was reconstructed after a 2008 fire. The building had been an old farmhouse dating to the early 1900s that was moved to the site by Sonny Hatfield after the original train depot burned down in the 1930s. (The original train station may have been one of the many robbed by Jesse James.) The diverse menu is a tribute to Kentucky traditions, as is the Depot's motto: "Never rush a supper-club experience—we won't." The motto seems to prove true the old joke that if you want someone from the south to hurry up, you are just gonna have to wait a minute. The Depot is located downtown at 201 East Main Street next to the railroad tracks and serves lunch and dinner daily. You can call (270) 369-6000 for reservations or more information or visit tonyyorksonmain.com.

For Amish crafts and goods including quilts, baskets, and flavor-packed fruit preserves, watch for horse-drawn wagons set up as roadside shops in and around town. Whether or not you are interested in buying, just stop in and enjoy a lazy stroll under the shade trees downtown. Or if you prefer to stroll on the web, have a look at glendalekentucky.com.

The *Official Kentucky State Championship Old-time Fiddling Contest* is an event for beginner and virtuoso musicians or for anyone who just likes to listen to bluegrass music. Fifteen to 20 different contests, including harmonica, flat-top guitar, mandolin, banjo, bluegrass band, and even jig dancing, are held annually at Freeman Lake Park in Elizabethtown during June. This is a recommended place to have a breakdown—take your choice of "Tennessee Breakdown," "North Carolina Breakdown," "Straw Breakdown," or "Cheatum County Breakdown." When the region's hottest fiddlers compete in the Governor's Cup Fiddle Off, you'll want to cry at the music's sweetness—but the wind from the musicians' lightning quick bow action will dry your tears before they can hit your cheeks. Camping is available, and folks are invited to come early for the informal jam sessions that go on all week prior to the main contest. For more information about the park or the contest, call (270) 257-2311 or check kentuckyfiddler.com. Also ask about the park's other special events such as the "Dulcibrrr" in February, a weekend for fans of lap and hammered dulcimers.

In the town of **Leitchfield,** 18 miles southeast of the State Resort Park, you can make an appointment to tour the **Jack Thomas House,** the oldest house in the county and a grand Federal-style mansion at 122 East Main Street. The original two-room house, built in 1815, became the south wing of the expanded building. Tours are given Tuesday through Friday from 10 a.m. to 4 p.m. Admission is charged. For information and tours, call the Grayson County Historic Society at (270) 230-8989 or check the website, graysoncokyhistsoc.org.

Not everything in the area is caught in the past. John and Lisa Brittain of the **Nolin River Nut Tree Nursery** have become famous for performing nutty modern-day miracles. Of the more than 100 varieties of nut trees grown in their nursery, most are grafted. You're not supposed to be able to graft most nut trees because the sap tends to run so much that the grafts don't take—that is, heal and fuse to the rooted tree—yet these growers make expert use of an obscure method called a coin purse graft. They also are able to dig and ship nut trees up to 5 feet tall—that's 4 feet taller than the "rules" claim to be possible without fatally damaging the taproot.

The Brittains can probably answer any question you have about nut trees and sell you just about any variety your heart desires. They now have more than 175 varieties of nut trees available, plus 15 kinds of persimmons and four varieties of pawpaw. For between $16 and $68 per tree, you can choose from a number of walnuts, heartnuts, butternuts, chestnuts, hickories, pecans, and hicans (a cross between hickory and pecan). Order as far in advance of spring as possible. For a catalog, write Nolin River Nut Tree Nursery, 797 Port Wooden Road, Upton 42784, or call (270) 369-8551. Or check out their website at nolinnursery.com. Be sure to call ahead if you want to visit.

Abraham Lincoln has put **Hodgenville** on the map and kept it there. From Elizabethtown take Highway 61 south to Hodgenville and follow signs to the **Abraham Lincoln Birthplace National Historic Site** (270-358-3137; nps.gov/abli), just south of town at 2995 Lincoln Farm Road. A humble log cabin like the one in which Abe was born on February 12, 1809, is enshrined in a huge, stone-columned building prefaced by 56 steps, which represent the years of Abe's life. The park is open from 8 a.m. to 4:45 p.m.

daily, with hours extended until 6:45 p.m. in summer. Go through town on US 31E to visit *Knob Creek Farm,* Lincoln's boyhood home. There is a replica of the cabin where young Abe's first memories were formed; this was the last place he lived in Kentucky. The farm is open year-round, with a ranger on-site to answer questions April through October. The buildings are closed for safety reasons. Call (502) 549-3741 for more information.

Downtown on Lincoln Square near the bronze statue at 66 Lincoln Square is the small *Lincoln Museum* (270-358-3163; www.lincolnmuseum -ky.org), open Monday through Saturday from 8:30 a.m. to 4:30 p.m., Sunday from 12:30 to 4:30 p.m. Admission is $3. The museum features twelve scenes from Lincoln's life (with wax figures) and a display of memorabilia. Ask about the *Lincoln Days Celebration* (270-358-8710; lincolndays.org) held in town during October. The festival features a few odd events, including Lincoln look-alike contests and a very manly rail-splitting tournament. Call the LaRue County Chamber of Commerce at (270) 358-3411 or visit laruecountychamber.org for more information.

Lakes and Knobs Region

Going east from Glasgow, the high road leads to Columbia, the low road to *Burkesville.* Take Highway 80 or the Cumberland Parkway to *Columbia.* Few people know that on April 29, 1872, Jesse James and his gang held up the Bank of Columbia and killed a cashier, R. C. Martin. Nor do most know that Mark Twain's parents, Jane Lampton and John Marshall Clemens, were married in Columbia in 1823. Fewer still realize that Maxwell House coffee was developed by a Burkesville boy named Joel Owsley Cheek. After a brief career as a traveling (by horseback) salesman, Cheek started experimenting in the late 1870s with roasting and mixing blends of coffee that were usually sold to the stores green and unground. The first place to sell the expensive blend was the Maxwell House hotel in Nashville, Tennessee. The rest is history.

On the campus of Lindsey Wilson College in downtown Columbia is an architectural treat worth taking a side trip to see, wherever you're going. The *John B. Begley Chapel,* at 210 Lindsey Wilson Street, was designed by E. Fay Jones, a Frank Lloyd Wright disciple who is said to be the world's foremost chapel architect. It looks like two silos made of brick with glass domes, and, in fact, was inspired by farm silos. But few farms could afford silos made using 180,000 bricks! It's open to the public Monday through Friday from 8 a.m. to 4 p.m. and on some weekends. For more information call (270) 384-2126 or visit lindsey.edu.

North of Columbia, just off Highway 55, is the **Green River Lake State Park** (270-465-8255; parks.ky.gov/park/recreationparks/Green-River/default.aspx) and the starting place for a self-guided tour of sites associated with the **Battle of Tebbs Bend,** fought in early July 1863. This battle marked the beginning of Confederate general John Hunt Morgan's daring campaign, known as the Great Raid into Indiana and Ohio, which ended later in July when he and his men were captured in Ohio. The battle at this site ended when the Confederates were demoralized by what they mistakenly thought to be Union reinforcements arriving. The Union commander, Col. O. H. Moore, had fooled the Rebels into thinking backup troops were arriving all night by having his men go back and forth over a bridge crossing the Green River. One other fascinating deception in this battle was revealed afterward when one of the Union wounded turned out to be a 16-year-old girl named Lizzie Compton, from London, Ontario, who was posing as a man. There have been reenactments of the battle in years past, but they were suspended a few years ago after, as one observer put it, "the North and the South *really* got into it with each other." Disagreements over whether to stage the battle authentically or to have the Rebels win led to the event's demise. You can get information about the battle at the park or at the Taylor County Tourist Commission, 325 East Main Street in Campbellsville. The commission's phone number is (270) 465-3786 or visit campbellsvilleky.com.

In the park, stop by the interpretive center and request the key to the **Atkinson-Griffin House** (tebbsbend.com), a 1½-story double-pen log building used by the Confederates as a hospital after the battle, which now houses some Civil War exhibits and even has bloodstains on the upstairs bedroom floor. Also, get the little map and list of other battle sites.

In **Campbellsville** there are two relatively obscure historic sites that are worth a stop. At 1075 Campbellsville Bypass, visit the **Jacob Hiestand House,** an exquisite Federal-style stone house built in 1823 by a German tanner who had moved to Kentucky from Pennsylvania. The house that is there now was moved (try to imagine that task!) from its original site because it was endangered by sprawling development. Though there are many stone houses in this state, this one was particularly well crafted. The house is open 8 a.m. to 4 p.m. Monday through Friday. Saturday by appointment only. Admission is $3 for adults, $2 for seniors and $1 for students. Call (270) 789-4343 for more information.

Another building that was moved from its original location for the sake of preservation is the *Friendship School,* a humble little one-room schoolhouse built in 1918 and now located behind the Taylor County High School at 300 Ingram Avenue. People are welcome to visit the schoolhouse on Sunday afternoon between 1 and 4 p.m. from July through December, or by appointment (800-738-4719). This little school is a classic example of Kentucky's one-room schoolhouses, which were built inexpensively and run by teachers who were legendary for their level of devotion and self-sacrifice. The Friendship School, like many of its kind, had a class size of between eight and 40 students, ranging in grade from first to eighth. Like the current hours Friendship School is open, the school year ran from July through December from 8 a.m. to 4 p.m. regardless of weather conditions. Such tiny schools were located within walking distance of a few families who could pay the teacher. (This may come back into vogue and would certainly be considered radical.)

trueblue

When Taylor County's Friendship School was built in 1918, there were 7,067 one-room schools operating in Kentucky. Most had closed by the 1950s.

Campbellsville is a great place to visit if you're in the market for fine handmade cherry furniture. There are three companies in town that manufacture the furniture: *Campbellsville Cherry Reproductions, Inc.,* at Saloma Road (270-465-6003; campbellsvillecherryreproductions.com); *Campbellsville Handmade Cherry Furniture,* at 600 Water Tower Bypass (270-789-1741; cvillecherry.com); and *Gary Humphress & Sons,* at 303 East Main Street (270-465-2786; humphresscherryfurniture.com). All welcome visitors and have showrooms of beautiful beds, chests, tables, and other pieces. If what you want is not in stock, you can order it and have it shipped. "Campbellsville cherry" graces houses all over the world.

In a little town called *Mannsville,* east of Campbellsville about 8 miles on Highway 70, is *Penn Country Hams,* at 8850 Liberty Road, a place that might be familiar to a ham fan since it sells more than 50,000 a year. You can tour the facilities and do some taste testing before you purchase. Call (270) 465-5065 for information. Hours are 8 a.m. to 6 p.m. Monday through Saturday.

West of Campbellsville about 13 miles in the town of *Greensburg* stands the oldest existing courthouse west of the Alleghenies. It was built in 1803 and now houses a regional museum. Around town you can see a number of other historic buildings, many of which are on the National Register of Historic Places, including a log cabin, circa 1796; an old railroad depot; and a 445-footlong pedestrian bridge. South of the Campbellsville/Columbia/Greensburg area is *Dale Hollow,* a large man-made lake that straddles the Kentucky-Tennessee line. Take Highway 61 to Burkesville and watch for signs to 5970 State Park Road. The area is full of small marinas, motels, and fishing camps. It is said to be one of the cleanest lakes in the state, and since there are myriad inlets and islands, Dale Hollow is good place to swim. Dale Hollow Lake Resort Park has a lodge and offers horseback riding and hiking. Call (270) 433-7431, or visit parks.ky.gov/parks/resortparks/Dale-Hollow/default.aspx for reservations or information.

Northeast of Dale Hollow is *Lake Cumberland,* one of the largest fabricated lakes in the United States; its peak surface area is more than 55,000 acres. It is also said to have more walleye, bass, and crappie than any other American lake.

Although there are water-oriented businesses all around the lake, you may want to stop by the headquarters of the Lake Cumberland State Resort Park (off US 127 just south of Jamestown at 5465 State Park Road; 270-343-3111; parks.ky.gov/parks/resortparks/Lake-Cumberland/default.aspx) to get specific information. If you boat around the big, clear lake, you'll find endless little coves to explore, places to swim, fossils over which to ponder, and almost no commercial

trueblue

Besides Dale Hollow lake, another thing shared by Kentucky and Tennessee is a little town with a rowdy reputation called *Static,* which sits directly on the border where US 127 goes through. Kentucky says Static belongs in Tennessee, and Tennessee says the town is all Kentucky's. With a town name that means "showing little change," it's no wonder no one claims the place. To make things worse, legend has it that Static was named after a local farmer's one-eyed bulldog.

development to distract you. The park also has a lodge with a restaurant, cottages, an indoor pool, campgrounds, and a marina.

Don't you want to know where all those fish in the lake come from? (Well, not all the fish—birds transport some.) Follow US 127 south from the park and watch for signs for the **Wolf Creek National Fish Hatchery** (270-343-3797; fws.gov/wolfcreek), where thousands of rainbow and brown trout are raised. Auxiliary pleasure begins if you take time to watch wild birds, such as the ever-so-svelte great blue heron or the sassy belted kingfisher, feast on the easy pickings. Deer feed near the dam daily at dusk. The hatchery at 50 Kendall Road has some interpretive displays that explain the process of mass-raising fish. Open from 7 a.m. to 3:30 p.m. daily.

Starting from the state park, take Highway 1058 west, then Highway 379 south through Creelsboro; when the road almost touches the Cumberland River, watch for signs for the **Creelsboro Natural Bridge.** Though there are many rock bridges in Kentucky, this 75-foot arch has been designated

The Bigger Apple!

Fast-food restaurants really weren't the first to "supersize" it. As evidence, there's the annual **Casey County Apple Festival** (caseycountyapplefestival.org), held in Liberty the last full week in September.

This festival has been an annual event since 1974, often attracting up to 50,000 visitors. Undoubtedly they follow their noses to this small south-central Kentucky town, because cookin' big is a centerpiece of the event.

The folks in Casey County, you see, have a special supersize oven, and they set it up in the city parking lot at festival time. The feasting begins Wednesday night, when they bake a giant chocolate chip cookie. Then on Thursday night, guests can share in a giant pizza. All of this is just a warm-up, however, for the main course, which gets under way Saturday morning when volunteers start assembling "the world's largest apple pie." Mix 30 bushels of apples, 200 pounds of sugar—you get the idea. The result: a 1,200-pound pie with a buttery crust 8 feet in diameter. (It takes a forklift to get it into the oven.) The pie bakes and bakes until noon Saturday, when it is scooped into bowls for the drooling crowd. Got a major sweet tooth? Call the Liberty & Casey County Chamber of Commerce at (606) 787-7106 or visit libertykentucky.org for more information about this all-American feast and the city.

Mysteries of Dark Skies

If you happen to be driving along KY 78 near Liberty after dark, take a few moments to glance skyward. You are at the site of a true unsolved mystery. It happened on January 6, 1976. Three Casey County women, two of them grandmothers and all avid churchgoers, were returning from dinner at a Stanford restaurant. Between Hustonville and Liberty, they saw what they thought was a plane about to crash. Next thing they knew, it was an hour and 25 minutes later and they were 8 miles down the road, with severe headaches and burnlike red marks on the backs of their necks. The car's electrical system was malfunctioning, and the paint on the hood was blistered. Shaken and confused, the women returned to Liberty, where a neighbor asked them to draw what they had seen, and their aircraft looked suspiciously like a UFO. Soon, a veritable army of UFO investigators, and the national tabloids, descended upon this small Kentucky town. Under hypnosis the women told a story that seems almost commonplace today, but was then quite rare: They had been taken aboard a spacecraft and examined by creatures with huge, pale blue eyes. Later they even passed a polygraph test. These unlikely UFO abductees have long since moved away from Liberty, Kentucky; they grew tired of hearing the ridicule and laughter. The case, however, remains unsolved, a mystery to be pondered by those who gaze upon the night skies of Casey County.

a National Natural Landmark because it is limestone rather than the more common sandstone.

To get to Mill Springs, go to Monticello in Wayne County and follow Highway 90 to Touristville. Turn west on Highway 1275 and you'll see signs for the *Mill Springs Mill*, "largest overshot waterwheel in the world." That's a slightly overrated waterwheel, but as it turns out, the wheel is 40 feet, 10 inches in diameter, making it the third-largest in the nation and among the top 10 in the world. It may be the only one of the biggies to still be functioning as a gristmill. The first cereal grinding mill was built around 1817 at this site, where 13 springs gushed out of the hillside. The waterwheel also powered a cotton gin, carting factory, and wagon production line. After a fire and several remodelings, in 1908 the Diamond Roller Mills's 40-foot wheel was installed. Today the mill is open at no charge to the public from May through October, 9 a.m. to 5 p.m. daily. On weekends cornmeal is ground with the old equipment. For specifics call (606) 348-8189.

The mill is the site of a tide-turning Civil War battle in January 1862. Confederate general Felix Kirk Zollicoffer set up camp at a house near the mill, the Metcalfe House. Zollicoffer lost the Battle of Logan's Crossroads and thereby left the first gap in what was a long, strong Rebel defense line in Kentucky. Just west of Somerset on Highway 80 in a town called Nancy arc the *Mill Springs Battlefield* (606-636-4085; millsprings.net) and the Zollicoffer Park and burial site, where more than a hundred rebel troops are buried under one stone, all from the Mill Springs battle. Driving tour maps of the battlefield are available at the park. From the cemeteries you can see (and smell and taste and climb) the fruit trees at the adjacent *Haney's Appledale Farm* (606-636-6148; haneysappledalefarm.com), one of the state's best and largest apple and peach orchards, located 1 mile east of the battlefield (west of Somerset 8 miles) at 8550 West Highway 80. July through Christmas the orchard is open Monday through Saturday from 9 a.m. to 5 p.m. and on Sunday from 1 to 5 p.m. Some of the time "U-pick" is available, and you're always welcome to buy any quantity of fruit you want—the owner says, "Heck, I'd even cut an apple in half if that's all you wanted."

If you venture into *Somerset,* you'll not be excited by the seemingly endless strip-type development, but there is one place that may be worth stopping: Call (606) 677-6000 for a schedule of performing arts events at the *Center for Rural Economic Development* at 2292 South Highway 27 (centertech.com).

When you leave Jamestown, you leave the lake area and enter the Knobs again. Take US 127 north into Casey County, known as the *Gate Capital of the World.* Most gates, truck racks, and round-bale feeders are made of tubular steel, a concept first developed in 1965 by Tarter Gate in Dunnville, the first and largest of the gate companies in the county, producing more than 1,000 gates a day.

Due to the isolation and beauty of this hilly country, a large number of Mennonites have moved into the area. It's always inspirational to see their neat, well-tended farms, but these people are not interested in intrusion from the outside world. This community has two businesses that are open to the public. Going north on US 127 from Russell Springs at Highway 80, turn southeast on Highway 910. Go about 3½ miles and turn east onto South Fork. This is a beautiful drive past both secular and Mennonite farms (watch for "shocked" corn and draft horses in the field). It's hilarious to see the contrast in styles: Watch to the right side of South Fork for the gaudiest house in the world; the obviously secular yard is thick with whirligigs, holiday yard art, and endless junk.

At the other extreme and just a few miles away, *Bluegrass Wood and Leather Craft* (furniture, chairs, tables, harnesses, and leather goods) is a remarkable place run by remarkable people. The store is a large building on the right filled with furniture (mainly oak) upstairs and leather goods downstairs, all of excellent quality. Because the Mennonites in the area do much of their farming with horses and mules, the leather items are primarily horse-related, but there aren't many limits to these craftsmen's abilities. The fellows in the shop are more than willing to answer questions, and if you're serious about a purchase, they are glad to take a special order as long it falls within their way of working. There's no phone, but they are usually open on weekdays during business hours.

Back on Highway 910, go "just a little piece" farther south to *Dutchman's Market*, a small Mennonite general store in the basement of their community elementary school. To remain apart as much as possible from the corrupt aspects of today's culture, these Mennonites often employ low-technology methods for farming, building, and living in general. So, if you are in search of something unusual, a modern instance of an old model of any kind of equipment, like a hand pump for your cistern, inquire about it at Dutchman's. Let me also recommend the local sorghum molasses. Alan Oberholtzer, the local molasses meister, keeps this store well stocked. You'll want to speed home to make a mess of biscuits just to have an excuse for draining what promises to be the first of many jars.

The Underwater World of "Atlantis"— in Kentucky

Burnside, just south of Somerset on US 27, is not only the only town on Lake Cumberland—it is the only town under the lake. In the late 1940s the U.S. Army Corps of Engineers moved the entire town to higher ground because the lake area was being impounded. The durable remains of old Burnside become visible during the winter when the lake's level lowers. It's eerie seeing foundations, porch steps, and sidewalks emerge from the mud and debris.

Nearby in **Burnside,** on US 27 south of Somerset, is **General Burnside Island State Park,** a 430-acre island that's right in the middle of a deep bend in the Cumberland River as it's widening into lake status. You can camp here, launch a boat, even play golf. What the heck?! You're on an island in Kentucky! Call (606) 561-4104 for any information (parks.ky .gov/parks/recreationparks/General -Burnside/default.aspx). At Christmas the park sponsors a lavish 3½-mile drive-through light show with several hundred displays and more than a million lights.

trueblue

The last stagecoach line in Kentucky ran the 20 miles between Monticello, a town named for Thomas Jefferson's home, and Burnside.

The **Natural Arch Scenic Area** was once Cherokee country and is now a beautiful place to take a few short but spectacular day hikes. (If you're feeling energetic, you could actually cover all the trails in one day.) From Somerset take US 27 south for 21 miles, then turn right (west) on Highway 927 and follow the signs for 4 miles. The natural arch for which the area is named is a majestic 50-by-90-foot span of sandstone that curves above the forest below. Short trails go to some spectacular overlooks and fertile deep valleys. Early spring is a great time to go; every week brings a different set of wildflowers, including the rare lady's slipper. For trail maps or trail condition reports, contact the Somerset District Office, 135 Realty Lane, Somerset 42501, or call (606) 679-2010.

You must pay a visit to some or all of the Appropriate Technology Demonstration centers owned and operated by **Appalachia—Science in the Public Interest,** or ASPI. Make your way toward Mount Vernon via I-75, exit 59; US 150; or any of the small but beautiful and navigable roads that wind that way. This place marks the western edge of one of North America's most diverse eco-regions, the Mixed Mesophytic Forest, a highly varied hardwood forest. This also marks a theoretical borderline into the foothills of Appalachia, a region much beset by economic and ecological abuse. ASPI's vision is to demonstrate and promote the economic and political power found in self-sufficient living, simple living that is healthy for people and for the environment. Although Appalachia desperately needs this vision, the sustainable practices promoted by ASPI apply to everyone

The Shortest Creek in the World

Stab, a short name for a small town with a short creek, is 10 miles east of Somerset along Highway 80 near the Pleasant Run Baptist Church. Short Creek emerges from a hillside cavern at an impressive width of about 25 feet. It flows in a semicircle for maybe 150 feet and ducks back underground in a small cave. There's no doubt, this is the shortest creek in the world. The family that owns the creek says that there was a gristmill at one end and that the creek formerly was used for wintertime baptisms because the water is always 54 degrees Fahrenheit. The Taylors own the small grocery at Stab, too. Stop by their store and ask permission to have a picnic by the creek. You may hear some good stories.

in every situation: Use locally available materials and apply good science in order to live compatibly with your natural surroundings. In the 1970s there were many demonstration sites like this across the nation. This is one of the few remaining centers, and it's more active than ever.

Downtown Mount Vernon is ASPI's main headquarters and houses a small-town demonstration site with a wonderful intensive garden nestled surprisingly right in the midst of asphalt parking lots. The office at 50 Lair Street is open from 8 a.m. to 4 p.m. on weekdays. Call ahead to make an appointment to visit the demonstration center; (606) 256-0077; appalachia -spi.org.

Cumberland Falls is not really off the beaten path, but it's such a flamboyant, unusual cataract that it must be recognized. Follow I-75 to Corbin, get off on US 25W, veer west on Highway 90, and follow the signs to **Cumberland Falls State Resort Park** (606-528-4121 or parks.ky.gov/parks/resortparks/Cumberland-Falls/default.aspx) at 7351 Kentucky 90. The wide, humble Cumberland River explodes dramatically as it crashes over the curving precipice and becomes the largest American waterfall east of the Rocky Mountains, except for Niagara. When the entire disk of the moon is illuminated and the skies are clear, a long moonbow arches from the top of the falls to the turbulent waters

trueblue

Cumberland Falls near Corbin is the second-largest waterfall east of the Rockies (only Niagara is bigger).

below. The only other moonbow in the world is at Victoria Falls along the Zambezi River in southern Africa. The Cumberland Falls is so powerful that the mist fans way out and above the water; when the wind is right, you get a gentle shower on the rocks at the top. More than 65 feet high and 125 feet across, the waterfall is believed to have retreated as far as 45 miles upstream from its original position near Burnside. In a process that takes many millennia, the water wears away the soft sandstone under the erosion-resistant lip at the top.

The park, which is open all year, has another smaller but beautiful falls called **Little Eagle Falls.** If it's hot, the pool below Little Eagle Falls is a divine swimming hole. Ask for information at the park lodge about hiking trails, rooms, cabins, and special events. Within the park is a state nature preserve left to its wild state. It boasts more than 15 species of rare plants and animals including endangered mussels and plants like the box huckleberry, brook saxifrage, goat's rue, and riverweed. A guided hike can be a real education.

Another way to "get into" the river, and to have a rip-roaring good time, is to hook up with a guided canoeing or white-water rafting trip down the river. Write to **Sheltowee Trace Outfitters,** 2001 Kentucky 90, Corbin, 40701, call (800) 541-7238, or visit ky-rafting.com.

The other big playground in this region is at the **Big South Fork National River and Recreation Area** (nps.gov/biso) in McCreary County and below the border. Take US 27 or I-75 south to Highway 92 and go west to Stearns. If you're arriving via US 27, check out the natural rock bridge just off Highway 927, which goes to Nevelsville. You can also get to Big South Fork on Highway 700, which intersects US 27 near Whitley City. The latter route brings you directly to **Yahoo Falls,** Kentucky's highest at 113 feet. The designation is a little misleading, though. Yahoo is by no means a massive waterfall. In fact, it's just a thin stream of water that drops a great distance. In dry summers it virtually disappears. But water quantity aside, the hike to the bottom is pleasant and well marked.

The whole Big South Fork area is beautiful. Deep, jagged gorges are frequent surprises, and the variations in the landscape, from cool woods to hot, high, open-faced rocks, are endlessly pleasing. That the area was once extensively logged and mined is apparent. From early April through the end of October, the USDA Forest Service operates the **Big South Fork Scenic**

Railway, which takes visitors on a three-hour trip through the Stearn Coal and Lumber Company's former logging and mining empire, now mostly second-growth woods. Call (606) 376-5330 or check bsfsry.com for information and excursion times. You can also drive or take the railway to an abandoned coal mining camp called *Blue Heron,* or Mine 18. This isolated company town was built in 1937 and nearly abandoned by the late 1950s, and the original buildings were ingeniously rebuilt as "ghost structures" in 1989. Life-size photographs of miners and their families occupy the skeletal structural and corrugated-steel spaces, and recorded voices depict life in the camp through a kind of time-delay oral history. The walk across the coal tipple bridge is breathtaking—you can't help but appreciate the engineering. Another camp, circa 1910, called the *Barthell Mining Camp,* is accessible only by train. You can even lodge overnight in one of the mining cabins. The appointments have improved over the days when miners slept here, however: Each cabin includes two bedrooms with queen-size beds, and kitchens with microwaves. Call (888) 550-5748 for information (barthellcoal camp.com).

At the peak of a hill in Stearns is the *McCreary County Museum* (606-376-5730; mccrearymuseum.com), located in the nearly century-old former Stearns Coal and Lumber Company office building. The history, depicted by displays, begins with pre-European Native American culture and ends in the present with a gallery devoted to local contemporary artwork. Museum hours vary so call ahead. Museum is open December through March by appointment only.

Take exit 11 off I-75 and keep an eye peeled for a new brick colonial-style building on the campus of Cumberland College in *Williamsburg.* This is the *Cumberland Museum, Inn, and Center for Leadership Studies.* Students work in the facility to help pay for their tuition and to learn real-world skills in hotel management. The restaurant and lodgings have a great view of the surrounding mountains. Rates are around $94; call (606) 539-4100 for information (cumber landinn.com). Among other things, the eclectic Cumberland Museum has

trueblue

In 1818, while drilling for salt along the Big South Fork, workers inadvertently discovered oil. So began the first commercial oil well in America.

an Appalachian lifestyle exhibit, a Native American artifacts collection, a very unusual collection of more than 6,000 Christian crosses, and a "life science" collection that consists of actual, preserved animal specimens, such as polar bears and shrews, shown in displays that mimic their natural habitats. There is an admission charge. For more information call (606) 539-4050. Hours are 11 a.m. to 6 p.m. Monday through Friday and 10 a.m. to 6 p.m. Saturday.

Jellico, Tennessee, just across the border on I-75, is (or was) the number-one place for underage Kentuckians to get hitched. In Jellico they do it fast, legal, and without parental or priestly consent: "I do, and he does, too."

Corbin sits on the adjoining corners of Whitley, Laurel, and Knox Counties and serves as the commercial hub for the whole area. Although Corbin is not famous the world over, its native son, Col. Harland Sanders, is. From Tokyo to Moscow to London, England, and London, Kentucky, the Colonel's red-and-white portrait, complete with the almost sinister goatee, smiles out on chicken consumers everywhere going through the KFC doors. Corbin is the home of the original restaurant—it's even listed on the National Register of Historic Places. At The **Harland Sanders Cafe & Museum,** see Harland's kitchen as it was in the 1940s and eat in a dining area restored to resemble the original restaurant. To get there, go north of Corbin and take US 25E south; turn right at the second traffic light. Hours are 10 a.m. to 10 p.m. daily. Call (606) 528-2163 for information.

London, the next town to the north, is trying to get in on the chicken action, too, and holds an annual World Chicken Festival downtown at the end of September. In addition to the usual festival activities, all the great cooks in town compete for coveted cook-off prizes. The real winners are the tasters. Call (800) 348-0095 or visit chickenfestival.com for specifics.

If you think the interstate near London looks busy now in a postindustrial, highway-laced world, ponder the years between 1775 and 1800, when more than 300,000 people came into Kentucky from the east through this area when it was wild. The **Levi Jackson State Park** is situated at the intersection of the Wilderness Road and Boone's Trace, the two main frontier "highways." The park is just 2 miles south of London on US 25 at 998 Levi Jackson Mill Road. The Mountain Life

trueblue

The world's largest collection of millstones is found at McHargue's Mill near London, Kentucky.

Museum gives newcomers to the area a glimpse of pioneer history with a reproduction pioneer settlement stocked with period furniture and Native American artifacts. Also at the park is McHargue's Mill, a completely operational restored gristmill, circa 1812, that serves as a kind of mill museum and has what may be the world's largest collection of millstones. On park grounds is the only marked burial ground along the Wilderness Road (though historians believe that there are many other cemeteries lacking headstones). For questions about hiking, camping, or any park information, call (606) 330-2130 or visit park.ky.gov/parks/recreationpark/Levi-Jackson/default.aspx.

Ask at the area visitor center, off I-75 at exit 41 (800-348-0095), about *Camp Wildcat Civil War Battle Site.* The Battle of Wildcat Mountain, as it's also called, was four days of skirmishing that took place October 1861. Collectively, the encounters are considered the first major battle and Union victory in Kentucky. The battle site off Hazel Patch Road includes various monuments and rough terrain.

The Rockcastle River, the lower part of which has been designated a Kentucky Wild River, runs through some gorgeous country in the Daniel Boone National Forest. Riding its currents is probably the perfect way to see the land in this area. No matter what your skill in a canoe or kayak, you will be challenged. Between March and October three area outfitting companies offer trips along the Rockcastle, which, by the way, has rapids rated between Class I and IV. The next town to the north is *Mount Vernon.* Mount Vernon is considered a kind of gateway to the Knobs, the serious hills that skirt the Appalachian Mountains. For a double delight—beautiful mountains and wonderful people—take a drive straight uphill from the caution light in downtown Mount Vernon at the junction of US 150 and Highway 1249. Exactly 10 miles later you'll find yourself on a hillside in front of a redbrick ranch house on the left, home of *Betty Thomas Teddy Bears.* Betty works at home and welcomes visitors but requests that you call first at (606) 256-5378 to see her fine dolls and stuffed animals—everything from realistic Canada geese and goslings, decoy-size mallard ducks, debonair foxes dressed in traditional hunt clothing and hard hats, Old World–style teddy bears, mice, cats, dogs, unicorns, soft-sculpture baby dolls, and on and on. Most of her pieces have hinged joints, and all are stuffed so tightly that they stand independently; all are made of high-quality wool, satin, or cotton in delicious colors.

Ms. Thomas's patience, persistence, and skill with her hands come to her honestly. Her parents raised 13 children in a log cabin in a holler (hollow) just across the road from her present home. Her father, William McClure, is rightfully considered a kind of legend among folk-culture enthusiasts. For years his handmade wooden roof shingles were in constant demand in all the surrounding states, as were his handsome carved dough bowls. You can see some of his work on the roof of the Aunt Polly Hiatt house at Renfro Valley (coming up next). They say that although that roof has gaps in it so big you can see sky through them, it doesn't leak a drop. Long live the McClure family!

Here's the lineup: "Banjo Pickin' Gal," "Winking at Me," "Chicken Reel," "Cackling Hen," "Barbara Allen," "Poor Ellen Smith," "Tramp on the Street," "Matthew 24," and "Old Shep." These could be the names of thoroughbreds in the starting gate at the Derby but are, in fact, some of the best country songs ever written and some of the first ever performed at **Renfro Valley,** Kentucky's Country Music Capital. Many folks in the region remember when they first heard John Lair's silk-smooth voice in 1939 broadcasting an all-country-music radio show live from his big tobacco barn in Rockcastle County. Those humble beginnings have led to the establishment of a large complex of buildings and traditional music and entertainment programs at Renfro Valley; the radio shows are now transmitted to more than 200 stations in North America. In addition to performance events in the auditorium (a luxury barn), there are on the grounds a craft village with mountain craft demonstrators, a gift shop, the Renfro Valley Museum, a bakery, a hotel, and a restaurant. Go north from Mount Vernon a few miles on US 25; for the more scenic route, to the Renfro Valley exit. For more information, show tickets, or reservations, call (800) 765-7464 or check renfrovalley.com. Renfro Valley is open March through mid-December.

Next door to Renfro Valley is another attraction sure to get your toes tapping. And along the way you just might learn something about Kentucky history. The **Kentucky Music Hall of Fame and Museum** opened in 2002 to honor the state's musical heritage from country to classical. Exhibits include costumes from Kentucky stars such as Loretta Lynn, The Everly Brothers, and Rosemary Clooney; a time line with fascinating and beautiful antique instruments; and a hands-on area where you can explore pitch, tempo, and timbre. The museum also hosts special performances and offers weekly music lessons and an on-site sound studio for aspiring inductees. The museum is open 10 a.m. to 6 p.m. Tuesday through Saturday and 9 a.m. to 5 p.m. Sunday (606-256-1000; kentuckymusicmuseum.com). Admission is $7.50 adults, $6 seniors, $4.50 children ages 6 to 12.

More Good Lodging in South-Central Kentucky

BOWLING GREEN

1869 Homestead Bed & Breakfast
212 Mizpah Road
(270) 842-0510
1869homestead.com
Historic home on 55 acres, with three guest rooms and numerous hiking trails.

BURKESVILLE

Cabin Fever
243 Davidson Road
(270) 358-4415
cabinfeverky.com
Bed-and-breakfast in wooded setting.

CORBIN

Best Western
2630 Cumberland Falls Road
I-75, exit 25
(606) 528-2100

Cumberland Falls State Resort Park
7351 Kentucky 90
(606) 528-4121
parks.ky.gov/parks/resortparks/Cumberland-Falls/default.aspx
Rustic stone lodge and 16 cabins; open year-round.

GLASGOW

Four Seasons Country Inn
4107 Scottsville Road
(270) 678-1000
fourseasonscountryinn.com
Twenty-one guest rooms with private baths

JAMESTOWN

Lake Cumberland State Resort Park
off US 127
(270) 343-3111
parks.ky.gov/parks/resortparks/Lake-Cumberland/default.aspx
Two lodges and 30 cabins; open year-round.

LEITCHFIELD

Rough River Dam State Resort Park
Highway 79
(270) 257-2311
parks.ky.gov/parks/resortparks/Rough-River/default.aspx
Lodge and cottages.

MAMMOTH CAVE

Mammoth Cave Hotel
Mammoth Cave National Park
(270) 758-2225
mammothcavehotel.com
Rooms and cottages; pet kennel available.

RADCLIFF

Best Western Gold Vault Inn
1225 North Dixie Highway
(270) 351-1141
goldvaultinn.net

SMITHS GROVE

Victorian House Bed and Breakfast
110 Main Street
(270) 563-9403
bbonline.com/united
-states/kentucky/smiths
-grove/victorian.html
Four rooms with private
baths and fireplaces;
located in antiques district
10 miles north of Bowling
Green.

WILLIAMSBURG

Cumberland Inn
649 South Tenth Street
(606) 539-4100
cumberlandinn.com

More Fun Places to Eat in South-Central Kentucky

BOWLING GREEN

Brickyard Cafe
1026 Chestnut Street
(270) 843-6431
brickyardcafe.net
Italian trattoria in an 1860s
brickyard building.

440 Main Restaurant and Bar
440 East Main Avenue
(270) 793-0450
440main.com
Elegant dining in a
restored historic home.

Judy's Castle
1302 US 31W Bypass
(270) 842-8736
Country cooking. Well
loved breakfasts and daily
plate specials—meat-and-
three-veggies classics.

CAVE CITY

Water Mill Restaurant
Highway 70
(270) 773-3186
Large buffet or order from
the menu.

Sahara Steak House
413 Happy Valley Road
(270) 773-3450
Steaks, seafood, and
country-ham dishes.

CORBIN

Cumberland Falls State Resort Park
Highway 90,
southwest of Corbin
(606) 528-4121
parks.ky.gov/parks/
resortparks/Cumberland
-Falls/default.aspx
Wide variety of
sandwiches and seafood
entrees, plus regional
specialties such as
country ham, served in a
family atmosphere.

Dale Hollow Lake State Resort Park
Highway 1206, south of
Lake Cumberland
(270) 433-7431
parks.ky.gov/parks/
resortparks/Dale-Hollow/
default.aspx
Variety of American dishes
and regional specialties.
Dinner buffet Friday
through Sunday.

ELIZABETHTOWN

Ginza Japanese Restaurant
1705 North Dixie Highway
(270) 737-5536
Japanese food in casual
setting. Popular lunch.

Stone Hearth Restaurant
1001 North Mulberry
Street
(270) 765-4898
stonehearthetown.com
Home cooking.

LEITCHFIELD

Rough River Dam State Resort Park
Highway 79
(270) 257-2311
parks.ky.gov/parks/
resortparks/Rough-River/
default.aspx
Buffet and regional
specialties.

LIBERTY

Bread of Life Cafe

5369 South Highway 127
(4½ miles south of town)
(606) 787-6110
galileanhome.org/bread
-of-life
Pennsylvania Dutch–style
cooking. Proceeds go to
the Galilean Children's
Home. Freshly based
bread, rolls, desserts.
Buffet and menu. Except
Sunday, open daily for all
three meals.

RENFRO VALLEY

The Lodge Restaurant

I-75, exit 62
(800) 765-7464
renfrovalley.com/the-lodge
Country cooking, with
great soup, beans,
chicken and dumplings,
and chocolate pie.

SCOTTSVILLE

Harper's

3085 Old Gallatin Road
(270) 622-7557
Three meals a day served
Wednesday to Sunday,
but it's the catfish that
has made this second-
generation family-owned
place popular for almost
30 years.

Western Kentucky

The sky seems bigger in the vast, open land of this western region. Sunsets are beautiful, and you can see a storm coming for hours. There's plenty of room for everyone, and everyone's here, from coal miners and bluegrass musicians to Amish farmers and master quilters. There must be something in the soil here because legendary figures have sprung up like weeds: Robert Penn Warren, Edgar Cayce, Casey Jones, Jefferson Davis, and John James Audubon, to name a few. Western Kentucky also boasts some of the best museums in the state, such as Shakertown at South Union, the most southern of all Shaker communities; the Museum of the American Quilter's Society; and the Owensboro Museum of Fine Art.

Most dear to Kentuckians is the Land Between the Lakes, a clean, gorgeous, wild land surrounded by Lake Barkley and Kentucky Lake, a double paradise for fisher folks. There must be more resorts and marinas per square mile around the Land Between the Lakes area than anywhere else in the state. Stop and ask about camping, cottages, fishing, restaurants, or anything else your heart may desire. American bald eagles also find this region attractive

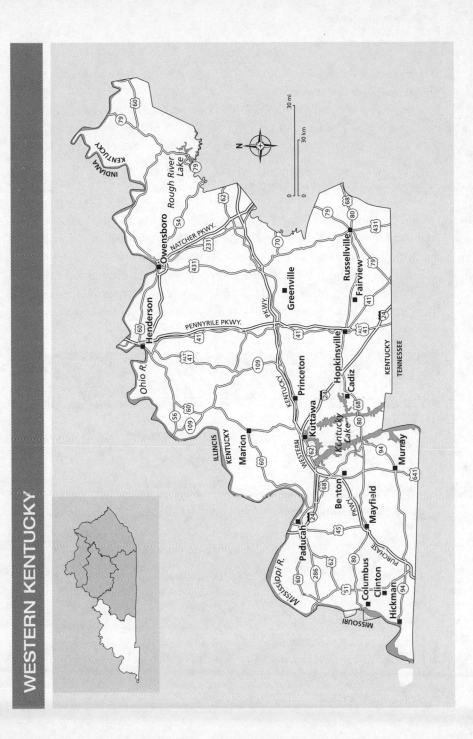

WESTERN KENTUCKY

and make their homes here and along the shore of the Mississippi River in the far southwestern region.

You'll find western Kentucky quiet, not overdeveloped, yet full of fascinating surprises. The fact that people here have uniquely open spirits gives the traveler a chance to absorb and deeply enjoy the culture of this place.

Jackson Purchase

On the fourth Sunday in May, if you are anywhere near **Benton,** west of the lakes on US 641, plan to attend **Big Singing Day,** the only American singing festival that uses the 1835 *Southern Harmony Book* of shape note tunes. (Shape note singing is a traditional form of a cappella that represents the four notes—mi, fa, sol, la—on the staff by a different shape; i.e., diamond, triangle, circle, square, respectively.) This wonderfully nonhierarchical group singing event has been happening here since 1843. There is no leader and no instrumental accompaniment, and the songs, usually traditional Welsh hymns, are arranged in parts such that no one sings beyond his or her range. Weather permitting, the singing happens outdoors on the courthouse lawn.

The other big event is Benton's *Tater Day,* held on the first Monday in April since 1843 and one of the world's few events dedicated to the delectable sweet potato. Pay your homage to a great food and enjoy a friendly small-town festival. Activities run the whole weekend, leading up to the day itself. For information on Big Singing Day or Tater Day, call the Marshall County Tourism Office at (800) 467-7145 or visit kentuckylake.org.

Just outside Benton in *Draffenville,* the music continues. On any Saturday night of the year and on Friday in June, July, August, and December, a live country music show is performed at *Kentucky Opry* at 88 Chilton Lane. Locals love this show, so if you're serious about getting to know this region, you've got to stop by and "give a listen." It's a family-oriented place, so children are welcome but alcohol is not. The specialties are country, gospel, and some really hot bluegrass. Admission varies according to the show. Call (270) 527-3869 or (888) 459-8704 or go high-tech and log onto kentuckyopry.com.

Going south on US 641 brings you to the peaceful town of *Murray,* which Rand McNally once ranked the "number one retirement location in the country" because of the proximity of outdoor recreational areas, the low crime rate, and the low cost of living.

Rudy's Restaurant (270-753-1632), on the west side of the courthouse square at 104 South Fifth Street, is so crowded at lunchtime that you may have to sit with a stranger if you're determined to have a fresh hamburger and homemade onion rings. This little place has been open since the early 1930s, when the original Rudy made it famous for its

trueblue

Kentucky is one of only four states to use the designation commonwealth, meaning government based on common consent of the people.

consistently good country cooking and cutting-edge gossip. Rudy, a short, roly-poly fellow whose lip never knew the absence of a cigar, collected money and spread the news of the day from a stool behind the big brass

Authentic to the End

Civil War reenactors (and Kentucky has a slew of them) often take their reenactment quite seriously, insisting on meticulous detail and authenticity in their uniforms and accessories and often adopting the total identity of soldiers from the past. Carrying this thought to its ultimate conclusion was one of the inspirations for **Bert & Bud's Vintage Coffins,** of Murray. Roy "Bud" Davis, the former director of the Clara M. Eagle Art Gallery at Murray State University, creates 19th-century "toe pincher–style" and other unique coffins at a studio in his garage. So far, business hasn't been exactly lively, but one Murray antiques buff ordered a coffin for use as a coffee table, and a Nova Scotia customer plans to use one in a theatrical production. Meanwhile, he is looking at lighter sidelines. He also built a whimsical coffin that looks like a dollhouse for his wife. "She has no intention of using it for a long time," he noted. "Our market is really not for people who need a coffin now, but for people who want something different and tend to plan ahead." Give Davis a call at (877) 371-9279 or (270) 753-9279 if you're interested in stopping by while you're in Murray. The website is fascinating too: vintagecoffins.com.

cash register. Monday through Friday breakfast starts at 5 a.m., and lunch ends at 2 p.m.

Potter Wayne Bates is known throughout the region for his meticulously crafted sgraffito porcelain vessels. My own favorites are the striking black-on-white radial designs on wide bowls, but he also makes use of brighter colors. You can see a wide selection of his pieces and usually watch him at work if you visit his studio and showroom called **Wayne Bates Studio & Gallery 121.** Because he works and lives at the same site, he's usually open daily, but it's a good idea to call ahead at (270) 436-5610. To get there from Murray, take Highway 121 South (in town it's Fourth Street South); drive 8.3 miles (if you measure from the courthouse square) and watch on the left for his gallery sign. He has a great website at waynebates.com that shows the work and gives information about upcoming events at the studio and so forth.

Take Highway 94 east from Murray and go about 8 miles. Look for a sign that says **Alfred Duncan House of Willow** (270-759-9595). Go another mile and turn right on Old Newburg Road and look for a sign that says **George Beard's House of Willow** (270-226-5536). In either place you'll probably see curving bent willow chairs in the yard by the signs. Each man has a workshop by his house. Each man is carrying on a "stick furniture" tradition that was probably started by the gypsies who sold willow chairs in this area in the 1930s. George Beard taught Alfred Duncan the craft and approves of his student's work so much that he claims he can't tell their work apart. Both men are extraordinary, thrifty chair makers. Regardless of the fact that this style of outdoor furniture is in vogue at the moment, this craft has lasting integrity. These chair makers go to riverbanks in Kentucky and all over swampy areas of the South to gather red and white willow branches that they bend and nail into place while still green. Nothing is wasted; the large stock is used for heavy supports, thin branches are twisted into decorative backs or armrests, and the very thinnest trees, some as young as six months, are used as "benders," pliable pieces that make accommodating seats. Sit in any chair, love seat, or rocker and your body will understand that the Shakers couldn't have designed them better. The choices of branch size and spacing create a simple and visually stunning effect. Beard has become something of a regional treasure. In 1978 the Smithsonian bought one of his hooded chairs in red willow for its permanent collection; a dark red Indian willow love seat is in a museum in Utah; and the Kentucky Museum in Frankfort exhibits a settee and child's chair. These are craftsmen

SELECTED SOURCES OF TRAVEL INFORMATION FOR THE JACKSON PURCHASE AREA

**Kentucky's Western Waterland
Tourist Information Center**
721 Complex Drive
Grand Rivers 42045
(270) 928-4411 or (800) 448-1069
kentuckylakebarkley.org

**Paducah/McCracken County
Convention and Visitors Bureau**
128 Broadway, Paducah 42001
(270) 443-8783 or (800) PADUCAH
paducah.travel

Murray Tourism Commission
201 South Fourth Street
(270) 759-2199
tourmurray.com

not to miss and nice folks to boot. They're usually around, but if you'd like to make sure they have some furniture in stock, call ahead.

Hazel, just south of Murray on US 641, was one of the towns that sprang up in the 1890s as the railroad connected western Kentucky with the rest of the world. The town may have been named for the daughter of the conductor of the first through train, although other Hazels are also in contention. Samuel H. Dees, who founded the Hazel Post Office, also had a daughter named Hazel. Some think the name refers to the thick hazel groves that grow in the area. In more recent times, Hazel has made a name for itself as an antiques lovers' haven. The town's charming turn-of-the-20th-century storefronts are now home to dozens of antiques malls and shops; one count placed more than 250 dealers active in the community. So bring your measuring tape, your magnet, your price guides, and your checkbook, and plan to spend all day wandering from shop to shop. Get back on Highway 94 and head west toward the Mississippi River and the little town of Hickman. If you're inclined to take a bizarre little side trip, take a brief detour onto Highway 97 south toward Bell City and watch for **Murdock Mausoleum,** a semiunderground building with a sign on the top that reads, "Stop See A Road Map To Heaven." Who wouldn't stop? On the wall of the porch is a large painted sign describing how one can get to heaven—the gospel of John is heavily quoted. Behind a decorative iron door and window one can view the burial area. The graves of two women take up perhaps a sixth of the burial space, leaving the rest free for future occupants.

As you pass through Cayce, know that this was the home of the legendary daredevil railroad engineer John Luther Jones (better known as Casey Jones), who was "yanked-up" here. When he got his first job with the Illinois Central, there were so many Joneses that his boss nicknamed him "Cayce." The legend that developed around him after his death somehow also corrupted the spelling to "Casey," but folks here haven't forgotten.

trueblue

Mark Twain called Hickman "the most beautiful town on the Mississippi."

From Hickman you can take the **Hickman-Dorena Ferry** across the Mississippi River to Missouri. The ferry runs daily except Christmas Day. The first run of the day is at 7 a.m. from the Kentucky side, 7:30 a.m. from the Missouri side, with the

Where, Oh Where Did Wolf Island Go?

Hickman County is missing a tooth. Sometime between 1820 and 1870, a channel of the Mississippi River shifted to the east, leaving a 9,000-acre chunk of Kentucky land stranded in Missouri, nearly a mile west of the rest of the county. Despite its new location, in 1871 the Supreme Court awarded the land, now called Wolf Island, to Kentucky, thereby denying the big daddy of all waters the power to move official boundaries.

last run at 6:15 p.m. from the Kentucky side and 6:30 p.m. from the Missouri side. During the day, runs are made by demand. There's a button to push on the telephone pole near the ferry entrance to signal the captain that you want to cross. Fare for an automobile is $16 one-way. Save your ticket and you get half fare for the return trip. Call the ferry boat itself at (731) 693-0210 or the main office at (731) 285-0390 for information (dorena -hickmanferryboat.com).

From Hickman you can also follow Highway 94 southwest to **Reelfoot Lake.** The part of the lake that is in Kentucky (most is in Tennessee) is wild, beautiful swampland. During the winter of 1811–12, a series of earthquakes along the New Madrid fault shook the whole region so violently that the tremors made bells ring as far away as Pittsburgh, Pennsylvania. Reelfoot Lake was created when the quakes caused the Mississippi River to run backwards; when it returned to its usual flow, it straightened out and left behind one of its old curves. Look at your map and the abandoned bend will become obvious. Admire the large stands of bald cypress trees. Their lower trunks are broad, flaring like upside-down flying buttresses; the needles are feathery and fine; and they're surrounded by their own "knees," or cone-shaped roots, which seem to emerge from the water independently. These roots make it possible for the large trees to remain upright in the muddy soils. Follow Highway 94 southwest to the Reelfoot Lake National Wildlife Refuge and talk to the rangers about the local wildlife.

The only way to go farther west in Kentucky is to drive down Highway 94 into Tennessee, where it becomes Highway 78. From Tiptonville, Tennessee, follow the signs to the Madrid Bend, also known as Kentucky Bend or Bessie Bend. A few families have the peninsula to themselves to farm however they please.

North of Hickman and "inland" a bit, on US 51, is the town of *Clinton,* home to the new *Hickman County Museum,* which is a testament to the spirit of local devotion to local history. Volunteers and a museum board renovated an 1870s house (once belonging to Capt. Henry Cruse Watson, who fought with the Confederate army) at 221 East Clay Street. Each of nine rooms presents thematically grouped artifacts (all of which were donated), from the College Room to the Medical Room. Items on display range from historic military uniforms, an early 1900s fire-hose cart designed to be pulled by two men on foot, political mementos associated with "local boy" Alben W. Barkley, pottery made by prehistoric peoples called Mound Builders, and all sorts of agricultural tools. Hours are 1 to 4 p.m. on Wednesday and Saturday, or by appointment. For more information call (270) 653-6187.

In the center of the Jackson Purchase region is the town of *Mayfield,* known to outsiders for *The Wooldridge Monuments,* "the strange procession that never moves," in the cemetery. The entrance to the Maplewood Cemetery is in town at the intersection of the US 45 overpass and North Seventh Street. The 18-figure group in sandstone and Italian marble was erected in the late 1890s by an otherwise inconsequential bloke named Henry G. Wooldridge. Though he is the only person buried on the site, the figures represent him on his favorite horse, Fop; him standing by a podium; two hounds, a fox, and a deer; and his three sisters, four brothers, mother, and two great-nieces, one of whom, rumor has it, actually resembles Henry's first love, Minnie, who died in her youth. Legend has it that when the statues were en route from Paducah, a drunk climbed on the flat railcar and mounted the stone horse behind the stone Wooldridge to ride into Mayfield, the drunk king of a mute parade. For information call the Mayfield/Graves County Chamber of Commerce at (270) 247-6101.

trueblue

Alben W. Barkley was born in 1877 in Graves County and raised there in relative poverty before his steady political climb from law clerk to county attorney to U.S. congressman, senator, and finally, in 1949, to vice president in the second administration of President Harry S. Truman.

Bobbie Ann Mason

Mayfield is the hometown of Bobbie Ann Mason, one of America's most percep-
tive and powerful writers. If you've read her work, you'll feel you've been in this
region before. Her fiction is intensely crafted and rich in realistic detail, and her
characters seem familiar, not at all larger-than-life. Mason says, "Like me, these
characters are emerging from a rural way of life that is fast disappearing, and
they are wondering where they're going to end up." Her novels include *Feather
Crowns, Spence + Lila,* and the powerful work about the effect of the war in Viet-
nam on rural Americans, *In Country,* which was made into a well-loved movie by
the same title. She has written many short stories and recently published a selection of her favorites called *Midnight Magic,* which will make you seek out all her
short fiction. Mason lives in Kentucky and still has family in Mayfield.

If you aren't sure whether you are really in the South, you will be
when you encounter another memorial in town right in the center of town
square, because it's dedicated to Mayfield's Confederate dead. More local
history is explained just blocks away in the **Western Kentucky Museum** at
120 North Eighth Street, at the corner of West North Street. The museum of
artifacts dating back to the late 19th century includes lots of regional business and agricultural paraphernalia, particularly pertaining to tobacco. Also
housed in the restored icehouse is the **Graves County Art Guild,** which
showcases local paintings and sculptures. Both are open Tuesday through
Friday from 10 a.m. to 4:30 p.m. and Saturday 10 a.m. to 1 p.m. For more
information call (270) 247-6971 or visit icehousearts.org.

Fiery debates and pit barbecue are at the heart of the **Fancy Farm
Picnic** (fancyfarm.net), perhaps the sole survivor of grassroots political-
campaign picnics in America. *The Guinness Book of World Records* lists it as
the world's largest one-day picnic, not surprising when more than 15,000
pounds of fresh pork and mutton are cooked annually. The first Saturday in
August at 10 a.m., games and entertainment begin, country-goods booths go
up, and local, state, and national political figures rile the crowds, one way
or another. Speeches are given from a red, white, and blue bunting–covered
flatbed wagon, just like in 1880, when the picnic was established as the last
opportunity for candidates to meet before the August primaries. Because the
primaries are now held in May, the picnic functions as a debate forum for

the final candidates. Fancy Farm is 10 miles west of Mayfield on Highway 80, at its junction with Highway 339.

Due west on Highway 80 in Hickman County is the low-lying river town of **Columbus.** Slightly upriver, between Columbus and Clinton, the **Columbus-Belmont Battlefield State Park** (270-677-2327; parks.ky .gov/parks/recreationparks/Columbus Belmont/default.aspx) perches on 200-foot-high palisades. The park marks the Civil War site of the western-most Confederate fortification in Kentucky. Rebel soldiers installed a whop-ping mile-long chain, held afloat by wooden rafts, across the Mississippi River to prevent Union gunboats from moving south. Each link of the chain weighed 15 pounds, and the anchor attached to it was six tons. Cannons were lined up on the face of the bluffs. Shortly after the fortification was complete, Union forces led by Ulysses S. Grant took the town in 1861 when Confederate forces were crumbling everywhere. The park's high bluff is a pleasantly dizzying picnic and camping site. The huge anchor with its chain

A Festival Whose Ap-peel Is Remembered

Fulton, Kentucky, a fence-sitting town on the Kentucky-Tennessee border (South Fulton is in the Volunteer State), reminds me of that old song, "Yes, We Have No Bananas." Once, Fulton had plenty of 'em. For decades, wholesalers from all over the country came to Fulton to buy bananas, which were shipped from South America via New Orleans to the largest icehouse in the United States in, you guessed it, Fulton. In 1962 the town started the annual International Banana Festival, which featured the "world's largest banana pudding." One year the publicly made pudding topped two tons in order to make it into *The Guinness Book of World Records.* Changing times, however, were catching up with Fulton, and in the festival's last years, the town had to practically beg for bananas. So in 1992 the festival was disbanded. In a way, though, you can still experience it, in a children's illustrated story published online by Indiana author and illustrator Jerry Jindrich. Through tales and drawings, Jerry and his wife, Susan, have cre-ated an educational fantasy world online called the "Island of Meddybemps, home of Chateau Meddybemps." One of the stories, titled "But That Wasn't the Best Part," was inspired by the International Banana Festival, which Jerry attended one year. Wonder what the best part was? Visit meddybemps.com and find out a little about a Kentucky town's festival that will always *ap-peel* to the imagination.

The Most Debated Place Name in Kentucky

If you've become hooked on digressions, here's an opportunity to indulge. Continue from Barlow on US Highway 60 east to La Center and take Highway 358 north, then go west on Highway 473 through Ogden (once called Needmore) to *Monkey's Eyebrow,* the most debated place name in the state of Kentucky. There is no post office, hence no official name, but we argue nonetheless. Journalist Byron Crawford submits the idea that, if one looks at the shape of the northern boundary of Ballard County, the Ohio River forms a rough profile of a monkey in such a way that this community is just where the eyebrow would be. Others say that there was a store owned by John and Dodge Ray, the brothers who settled the sandy loam ridge in the late 19th century, and behind it was a berm that resembled a monkey's eyebrow because it was covered with tall grasses. New theories are welcome fuel for the fire.

is still on display, along with some cannons. Civil War buffs will also enjoy walking along the earthen fortifications and visiting the small but interesting Civil War Museum with its exhibits of cannonballs, documents, and other artifacts. The park at 350 Park Road is open year-round, but the museum is open April through October. There's a small admission fee.

Follow Highway 123 north to Bardwell, then take US 51 north to Wickliffe. Every Memorial Day weekend from Wickliffe to Fulton, on the Tennessee border, US 51 is lined with flea markets and yard sales. If you can't find junk to your heart's desire on that weekend, you ain't never gonna find it.

Go through Wickliffe as if you were crossing the river to Cairo, Illinois, and look for signs to the *Wickliffe Mounds Research Center* (270-335-3681). You'll understand why the Mississippian Indians chose this site as a town or ceremonial grounds when you stand on the highest mound and look out toward the wide sparkling junction of two massive rivers, the Ohio and the Mississippi. The scene is exhilarating. In addition to the intact, four-sided, flat-topped ceremonial mound, three excavation areas have been preserved and interpreted for the public.

One of the most significant displays is in the cemetery. Without being eerie or morbid, the space is moving. The bodies were buried close together, each surrounded by a few significant belongings, each facing east as if to remain in contact with the cycle of days and nights. The display explains how archaeologists determine diet, illnesses, typical injuries, and physical appearances by analyzing the remains of people who weren't radically different from us. All the actual human remains and burial goods have been replaced with plastic replicas in their original positions. This seriously self-examining display deals with various points of view, includ ing a Native American view, about the appropriate study and treatment of human remains. The curators and Native American advisers are working toward making Wickliffe Mounds into a ceremonial site, as it was thousands of years ago. Hours are 9 a.m. to 5 p.m. Wednesday through Sunday from March to November. Admission is $5 for adults, $4 for seniors and children. Write to the Wickliffe Mounds Research Center, P.O. Box 155, Wickliffe 42087 or visit parks/ky.gov/parks/historicsites/Wickliffe-Mounds/default.aspx.

About 6 miles northeast of Wickliffe on US 60 is the town of Barlow, and in it a museum called the **Barlow House Museum,** on the corner of Broadway and Fifth Street at 509 Broadway Street, which pays tribute to the early history of Ballard County by preserving the home and belongings of a family that helped settle the region. In 1849 Thomas Jefferson Barlow bought land but didn't want to farm, so he opened a general store and started selling lots for houses. Like many an American town, that's how Barlow was born. The fully restored 1903 Victorian home belonged to Thomas's oldest son, Clifton J. Barlow, and remained in the Barlow family until 1989. The house is open to the public for tours Monday, Friday, and Sunday from 1 to 4 p.m., or by appointment, and also for meetings, receptions, and so forth. For more information, call (270) 334-3010 or visit barlowgeneaology.com. Admission is $2 for adults.

To get in touch with nature, go east on US 60 until you reach Future City. Turn left (northeast) on Highway 996 and go almost 6 miles to where the road ends in a strange swampy landscape. The Kentucky State Nature Preserves Commission has purchased **Metropolis Lake** in order to protect this intriguing, naturally formed, little body of water and the surrounding river floodplain from destructive development. Fishing is permitted here because anglers drool over the lake's population of fish and because people take good care of the area. Although the lake area used to be a developed commercial recreation area, today it is more pure, an enchanted dreamscape with bald cypress and swamp tupelo trees casting strange shapes against the sky and even stranger reflections on the water. Beavers, kingfishers, wildflowers, and seven rare aquatic species are among the many living creatures that share this special space. If you have questions call the commission at (502) 573-2886; naturepreserves.ky.gov/naturepreserves/Pages/Metrolake.aspx.

Stay on US 60 and go east into **Paducah,** the urban center of the Jackson Purchase region. As you near the downtown area, look for Noble Park on the west side of the road. Stop when you come across an enormous, haunting sculpture of a Chickasaw Indian. The piece, called **Wacinton,** or "to have understanding," was carved from a 56,000-pound red oak tree by Hungarian-born sculptor Peter "Wolf" Toth in 1985. Toth donated the piece to the city of Paducah and the state of Kentucky in honor of the Native American people who lived in the area before the Jackson Purchase, in 1818. In 1972, at the age of 25, Toth decided to carve a giant Native American sculpture for every state in the Union. He refuses pay. His "trail of whispering giants" is his gift to our national conscience. He identifies with the suffering of Native Americans because he and his family lost everything when they fled Hungary in 1956 just before the communist revolution. Paducah's *Wacinton* is Toth's 50th sculpture. After the United States, he says he'll be carving in Canada, then Mexico.

The people of Paducah have renovated and preserved a once-dilapidated Classical Revival mansion at 1845 Lone Oak Road by making it into the **Whitehaven Welcome Center,** south of town on I-24, and filling it with antique furniture from the area. Get travel information here, or call the center at (270) 554-2077, or check paducah.travel. The lobby and information area are open 24 hours, with tours of the house offered from 1 to 4 p.m. daily.

In downtown Paducah between Broadway and Kentucky Avenue at 121 Market House Square is the Market House, the hub of business and trade since 1836. Today the building houses three arts organizations. The **Market House Museum** (270-443-7759; markethousemuseum.com) is a regional history museum that includes the reconstructed interior of an 1877 drugstore. Hours are noon to 4 p.m. Tuesday through Saturday from March through December. Admission is $1.50. The **Yeiser Art Center** and gift shop (270-442-2453; theyeiser.org) hangs traveling exhibits of contemporary and traditional art. Hours are 10 a.m. to 4 p.m. Tuesday through Saturday. Admission is $4 for adults, $1 for children. Also at 132 Market House Square is the *Market House Theatre* (270-444-6828; markethousetheatre.org), a not-for-profit community theater—check its busy production schedule.

true*blue*

Paducah was founded in 1827 by William Lewis (of Lewis and Clark).

When people think of Kentucky crafts, quilts are often the first things that come to mind. Since April 1991, Paducah immediately comes to mind as the quilt capital of America, thanks to the *Museum of the American Quilter's Society,* downtown at the corner of Second and Jefferson Streets at 215 Jefferson Street. Those of us who have grown up around (or under) handmade quilts and have taken them for granted can't help but be awestruck with the beauty and variety of the quilts in the museum. Unlike many collections in the region, this museum is primarily devoted to the modern quilt. Those who appreciate abstract painting may find a new passion in the bold shapes and colors of these "canvases."

In addition to the main display area of more than 150 quilts from the permanent collection and the two additional galleries with quilts from traveling exhibitions, the 30,000-square-foot building has a climate-controlled vault, classrooms, a gift shop, and an excellent bookstore that features more than 400 books pertaining to quilting and textiles. The museum is open Monday through Saturday from 10 a.m. to 5 p.m. year-round. From March 1 through November 30 it is also open Sunday from 1 to 5 p.m. Admission is $11 for adults, $10 for seniors, and $5 for students. For more information call (270) 442-8856. Three-day quilt-making workshops taught by renowned quilters from across the country are offered every year. For schedules write MAQS/Workshop Program, P.O. Box 1540, Paducah 42002-1540 or check quiltmuseum.org.

Also contributing to Paducah's position as Quilt City USA is the annual *AQS National Quilt Show and Contest,* sponsored by the Paducah-based American Quilter's Society. This national quilt extravaganza is held in late April at the Executive Inn Convention Center in downtown Paducah. More than 400 quilts from all over the world are displayed and judged to win a part of the $75,000-plus in cash awards. During that week the whole city is overflowing with quilts. Special workshops and lectures are offered, quilt supply vendors set up shop, and there's even a fashion show and contest. Hotel space is at a premium during the show, so plan ahead. For show information, write to AQS, P.O. Box 3290, Paducah 42002-3290, or call (270) 898-7903 or (800) 626-5420. Or visit the website at americanquilter.com.

And if you're saturated with looking and ready to get to work, continue up the street to 420 North Fourth Street, where *Quilter's Alley* offers a plethora of quilting supplies and gorgeous fabrics. Classes are offered regularly, and these knowledgeable folks can make appraisals. For more information call (270) 443-5673 or visit quiltersalleypaducah.com.

Right in the hub of old downtown Paducah at 118 South Second Street is the business you wish was next door every day. Five generations of German bakers have titillated taste buds at *Kirchhoff's Bakery and Deli* since it was established in 1873. Traditional as the skills are, the owners have stayed current and now offer a range of gourmet market items, deli cheeses, and fresh vegetables, as well as to-die-for breads and pastries. Hours are Monday through Friday from 7 a.m. to 5 p.m. and Saturday from 8 a.m. to 5 p.m. The phone number is (270) 442-7117. One of Paducah's most unique and geographically relevant institutions is the *Seamen's Church Institute/Center for Maritime Education Paducah* at 111 Kentucky Avenue, which is perched just to the dry side of the confluence of the Tennessee and Ohio Rivers. The Seamen's Church Institute began in the early 1800s as a floating church serving keelboat captains and other river workers. Today the Center for Maritime Education trains barge and riverboat captains and pilots to navigate freshwater inland rivers. In addition to the educational component, there is a nondenominational ministry based here that serves river workers in a variety of ways, from providing Christmas and Easter gifts to running a crisis hotline and coordinating services with "river-friendly" churches. Call (270) 575-1005 or visit seamens church.org.

The *River Discovery Center* is located next door at 117 South Water Street. This museum is housed in a beautifully restored 19th-century bank building, thought to be the oldest surviving structure in downtown Paducah. The museum's exhibit hall tells the story of inland navigation history through artifacts, maps, video, and interactive computer stations. The focus is on the cultures of the region shaped by the Ohio, Tennessee, Mississippi, and Cumberland Rivers, from the early indigenous peoples and their bark canoes to life and industry on the river today. Hours are 9:30 a.m. to 5 p.m. Monday through Friday year-round, and on Sunday from 1 to 5 p.m. from April through November. Admission is $8 for adults, $7 for seniors, and $5 for children under 12. For information call (270) 575-9958 or visit riverdiscovery center.org.

When you step outside the front doors of the museum, you're facing the confluence of two of the four rivers, the Ohio and the Tennessee. You're also facing a marvelous artistic vista that was created along the city's flood walls—some 22 murals showing scenes from Paducah history. The **Paducah Flood Wall Murals** were all created by Robert Dafford, a Louisiana artist noted for his large-scale public works in the United States and Europe.

Downtown Paducah seems somewhat larger than life itself during the summer **Downtown After Dinner** events. Each Saturday night from the first Saturday in May through September is like a mini festival, with music on the street corners, antique car displays, carriage rides, and late shop hours. The events attract lively crowds. Contact the tourism office at (800) PADUCAH or visit paducah.travel for more information.

Even when it's not Quilt Festival or After Dinner time, downtown Paducah is a lively and enjoyable place to be. There are numerous antiques shops and restaurants within easy walking distance of the museums and flood wall murals. In fact, the downtown revitalization has been so successful that city leaders are using it as the model for the revival of another city neighborhood, **Lower Town.** LoTo, as locals call it, is a historic district bordered by Park Avenue, Jefferson Street, Fifth Street, and Ninth Street, with houses from the 1820s through 1920s in various stages of renovation. An organization was founded in Paducah to foster this area as an arts district, and the city has advertised special incentives, from low-cost mortgages to marketing support, to attract both local and nonlocal artists.

Civil War buffs, take heed! The taking of Paducah by the Union in 1861 marks a significant moment in the war—when Kentucky finally lost its neutrality. The Union was responding to the recent Confederate victory at the nearby Mississippi River town of Columbus. This and other war stories are explained through artifacts, documents, and photographs at the **Tilghman Civil War Museum,** at the corner of Seventh and Kentucky

Avenues. The restored house was once home to a Confederate general, Lloyd Tilghman, who defended the Tennessee and Cumberland Rivers and was finally killed in action near Vicksburg. The center is open Tuesday through Saturday from noon to 4 p.m. from April through November or by appointment. Admission is $3 for adults and $1 for children ages 6 to 12. Call (270) 575-5477. Eight other relevant Civil War sites in downtown Paducah can be seen on a free walking tour. Stop by the visitor bureau at 128 Broadway for a map.

trueblue

Both Civil War presidents—Abraham Lincoln and Jefferson Davis—were born in Kentucky, one year and 100 miles apart.

For a worthwhile side trip from Paducah, head south of town on Highway 994, then east on Highway 348 toward the town of Symsonia where you'll find the *Henson Broom Shop Museum.* With a few simple pieces of equipment, three generations of skill, piles of sticks, heaps of broom straw, and lots of energy, Richard N. Henson makes hundreds of graceful, functional brooms. His grandfather, also Richard N. Henson, started making brooms in 1930 when the American economy was faltering and the family needed more income. The elder Henson liked to say, "A Hoover put me into business, and a Hoover put me out of business," referring to the president and the vacuum cleaner, respectively.

Today the third-generation broom maker is rarely out of work. During the summer and fall, Henson converts his horse trailer into a portable workshop, dons a costume, and travels to festivals where he does historic craft reenactment, educating the public while he works. (He has been winning blue ribbons for his craftsmanship all over the country.) Brooms have changed very little during the past hundred years. If you used to watch the television show *Dr. Quinn, Medicine Woman,* you probably saw Henson's brooms for sale in the show's general store and in use by the characters. To his array of old-fashioned kitchen, shop, whisk, cabin, colonial hearth, Shaker, and parlor brooms, Henson has added a fancy, twisted-handle design he calls the Jane Seymour Broom in honor of the show's star. Prices range from $5 to more than $50. He's glad to have visitors, so stop by anytime. You can call him at (270) 851-8510 or write him at 1060 State Route 3100, Symsonia 42082 (hensonbrooms.com).

Pennyroyal Region

Tennessee Valley Authority's (TVA) *Land Between the Lakes* national recreation area is considered the "crappie fishing capital of the world," not to mention the huge populations of largemouth and smallmouth bass—an angler's dream come true. The Tennessee River was dammed to make Kentucky Lake, and Lake Barkley was formed from the mighty Cumberland River. Together they comprise 220,000 acres of clean, safe water and form a 40-mile-long peninsula, which the TVA has developed for recreation and education.

For bird lovers, Land Between the Lakes, or LBL, is one of a scant handful of places where one can get a glimpse of wild bald eagles. In the 1960s poaching and the use of chemicals such as DDT reduced the number of breeding eagles to fewer than 600 pairs, making our national mascot nearly extinct on this continent. The wildlife management people at LBL successfully got the numbers back up by returning raptors to a natural habitat with very little human contact. Ask about eagle and wildlife programs at the Woodlands Nature Center. During the winter, eagle field trips are scheduled for the weekends.

trueblue

Kentucky Lake and Lake Barkley together form one of the largest engineered lakes in the United States.

Photographers can get close-up pictures of these marvelous creatures in captivity at the nature center or, if you're lucky and very patient, in the wild. Throughout the year there's plenty for nature enthusiasts to see and do. In addition to plenty of lake access ramps, there are great hiking trails, ranging from 0.2 to 65 miles in length. (The easy *Center Furnace Trail* goes past a historic iron furnace.) You can also rent a bicycle or a canoe. One of the natural programs has been an effort to reintroduce endangered wildlife species. LBL is home to the nation's largest public herd of bison, and in 1996, elk were released into the area. You may be able to see these animals along a self-guided driving tour of the *Elk & Bison Prairie.* At the Golden Pond Visitors Center, there's a small planetarium. And if you drive to the southern end of LBL (actually in Tennessee), you can walk around *The Homeplace 1850,* set up as a working 19th-century homestead. Enter the park from any direction—US 68 and US 641, Highway 94, or I-24, or in Tennessee, US 79 or TN 76—and go to the North, South, or Golden Pond Visitors Centers for directions and information about the park. For information about any of the attractions in Land Between the Lakes, call (800) LBL-7077 or (270) 924-2000 or go online at landbetweenthelakes.us.

true**blue**

The Land Between the Lakes area was once known as the Moonshine Capital of the World.

If you're hungry and caught smack-dab between a lake and a wet place, pull into **Patti's 1880s Settlement,** home of the Mile-High Meringue Pie, the 2-inch-thick pork chop, and bread baked in a flowerpot. With five gift shops, two restaurants, a miniature-golf course, and an animal park, Patti's seems like a continuation of the dream that a young multimillionaire, Thomas Lawson, had for the town in the 1880s when he found it nestled between the Cumberland and Tennessee Rivers. Lawson changed the town's name from Nichols Landing to Grand Rivers and built himself a resort town with the theme of Southern hospitality. Now that the rivers have been dammed, it should be renamed Grand Lakes, but . . . Patti's Restaurant, owned by the Tullar family, and a perennial favorite with both seasonal

Living Near the Pokey?

If you stand on the lakeside near Kuttawa and look across the water, you will see a massive monolithic stone fortress perched on a peninsula that is reminiscent of Alcatraz. This is the Kentucky State Penitentiary at Eddyville, Kentucky's only maximum-security prison. Growing up, whenever kids were reprimanded, someone would say, "Keep that up, and we'll be coming to visit you in Eddyville." A woman who actually grew up in Eddyville in a house just up the hill from the pen told of being in the kitchen and hearing prisoners bang chains against their bars as a form of protest and seeing the men hang white sheets out prison windows with written pleas to the outside world stating their dire need for a new warden. It spooked her to think that the prisoners could see their free neighbors and were bold enough to attempt communication. She also remembered the more trusted old lifers being allowed to sell trinkets by the front gate on Sunday afternoon. One old man gave her a shellacked peach-pit necklace because she reminded him of his own little ones far away.

and 12-month diners, is open year-round from 10:30 a.m. to at least 9 p.m. every day. Other activities vary some. Call (270) 362-8844 or (888) 736-2515 or visit pattis-settlement.com for specifics. Dinner reservations are strongly recommended. Located at 1793 JH O'Bryan Avenue in Grand Rivers, Patti's is usually packed.

At the Grand Rivers exit, number 31 off I-24, Kentucky's Western Waterland regional tourism information center (270-928-4411, 800-448-1069; ken tuckylakebarkley.org) is an important spot to stop and gather information. While you're there, look carefully at the pasture across the highway—there's a small herd of buffalo just like those that roamed these plains in the hundreds of thousands before European settlement.

An interesting loop drive in this area is along a bit of Lake Barkley's shore. Go to *Kuttawa,* a town with a name that means "beautiful" in Shawnee: From I-24 take exit 40, turn south on US 62, then turn south on Highway 295. You'll curve along the rim of the lake (gorgeous at sunset) toward Kuttawa. Just as you get to town, look for a public parking area on the lakeside and, if it's summer, stop for a little walk along the "Kuttawa cliffs," where you may be lucky enough to watch daring locals do some cliff diving into the deep water. In downtown metropolis Kuttawa there's a beach, marina, and harbor with a restaurant famous for its generous "Rudyburger." To complete the loop, stay on Highway 295 until it intersects with US 62, at which point you can go whichever direction your trip is taking you. Both the Western Kentucky Parkway and I-24 are nearby. For more information, try the Lake Barkley Tourist Commission at (270) 388-5300 or lakebarkleychamber.com. One bed (no breakfast) that is worth a visit ranks among Kentucky's most unusual grave markers. Stay on Main Street (also Highway 295), going north until the road splits into separate high and low lanes, and look to the left for the entrance to the city cemetery. When the cemetery driveway forces you to go either right or left, go right. In about 100 feet you will reach a grave that is on the left under a large oak tree and next to a tall obelisk. The marker is a life-size double-bed frame made of stone, beneath which are buried Eliza Jane and Charles Anderson. Married for 60 years, they moved to this marriage bed in 1901 and 1895, respectively. It's a beautiful marker and eerie, too. You'll see.

Due north of Eddyville, if you were to drive aboveground on US 641, you'd pass through Fredonia and Crayne before entering the busy little town of *Marion.* If you were to drive several hundred feet underground, you might just pass through sparkling veins of the amazingly beautiful mineral, fluorspar. Unlike diamond, fluorspar is beautiful in its natural state, just as you'd find in the walls of the underground highway on which you're traveling. Fluorspar, the industrial name for fluorite, the nonmetallic mineral calcium fluoride, is the primary source for tooth-decay retardant, as well as an important material used in the production of aluminum, zinc, some ceramics, and a whole range of chemicals. During and after World War II, Kentucky was the largest producer of the mineral in the United States.

For an actual tour (not virtual or imaginary) of some of the most interesting and varied samples of these crystals to be found anywhere, head down Main Street in Marion, then right on First Street, and watch for the signs to the *Ben E. Clement Mineral Museum,* 205 North Walker Street, in a former elementary school building. Hours from October through May are 10 a.m. to 3 p.m., Wednesday through Saturday, and June through September from 10 a.m. to 3 p.m. Monday through Saturday. Admission is $3 to $5. Someone knowledgeable will be on hand to guide you through this stunning array of fluorite crystals as well as other minerals and geological and archaeological specimens (petrified dinosaur dung, eggs, Mastodon teeth, and so forth) collected by Ben Clement over his 60-year career in the mining business. Most unforgettable is the room full of optical fluorite mounted in vitrines that light the crystals from beneath. For more information call (270) 965-4263 or visit clementmineralmuseum.org.

Another little museum in town deals strictly with objects made and used by the human hand. The *Crittenden County Historical Museum* at 124 East Bellville Street, just downhill from the Crittenden County Public Library, is open from April through October, Tuesday through Saturday from 10 a.m. to 3:30 p.m. or by appointment. Admission is free. Next to the white concrete-block building that houses an enormous range of regional artifacts is a reconstructed log cabin with period implements. It's delightfully out of sync with the rest of the neighborhood. Call (270) 965-9257 for more information (crittendenhistorymuseum.org).

The region north of Marion and south of the Ohio River has been settled in recent years by Amish families whose farms and houses might not strike you as much different than the surrounding non-Amish farms, but for a few subtle signals—and not just black buggies, either. See what you notice.

For an interesting driving loop, take US 60 north, then turn left (northwest) onto Highway 654 at the community of Mattoon. On the left is a very large, active Amish farm where there is a harness shop that's open to the public. Look across the road for a sign that says "Most Family Baked Goods" and definitely stop if it is open. Continuing north (watch for a flock of emus at a farm on the right with a sign in the yard for "Ray's Small Engines"), make another stop 1 mile beyond the Mount Zion Church Road at The Dutch Way Store, a tiny, family-run general store that's primarily stocked with goods for Amish use: inexpensive footwear; spices; all sorts of dry, bulk foods; and plenty of sewing supplies. It's open from 8 a.m. to 5 p.m. every day but Sunday. One overall-clad, non-Amish man shopping there bought two pounds of powdered sage leaves. He was slaughtering hogs and thinking about sausage spices. Seasonally, you can dig your own mums at the farm next to the store. Other signs along the way might alert you to the availability of lye soap or sorghum, fresh eggs or apple butter.

To continue the loop, go back and take the Mount Zion Church Road west and turn left (south) onto a tiny gravel road called Turkey Knob. When you meet Fords Ferry Road, either turn left (south) to get back to Marion or turn right, then right again onto Highway 91 and head toward Illinois.

To cross the wide and mighty Ohio River, you'll have to ride the *Cave-in-Rock Ferry,* unless the water's high, in which case you're up a creek. There's no place to cross closer than Paducah. The ferry runs daily from 7 a.m. to 10 p.m. The ride is free.

trueblue

The Albany, New York, setting of the movie *How the West Was Won* was filmed in Smithland, Kentucky, in 1961 by Metro-Goldwyn-Mayer.

There was no way to cross the mighty waters in the bitter winter of 1838 when thousands of Cherokee traveled on foot during the forced march from their homelands in southern Appalachia to what would eventually become reservation lands in Oklahoma. This devastating march, known as the Trail of Tears, included a winter spent at a site called *Mantle Rock.* Now owned by The Nature Conservancy and preserved for its rare biological community as well as for its historic importance, this gorgeous site is open to visitors year-round. From Marion take US 60 southwest to Salem, then turn north on Highway 133. Continue through the community called Joy;

when you have passed the junction with Highway 1436, go exactly 1.1 miles and look on the left for a bronze historical marker with the number 1675 painted on the post. It's very easy to overlook. If you pass the Cave Spring Church, you passed Mantle Rock. Park your car and take the short (¾-mile) hike in to the most dramatic natural feature of the preserve, a 30-foot-high sandstone arch with a 188-foot span and some fabulous honeycombed weathering patterns. It was here that the Cherokee waited for the ice in the river to melt. Over 4,000 died of cold and starvation, since they were not prepared for winter. In the spring they finally crossed into what is now Galcouda, Illinois.

Preceding this bleak event by almost 10,000 years, Archaic peoples camped on this site. Between AD 600 and 800, Lewis peoples, who were hunter-gatherers, had a village here. Archaeologists have discovered more than 100 stone burial mounds. Today the site is home to some rare and fragile plants, like June grass. The site is lush and quiet and so isolated that you might be able to let your mind travel to other times. If you want more information about the site or would like to arrange guided tours of the fragile glades (normally off-limits to hikers), contact The Nature Conservancy, 642 West Main Street #1, Lexington 40508, or call (859) 259 9655; nature.org. You are also welcome to visit the new ***Mantle Rock Native Education and Cultural Center*** at 110 South Main Street in Marion (270-965-5882; mantlerock.org).

The first major town east of the lakes on Highway 68 is ***Cadiz*** (pronounced KAY-dizz), named, perhaps, after the hometown of an early Spanish surveyor. Since the creation of Land Between the Lakes, people say that the name means "gateway" in Spanish, since Cadiz is at the southeastern entrance to the area. Saxophone lovers pay homage here to the inimitable Boots Randolph, who was born in Trigg County. (The question is, should a golf course be named after a musician? Poor guy.) Ham lovers must have a meal in town; prize-winning hams are served everywhere. During the second weekend in October, follow your nose to the ***Trigg County Country Ham Festival,*** which features the *Guinness* record holder for the world's biggest ham and biscuit. Non-Southerners may learn that not all country ham can be safely compared to the salt-drenched tongue of your big brother's hiking boot. Call (270) 522-8756 or visit hamfestival.com for festival information.

In downtown Cadiz, visit the *Janice Mason Art Museum,* 71 Main Street. A former post office building has found new life as an arts center, thanks to the efforts of a dedicated group of community volunteers. There are changing regional exhibits in various mediums, as well as a small gift shop. Hours are 10 a.m. to 4 p.m. Tuesday through Saturday and 1 to 4 p.m. Sunday. Call (270) 522-9056 to find out what's on display (jmam.org).

For more information about local attractions, including walking tours of historic homes and the Little River area, stop by the log cabin tourist center on Main Street downtown, call (270) 522-3892, or go to gocadiz.com.

trueblue

Musician Boots Randolph was born in Trigg County, Kentucky.

There is something eerie and irresistible about stepping into a person's space and looking at the way that individual's daily life is shaped and revealed by his or her personal belongings. The *Adsmore Museum* in *Princeton* draws visitors into the lives of its early-20th-century residents in that almost taboo way by presenting the house intact, changing detailed decorations and personal accessories eight times a year, and building the tour around stories of the family. The interpretive staff reenacts weddings, birthday parties, and wakes (complete with wailing mourners dressed in period clothes). Details make this place a treat. That the Victorians in Europe were not morally able to utter the phrase "chicken thigh," for example, comes as no surprise when you find that the piano's legs, like a lady's, were always chastely covered with a shawl.

Built in grand late-Victorian style in 1857, Adsmore was fully restored in 1986 by the local library board to which Katharine Garrett, the last family resident, donated the building and its contents. Adsmore could have also been called "Collectsmore," for it is furnished lavishly with items from all over the world. Also on the grounds is the Ratliff Gun Shop, a restored 1844 cabin filled with antique tools. The museum and grounds are open Tuesday through Saturday from 11 a.m. to 4 p.m. Admission ranges from $2 to $7, according to age category. Group rates are available. Call (270) 365-3114 or visit adsmore.org. Adsmore, at 304 North Jefferson Street in downtown Princeton, has been called the Natchez of West Kentucky because of its grand homes. From Cadiz the quickest route is Highway 139 north. From the Land Between the Lakes, take US 62, or take exit 12 from the Western Kentucky Parkway.

Princeton's oldest building, the circa 1817 Federal-style Champion-Shepherdson House at 115 East Main Street, has been renovated and is now home to the ***Princeton Art Guild.*** Like so many early settlements, Princeton began with a general store located near a big, dependable spring. A lean-to money counting room, also used by fur traders, is now an artist-in-residence studio. The main building houses a gallery, a gift shop, and space for special events and workshops. Hours are 11 a.m. to 2 p.m. Tuesday through Saturday. For more information, write the guild at 115 East Main Street, Princeton 42445, call (270) 365-3959, or visit princetonartguild.org.

In the not-so-distant past, the change of seasons was reflected in retail stores, and not just by "fall fashions" or seasonal decorations. Nowadays we often are offered the same things year-round. Not so with ***Newsom's Old Mill Store*** at 208 East Main Street. Garden plants are available in the spring and fresh produce is available as it comes in during the growing season. Gifts and specialty foods are offered year-round, with a special emphasis on

Fire?

Early one morning, during recent travels through western Kentucky, I was driving down an old highway in that trancelike state of the traveler. Moisture was rising like liquid smoke from low places, and silver frost traced grassy meadows where shadows lingered. Everything was beautiful and slightly surreal. My eyes snapped wide open at the sight of a tall, skinny barn from which real smoke was pouring out of every crack as if it was about to lift off its rubble stone launch pad foundation and head to Mars. It was sided with a hodgepodge of corrugated roof tin, galvanized here, rusted or painted there, and long boards were leaning at steep angles against any panel that opened or was loose enough to flap in the wind. Nearly driving off the road, I looked hard. The structure was not burning, but it sure as heck was smoking. Throughout the day I saw dozens more tall skinny barns made of just about anything, uniformly and calmly smoking away. These, I realized, were curing barns for dark-fired tobacco, unfamiliar to a bluegrass resident for whom Burley tobacco, which is air-cured in sievelike open-slatted black barns, is standard. Dark-fired tobacco is hung in these tall barns and carefully dried by use of slow-burning, smoldering fires usually built in pits in the floor. This year, late October was curing time. And for the traveling outsider, time not to call 911 at every puff of smoke.

country ham. The Newsoms sell their own aged hams, bacon, sausage, and, the favorite, hickory-smoked barbecue ham. The barbecued ham sandwich is a local favorite. Store hours are 9 a.m. to 4:30 p.m. Monday through Saturday. Call (270) 365-2482 or visit newsomscountryham.com for mail-order information.

For a historic picnic spot, stop just 1 block south of the Princeton courthouse at *Big Spring Park,* the original settlement's water source and a site where the Cherokees camped on the Trail of Tears. Also noteworthy is the Black Patch Tobacco Festival, which Princeton hosts in early September to commemorate the times when dark-leaf tobacco was harvested in the area in massive quantities. Accompanying this event is a dark and touchy history involving tobacco price wars and the night riders, a movement of farmers (made nationally famous by writers such as Robert Penn Warren) who turned to a sophisticated form of organized violence to ensure the viability of their way of life. Local historians explain the events during the Black Patch tour.

Take Highway 91 south from Princeton to downtown *Hopkinsville.* In the grand old Federal-style post office building at the corner of East Ninth (US 68) and Liberty Streets is the *Pennyroyal Area Museum* (270-887-4270; museumsofhopkinsville.org), an impressive regional-history museum.

The main display area is in the huge mail-sorting room. Notice the enclosed catwalks overhead, secret vantage points from which postmasters watched postal workers handle the mail, not to enforce efficiency (it is after all, a federal institution), but to prevent workers from stealing cash from the envelopes in a pre-checking account era.

The museum's displays address many facets of the Pennyroyal region's history, from agriculture and the Black Patch wars to reconstructed pioneer bedrooms and an 1898 law office. In the middle of the room sits a beautifully preserved original Mogul wagon, made just 2 blocks away in a large factory that manufactured every imaginable type of wagon. Mogul Wagon Company's ads in the 1920s read "Easy to Pull, Hard to Break" and "Buy a Mogul and Will it to your Grandson." Railroad and early automobile artifacts compete for your attention with a miniature circus made by John Venable, which is said to have inspired Robert Penn Warren's *The Circus in the Attic,* the title piece of an early collection of short stories. Museum hours are

9 a.m. to 5 p.m. Monday through Friday and 10 a.m. to 3 p.m. Saturday. Admission is $1 for children under 12 and $2 for adults.

The Edgar Cayce exhibit is one of the most popular in the museum. The display case contains a few photographs and significant personal objects, like Cayce's dog-eared desk Bible. Cayce, who was born in 1877 in southern Christian County near Beverly, was a "strange" child who preferred meditating on the Bible to playing baseball. In 1900, after a severe illness, Cayce mysteriously lost his voice. When put under hypnosis by "Hart—The Laugh Man" in 1901, Cayce diagnosed the problem and restored his own voice by using a treatment he discovered during hypnosis. That was the beginning of his career as an internationally known clairvoyant, "the sleeping prophet." He gave 14,256 psychic readings in which he diagnosed medical problems and predicted world affairs, including natural disasters and economic changes. Today the Association for Research and Enlightenment, based at Virginia Beach, Virginia, where Cayce spent the last 20 years of his life, continues "The Work," as Cayce called it, by providing a library and educational programs related to his readings.

Many of Hopkinsville's visitors from the west, passing through town en route to Virginia Beach, stop to see the place where Edgar Cayce and his wife, Gertrude Evans, are buried in the Riverside Cemetery on the north side of town, just east of North Virginia Street. Seven miles south of town on the Lafayette Road (Highway 107) in Beverly are Cayce's church, the Liberty Christian Church, which is open to the public at no charge, and his school, the Beverly Academy, which is now on private property. If you're a Cayce fan, ask at the museum about other significant sites.

Hopkinsville has done more than any other town in the state to pay tribute to the Native American people who were forced to move from their southeastern homelands across the Mississippi River to Oklahoma on the infamous Trail of Tears during the winter of 1838–39. More than 13,000 Cherokees camped in Hopkinsville and received provisions for their forced migration, during which thousands of people died.

The Trail of Tears Commission Inc. has developed the ***Trail of Tears Commemorative Park*** at Ninth Street and Skyline Drive on the west edge of town. The park includes impressive, larger-than-life statues of Cherokee chiefs White Path and Fly Smith, who are buried on the property. Near the banks of the Little River is a log cabin that serves as an education center.

Although the Cherokee people fought alongside the colonists during the American Revolution and later with Andrew Jackson in the War of 1812, Jackson, as president in the late 1820s, insisted that Native Americans of numerous tribes yield and leave their homelands east of the Mississippi. The forced removal spanned a decade, causing tremendous loss of lives in the process and leaving the survivors a legacy of hardship on barren reservations in the West. It should also be noted that gold was discovered on Cherokee land in Georgia in 1828, 10 years prior to the Native Americans' forced migration. The park includes a heritage center. Hours are Monday through Saturday from 10 a.m. to 4 p.m. April through October, and Tuesday through Saturday from 10 a.m. to 2 p.m. November through March (trailoftears.org).

The *Trail of Tears Intertribal Indian Pow Wow* has become an annual event, held the first full weekend in September. Although the recent history of the Native American people is tragic, this public festival is meant to commemorate the beauty and integrity of their culture. The pow wow features Native American crafts, food, storytelling, blow-gun demonstrations, and a very competitive Indian dance contest. Contact the Trail of Tears Commission Inc., 100 Trail of Tears Drive, Hopkinsville 42240, or call (270) 886-0701, or check trailoftears.org.

Ferrell's Hamburgers, 1001 South Main Street (270-886-1445), is a local landmark and a great place to get a classic grilled burger and fries. David S. Ferrell and his wife, Cecil Doris, opened the restaurant in 1936. Originally it offered curb service. Although Ferrell died in 2001 at age 87, his famous burger with pickles and onions continues to be one of Western Kentucky's most delicious traditions. Ferrell's is open 24 hours Monday through Saturday, but closed Sunday.

South of Hopkinsville, on the Tennessee border, is a small portion of the large Fort Campbell Military Reservation. Generally it's a private, no-trespassing kind of place, but the public is welcome to visit the *Don F. Pratt Memorial Museum,* a showcase of sorts for the history of the 101st Airborne "Screaming Eagles" Division (Air Assault), which is based here. Indoors one can see exhibits from the Civil War through Desert Storm, a restored World War II Cargo Glider, and other war-related artifacts. Outdoors are a number of army aircraft, including helicopters. Admission is free, and the hours are 9:30 a.m. to 4:30 p.m. Monday through Saturday, except Christmas and New Year's Days. To get there from US 41A, go through the fort's main gate and

Amish Ingenuity

Just to illustrate how the Amish in the area (there are many kinds of Amish communities) adjust their lives to both the community rules and the modern world, let me tell you how Betty Miller gets to work at Schlabach's Bakery every morning. Her community uses tractors and horse-and-buggy rigs, but not cars or bicycles. If she were male, she might hop on her Massey Ferguson and drive; if she were a child, she might sprint. Instead, she gets on her small tractor (a ride-on lawn mower) and commutes through yards and along the shoulder of the highway. Some churches won't allow use of any vehicle with rubber tires, so the members own steel-wheeled tractors. Other churches allow cars and trucks but insist they be painted black, even the chrome parts. Others allow congregation members to have cars and attend graduate school. And, at the other extreme, very orthodox communities use only horses and oxen.

stop at the visitor center, where you have to get a pass. Then continue on the same road, turn right on Tennessee Avenue, and left into the museum at 5702 Tennessee Avenue. For more information call the museum at (270) 798-4986 or visit campbell.army.mil/campbell/PrattMuseum/Pages?PrattMuseum.aspx.

As soon as you drive east from Hopkinsville, you are in an area heavily populated by Amish and Mennonite people. Nationally there are about 85,000 Amish, many of whom live in Pennsylvania, Ohio, and Indiana in communities that are being encroached upon by rapidly widening urban edges. Rural Kentucky has become a popular place for Amish families to relocate because the land is beautiful, isolated, and relatively inexpensive. When you visit Amish and Mennonite businesses, keep in mind that they are committed to their way of life in part because they want isolation from the rest of the world. Respect their privacy. Observe their work practices, for they are good stewards of their land and of all their resources. We could stand a little education.

About 6 miles east of town on US 68, at a big farmhouse with rock pillars by the driveway, Henry Hoover runs an unadvertised bulk food and farm supply business primarily meant to serve an orthodox community known as Horse and Buggy Mennonites, folks who have no cars or telephones. He will sell to the public, so stop in if you need flour, cereals, bread, cheese, and so forth. It's a great way to avoid excessive packaging and higher prices due to expensive advertising. Hours are by chance.

Pete's Custom Saddle Shop is an orderly, productive (secular) one-man leather operation at 9728 Jefferson Davis Highway (Old Highway 68) about 8 miles east of Hopkinsville. In addition to making and refurbishing more than a hundred saddles a year, Russell (Pete) Harry makes holsters, halters, and bridles, not to mention guns, tomahawks, and an occasional painting. Although he's geared primarily to custom work, there are always a few items for sale in the shop that will knock your socks off. Pete's original saddle designs range from a sleek bird hunting saddle to variations on Civil War styles to a western pleasure show saddle with special braces for a local woman who is paralyzed below the shoulders. One claim to fame is that he has built maybe 80 percent of the sidesaddles used in the United States, most of which are distributed by a company called Hundred Oaks. Even if you are not in need of tack, his stunning work and positive spirit are unique and inspirational. Because his hours are not regular, call him at (270) 886-5448 before visiting. petescustomsaddles.com.

About a mile and a half past Pete's is ***Fairview,*** a tiny rural town you can't miss, thanks to the ***Jefferson Davis Monument State Historic Site*** looming overhead at a height of 351 feet. From miles away in any direction, the incongruous tower, said to be the tallest unreinforced concrete-cast obelisk in the world, is visible poking into the sky. During summer months you can ride an elevator to the top for an impressive view of surrounding countryside. The obelisk has recently been renovated. You can also tour the visitor center, which includes a variety of exhibits on Civil War Kentucky. Davis, the first and only president of the Confederate States of America, was born in March 1808 in a house called Wayfarer's Rest in Fairview. The house was located on the site of what is now the Bethel Baptist Church. The Jefferson Davis Monument is located at 258 Pembroke-Fairview Road. Call (270) 886-6100 for hours and information or visit parks.ky.gov/parks/historic sites/Jefferson-Davis/default.aspx.

trueblue

The Jefferson Davis monument in Fairview is the fourth largest concrete obelisk in the world (351 feet).

Adjacent to the monument is the ***Zimmerman Farms produce stand.*** From late May to mid-October, you can buy delicious, organically grown fruits and vegetables. You can trust the Amish when it comes to wholesome, flavorful produce.

At *Elkton,* 8 miles east of Fairview, take Highway 181 south for about 10 miles and look to the right at 6225 Guthrie Road for *Schlabach's Bakery* (270-265-3459), an Amish bakery specializing in satisfaction. Its sourdough bread, sweet rolls, pies, cakes, cookies, and yes, even granola are delicious and always fresh. Hours are 8 a.m. to 5 p.m. every day but Thursday and Sunday. Although the owner is Abe Schlabach, you'll be more likely to meet one of his bakers, who live nearby.

Another mile or so south, at the intersection of Highways 181 and 848, is the *Penchem Tack Store* (270-483-2314), a large Amish tack and farm supply store also patronized by the general public. John H. Yoders and his sons work in the leather shop in the basement while another family member tends to retail sales upstairs. It's a great place to browse, especially if you're in the market for good functional suspenders, straw work hats, Redwing shoes, veterinary supplies, tack (commercially and locally made), or just a soft drink and candy bar. Hours are 8 a.m. to 5 p.m. Monday through Saturday.

If you are in the area in early summer and get that unbearable craving for strawberries (it's best to gorge), check out one of the local *strawberry kings* (there are several!) to see if they are open for picking. They'll direct you to the field on which you may sweetly graze.

Due south on either US 79 or 41, nestled right next to the Tennessee border, is the town of *Guthrie,* birthplace of Robert Penn Warren, poet laureate of the United States and Pulitzer Prize winner for both poetry and fiction. For those who have read his work, it is enriching to walk the streets and drive by the endless fields, an environment that obviously influenced his writing. Once in town, if you want details or if you'd like to tour the *Robert Penn Warren Museum,* the house in which Penn Warren was born, contact Mrs. Dean Moore at (270) 483-2683. Tours are given 11:30 a.m. to 3:30 p.m. Tuesday through Saturday and 2 to 4 p.m. Sunday. The house is at the corner of Third and Cherry Streets. For a biography or to read some of Penn Warren's work, check robertpennwarren.com. You can even hear him read from his work in his amazing voice.

In Russellville an impressive four-story brick building houses the *1817 Saddle Factory and Museum* (South Breathitt Street at East Fourth Street; 270-726-4181). The structure is considered one of the earliest industrial

Stick 'Em Up

The **Southern Deposit Bank** in downtown Russellville, on the corner of Main and Sixth Streets, was the scene of a great crime, the Jesse James gang's first out-of-state robbery. Prior to that day the gang was just a handful of local hoodlums. On May 20, 1868, the gang held up the bank for $9,000, shot and wounded bank president N. Long, and galloped away to join the ranks of America's famous federal fugitives. (What old Jesse didn't know was that there was an additional $50,000 in the vault.) Today the building has been restored into a classy apartment building.

buildings constructed in Kentucky. Historic records show that by 1820 there were 44 people living and working at the factory, most of whom were slaves and indentured servants. The museum exhibits objects that they manufactured—saddles, bridles, saddlebags, girths, suitcases, shoes, and so forth. You can see the workers' living quarters in the attic; there's graffiti on the plaster walls that somehow makes one's skin crawl. One object with West Kentucky mythic status is the weathervane in the shape of a fish, which was supposedly shot in 1868 by a member of Jesse James's gang. Tours begin at the Historic Russellville Visitor Center (280 East Fourth Street). For more information, call the center at (270) 726-4181 or check out visitlogancounty.net.

Three miles east of Auburn on US 68 at 850 Shaker Museum Road is *South Union Shaker Village,* now a wonderfully curated museum marking the site of a once-thriving village comprising more than 6,000 acres and 200 buildings. Members of the United Society of Believers in Christ's Second Appearing, more commonly known as Shakers, lived at the South Union community from 1807 until 1922. They supported themselves with sophisticated enterprises in garden seed, fruit preserves, fine colorful silk handkerchiefs, and farming. They also ran a large, steam-powered mill, hired out some of Kentucky's first purebred bulls for stud all over the state, and built and leased out (to "the World") a train depot, post office/general store, and tavern.

The 40-room building that now serves as the main museum was the Center House, a dwelling complete with kitchen, communal dining room, and bedrooms—men on one side, women on the other. The structure fulfills your basic expectations of a Shaker building, but in a slightly showier way—some of the trim boards are beaded, there is a nook for a clock, the first-floor window casings flare, and arches abound. From the woodstoves to the cooking utensils to the hat molds, South Union is filled with original Shaker objects, not reproductions. Even the brick dust and mustard-ochre stains on the woodwork are original (let's hear it for organic paint!). This Shaker museum also boasts the largest collection of western Shaker furniture in the United States.

The museum and gift shop are open from March 1 through November 30, Thursday through Saturday from 10 a.m. to 5 p.m. and Sunday from 1 to 5 p.m. Hours from December 1 through February are 10 a.m. to 4 p.m. Tuesday through Saturday. Admission is $8 for adults and $4 for children ages 6 to 12. Children age 5 and under are admitted free. Call (800) 811-8379 or (270) 542-4167, or write South Union Shaker Village, P.O. Box 30, South Union 42283, for information and a schedule of events. This and other info is also available at their website, shakermuseum.com. One mile east of the museum is Highway 73. Turn right (south) and go ½ mile to the **South Union Post Office** (270-542-6757), established April 1, 1826. This was the last building constructed in the Shaker community.

Directly across the road from the post office is the **Shaker Tavern Bed and Breakfast,** an ornate Victorian tavern the Shakers had built to house the overflow of railroad travelers stopping at the village for lodging. The tavern was always run by non-Shakers and still is. The tavern is a combined restaurant and bed-and-breakfast and gives this place the sparkle it deserves. Six classy bed-and-breakfast rooms are available for between $70 and $80 per night, and the chefs guarantee a full Southern breakfast in the morning. Guests also get a tour of the museum at South Union Shaker Village. Call (270) 542-6801 or (800) 929-8701 or visit shakermuseum.com/tavern for reservations or more information.

Yellow Banks, Green River

Daddy, won't you take me back to Muhlenberg County,
Down by the Green River where Paradise lay.
I'm sorry, my son, but you're too late in askin',
Mr. Peabody's coal train has hauled it away.

John Prine's famous lyrics give us a glimpse of Muhlenberg County's history, while traveling through the area gives us an update. *Paradise* is an enormous steam-generating power plant, the largest of its kind when it was built in the late 1950s. The county has not been hauled away completely, but you may think they're trying to do so when you see some of the monstrous earthmoving machines in the surface mines visible from several major roads. (The term strip mine is taboo.) Just driving through will convince you that this was the largest coal-producing county in the United States for 23 consecutive years until Environmental Protection Agency (EPA) regulations reduced the market for the area's high-sulfur coal. Seeing Paradise for yourself is worth the effort. From Central City (at US 431 and US 62), take Highway 70 south to Highway 176 and go east until you get there. Don't worry, you'll know it because the landscape changes dramatically as you approach the Green

true*blue*

The first commercial mine for bituminous coal in the entire state was opened near Paradise, in Muhlenberg County, in 1820. From 1973 to 1987 Kentucky led the nation in coal production.

River. First, there are the long train tracks with car after car of coal. There are the strange swampy lowlands, some of which are reclaimed mining areas. If you follow some of the side roads, you'll see eerie little pockets of undisturbed areas, mostly cemeteries, where no mining was allowed. Eventually you arrive at the power plant, announced by massive, curving cooling towers and a horizontal sulfurous yellow cloud, on still days. Aside from coal, great country music is this area's claim to fame. In front of the City Building in *Central City* is a monument to the town's native sons, Phil and Don Everly. To hear some of the Everly Brothers' great songs as well as other local entertainers, visit the *Muhlenberg County Music Museum* at 208 North First Street. Open Monday through Friday from 8 a.m. to 4 p.m. (closed for lunch from noon to 1 p.m.), the museum showcases artifacts and memorabilia from the Everly Brothers, Merle Travis, James Best, Spider and Dave Rich, Warren Oats, and Mose Rager. Take a trip back in time by choosing a song on a renovated 1953 jukebox. For more information call (270) 754-9603 or visit tourcentralcity.com. One of the most popular events is the International Thumb Picking Contest in honor of Merle Travis. Travis, who

One Interesting Town Mascot

What do bluegrass music, Scottish taxidermy, and barbecued mutton have in common? The Owensboro area. If you are approaching the area by the Bluegrass Parkway and still need convincing that Kentucky is far from mundane, head north on the Green River Parkway and take exit 69 to the tiny town of *Dundee.* When you get into town, keep your eyes to the sky. Standing stiffly above the Masonic lodge is a stuffed goat, imported almost 100 years ago from Dundee, Scotland. The town, which was once called Hines Mill, changed its name to commemorate this oddity.

was born in Muhlenburg County in 1917, was the son of a tobacco farmer and miner. According to music legend, he became friends with two coal miners, Mose Rager and Ike Everly (the Everly Brothers' father), who taught him how to use his thumb to play the bass strings while playing melody on the treble strings. Travis took the style and made it his own, becoming one of the first country players to demonstrate that a guitar could be a lead instrument. Pickers in the area continue to carry on his "Western Kentucky thumb picking" style. For festival information call (270) 754-9603 or log on to tourcentralcity.com or thumbpickers.org.

Greenville, just south of the Western Kentucky Parkway on US 62 or Highway 189, is home to several unique attractions. One is the *House of Onyx,* a mega mart of gemstones that promotes investment in precious rocks and discourages trust in the banking system. Beyond inventory and prices, its literature consists of an odd combination of claims that the House of Onyx is a real, honest business and fortune cookie–type moralistic quotes. One's curiosity is piqued. The business is primarily geared toward the wholesale and mail-order markets, but if you are in town on a weekday between 9 a.m. and 4:30 p.m., call ahead for a tour of the retail showroom. The mind boggles at the sight of rows of cases of rubies, sapphires, pearls, and myriad other stones. Though there is no sign, the office is in the Aaron Building at 120 North Main Street. Ring the doorbell and explain your interest, or call ahead for an appointment at (270) 338-2363; houseofonyx.com.

Fishing is fantastic in the *Lake Malone State Park.* The 788-acre lake is surrounded by a 388-acre park laced with middle-aged pine forests and sandstone bluffs and caves where the Jesse James gang supposedly hid out.

(Jesse James is to Western Kentucky what Daniel Boone is to the central and eastern parts—both hid everywhere, carved their initials on every historic tree and building, and are still receiving royalties for their freely interpreted deeds.)

This popular fishing lake is stocked with largemouth bass, crappie, bluegill, and channel catfish. Amenities include boat dock rental, camping, a swimming beach, picnicking, and playgrounds. Lake Malone is 22 miles south of Central City. From the Western Kentucky Parkway exit at Central City and take US 431 to Kentucky 973 to the park. From Greenville take Highway 181 south to Highway 973 and go 5 miles to the park. The park is open from early April until the end of October. For more information, call (270) 657-2111 or visit parks.ky.gov/parks/recreationparks/Lake-Malone/default.aspx.

Barbecue Doesn't Get Much Better

In mid-May Owensboro comes alive for the *International Bar-B-Q Festival,* during which time the local folks compete fiercely for culinary titles. A friend's father, "Pop Beers," concocted a darn good recipe for barbecued chicken that has won three festival championships. Because this generous soul has given me permission to pass on to you his secret recipe, I hereby command you to sensitize your palate before participating in the festival. I quote:

Bring the following ingredients to a rapid boil on medium high heat:

1 stick butter	1 teaspoon black pepper
Juice of 1 big lemon	1 teaspoon paprika
1 tablespoon Worcestershire sauce	1 teaspoon garlic powder
1 tablespoon soy sauce	1 teaspoon Accent meat tenderizer
5 shakes Tabasco sauce	1 teaspoon poultry seasoning

Cook until a brown scum forms and then goes away. Let cool and use. Won't spoil if kept. Makes enough for three 3-pound chickens. To use, cut fat (not skin) off chicken. Grill chicken on one side for 30 minutes, turn and repeat, then turn again, baste, and grill for 15 minutes; turn again and repeat. Eat!

On to the self-proclaimed *Bar-B-Q Capital of the World* and the third largest city in the state, *Owensboro.* In this town, where there's smoke, there's barbecue. Initiate yourself by eating at one of the many "smoking" restaurants where you can sample one version of honest-to-goodness Kentucky burgoo (a super-hearty meat-and-veggie stew that originated in Wales and came here via Virginia with the pioneers), to the famous *Moonlite Bar-B-Q Inn* (207-684-8143), a huge restaurant west of town on Parrish Street where the barbecue is all hickory-pit cooked. Moonlite is open 9 a.m. to 9 p.m. Monday through Thursday and 9 a.m. to 9:30 p.m. Friday and Saturday, and 9 a.m. to 3 p.m. Sunday. For more information about Moonlite, visit moonlite.com.

My favorite landmark in Owensboro is a *sassafras tree* in the front yard of E. M. Ford & Company on the corner of Frederica and Maple Streets. At a height of 100 feet and a circumference of 16 feet, this 250- to 300-year-old droopy-armed beauty is registered by the American Forestry Association as the largest of its kind in the country and probably in the world. A Mrs. Rash saved the tree from the merciless highway department by planting herself at the base of the trunk with a shotgun in hand. She then pulled political strings, and the governor immediately installed a retaining wall and lightning rod. (I'll bet Earth First! would recruit Mrs. Rash.)

The *Owensboro Area Museum of Science and History* (122 East Second Street; 270-687-2732; owensboromuseum.org) is a natural science and history extravaganza containing everything from live reptiles to a 100-plus-seat planetarium, a tobacco-store figure of Punch, dinosaur replicas, and artifacts illustrating events in Kentucky history. Kids and uninhibited adults love the hands-on science exhibits called *Encounter* and *The Owensboro Rotary Playzeum.* Though it is said that the museum started in a church building in 1966, the truth is that it began somewhat earlier in local storyteller and natural historian Joe Ford's backyard playhouse, where he stockpiled insects, rocks, and snakeskins, some of which are still in the museum collection. Open Tuesday through Saturday 10 a.m. to 5 p.m., Sunday 1 p.m. to 5 p.m. Admission is $3 per person.

Western Kentucky is almost as famous for bluegrass music as it is for barbecue. In fact, the Father of Bluegrass Music, Bill Monroe, was born and is buried in the little town of Rosine, one county over from Owensboro. The *International Bluegrass Music Museum* (117 Daviess Street, in

Owensboro's RiverPark Center; 270-926-7891 or toll-free 888–MY–BANJO; bluegrass-museum.org) honors Monroe and other bluegrass stars. The museum features vintage photographs along a time line of bluegrass history, instruments and interactive exhibits, and a Hall of Honor. Hours are 10 a.m. to 5 p.m. Tuesday through Saturday and 1 to 4 p.m. Sunday. Admission is $5 adults, $2 children.

One of Kentucky's largest fine art museums, the **Owensboro Museum of Fine Art** (901 Frederica Street; 270-685-3181; omfa.us) has an impressive permanent collection of works from 18th-, 19th-, and 20th-century American, English, and French masters and a decorative arts collection of American, European, and Asian objects from the 15th to the 19th centuries. The museum has completed a $1.6 million expansion, which includes a new Exhibitions Wing; an Atrium Sculpture Court; a restored Civil War–era mansion; the Kentucky Spirit Galleries, featuring rotating exhibitions of Kentucky folk art and crafts; and the Yellowbanks Gallery, for works by regional artists. One highlight is an early-20th-century German stained glass collection displayed dramatically in 25-foot towers in an atrium gallery. The Mezzanine Gallery contains religious art. Hours are Tuesday through Thursday from 9 a.m. to 4 p.m., Friday from 10 a.m. to 7 p.m., and Sunday from 1 to 4 p.m. Admission is free, but donations of $2 per adult and $1 per child are suggested.

trueblue

In addition to an official state song ("My Old Kentucky Home" by Stephen C. Foster), Kentucky also has an official bluegrass song, "Blue Moon of Kentucky" by Rosine, Kentucky, native Bill Monroe.`

There are times when rest can be found in activity. Do tennis (indoor and out), racquetball, swimming, horseback riding, fishing, canoeing, and weight lifting strike you as heavy labor? Joan Ramey, owner of Ramey Sports and Fitness Center and Ramey Riding Stables, has opened **Friendly Farms Bed & Breakfast** to all appreciative visitors. Several cottages are available. Cottages are 3 miles east of Owensboro on Highway 56. Call (270) 771-5590 or visit rameycamps.com

In all cultures, people set time aside to take retreats, quiet time for contemplation away from the bustle of everyday life. Whether or not you are Catholic or connected to any church or creed in any way, **Mount**

Saint Joseph Center and Community of Ursuline Sisters offers a quiet, respectful atmosphere to those of us yearning for space and time to absorb (or forget) life. Aside from retreats, the center offers all kinds of religious, cultural, and social programs. Call (270) 229-4103 for information or check ursulinesmsj.org. To get there, take Parrish Avenue (Highway 81) west out of town until it turns due south; take Highway 56 to West Louisville, turn right (west) on Highway 815, and look for the sign within 2 miles to 801 Cummings Road.

Go in the Maple Mount Farm entrance, find the Mother House, and ask to see the museum. Artifacts range from desks of the founders to gifts from foreign missions, musical instruments, religious articles, books, and displays, such as *The Madonna Room*, which houses a collection of reproductions of famous European Madonna paintings. The non-Catholic visitor learns that reliquaries are saints' shrines of all sizes that can be displayed anywhere from behind an altar in a massive gold frame to behind a pendant in a tiny glass locket. The idea of wearing a first-degree relic, usually a chip of a saint's bone hidden in the back of a ring, has endless implications.

From Mount Saint Joseph take an eastward drive on Highway 56 for 2 miles to the *Diamond Lake Resort and Campground* at 7301 Hobbs Road. Statewide catfish farming is on the rise because reclaimed surface mines are required to have settling ponds, which are appropriate places for raising fish. This farm is a successful, sophisticated business whose owners are more than happy to show people around. The resort has 270 campsites and 10 motel rooms for those who don't want to "rough it." Facilities include a pay fishing lake, pedal boats, go-carts, paint ball, laundry, grocery store, arcade, lakeside restaurant and grill. Open daily year-round 7 a.m. to 10 p.m. Call (270) 229-4900 or go to diamondlakeresort.net.

After the fish farm tour, you may be curious to know how the product tastes. The *Windy Hollow Raceway, Park, Restaurant and Museum* (270-785-4088) has a famous catfish buffet Friday and Saturday from 5 to 8:30 p.m. (and a big country-ham breakfast buffet on Sunday from 7 a.m. to 1:30 p.m. if fish isn't your dish). Every day is your lucky day at the pay lakes, and you don't even need a fishing license! Windy Hollow wins the contest for having the most going on at once: drag racing, water sliding, camping, pay-lake fishing, barbecuing, golf, and even old western movie viewing while you eat. Don't miss the cowboy museum. Yee-haw! From Owensboro follow Highway 81 south to Old 81 and exit west. Follow the signs.

Although the third weekend in October is the best time to visit **Reid's Orchard,** because it hosts a two-day harvest festival, any time during apple season in the fall is a good time to pick your own of whatever is ripe at that moment. The farm store offers cider, relishes, produce, and whatever else these industrious folks decide to make and sell. The orchard is located at 4818 Highway 144, off US 60, and is open spring through December with seasonal products. Call ahead (270-685-2444) or visit reidorchard.com for hours and information.

The **John James Audubon State Park** is about 20 miles west of Owensboro, along US 41 north of Henderson. Although Audubon is the

A Soldier's Story

An unusual and thought-provoking legacy of World War II is preserved at the **James D. Veatch Camp Breckinridge Museum and Arts Center** near the Western Kentucky community of Morganfield. In the 1940s this was a huge military training center. It was also the location of a United States prisoner of war camp, and among the prisoners was a young Czechoslovakian named Daniel Mayer, who had been conscripted into the German army and captured in Tunisia. Homesick, this self-taught artist began painting murals of his homeland on the walls of the prisoners' quarters. The scenes were so beautiful that Erick Zychowski, who was in charge of the camp's Officers Club, asked Mayer to paint murals to decorate the club's walls. It is thought that he painted more than one hundred scenes in buildings throughout the camp. Though most of Camp Breckinridge was torn down after the military vacated it in the 1960s, a local citizens group worked to save the Officers Club building. Today owned by the county, it features numerous displays of World War II artifacts as well as plaques and memorials to United States veterans. But the most striking artifacts line the main hall—more than 40 huge pastoral murals painted by Mayer between May 1943 and his death from pneumonia at the camp in July 1945. You can learn more about this fascinating wartime legacy by visiting Camp Breckinridge. Museum hours are 10 a.m. to 3 p.m. Tuesday through Friday, 10 a.m. to 4 p.m. Saturday, and 1 to 4 p.m. Sunday. Admission is $4 for adults, $2 for children. Call (270) 389-4420 for more information; breckinridge-arts.org. Camp Breckinridge is located near Morganfield at the intersection of the US 60 Bypass and Highway 2091 S. at 116 Village Square Road.

most famous American painter of birds, he was a failure as a business executive. While he lived in this area, from 1810 to 1820, Audubon got involved in several entrepreneurial projects, all of which failed because instead of working, he spent his days in search of rare birds. With nothing left but his portfolio of bird paintings, his talent, and an idea, Audubon dragged his poor family all over the South while he painted and searched for a publisher. Eventually he found an engraver in London, England, who printed his 435 hand-colored plates as *The Birds of America*. A complete bound set of the original folios and numerous individual prints are on display in the Audubon Memorial and Nature Museum, as is the largest collection of Audubon memorabilia in existence, including many of his original paintings, journals, correspondence, and personal items. Another treasure in the museum is a rare 3-by-5-inch daguerreotype of the elderly Audubon taken by the famous early photographer Matthew Brady.

The whole northern half of the park was donated as a nature preserve, with the stipulation that it be treated as a bird sanctuary and that the old growth beech and sugar maple woods be preserved. Ask the park naturalist what wild and amazing flora and fauna can be seen. The park also sponsors spring and fall migration bird walks.

Adjacent to the museum is the Nature Center, which features a glass enclosed Nature Observatory and a Discovery Center with exhibits on bird biology and psychology. Daily programs are offered in the summer, and special events are sprinkled throughout the rest of the year. Check for museum hours and admission. The park is open daily, sunrise to sunset. Call (270) 826-2247 for more information (parks.ky.gov/parks/recreationparks/John-James/default.aspx).

More Good Lodging in Western Kentucky

CADIZ

Lake Barkley State Resort Park
off US 68
(270) 924-1131
parks.ky.gov/parks/
resortparks/Lake-Barkley/
default.aspx
Two lodges and cottages;
golf and fitness center.

DAWSON SPRINGS

Pennyrile Forest State Resort Park
20781 Pennyrile Forest
State Park Road
(270) 797-3421
parks.ky.gov/parks/
resortparks/Pennyrile
-Forest/default.aspx
Lodge and cottages.

GILBERTSVILLE

Kentucky Dam Village State Resort Park
166 Upper Village Drive
(270) 362-4271
parks.ky.gov/parks/
resortparks/ky-dam-village
Lodge and cottages; golf
course.

GRAND RIVERS

Grand Rivers Inn
1949 JH O'Bryan Avenue
(270) 362-4487
grandriversinn.com
Rooms and cottages; ¼
mile from lake.

HENDERSON

John James Audubon State Park
3100 Highway 41 North
(270) 826-2247
parks.ky.gov/parks/
recreationparks/John
-James/default.aspx
Lakeside cottages with
fireplaces.

L&N Bed and Breakfast
327 North Main Street
(270) 831-1100
lnbbky.com
Historic home overlooking
the river.

Victorian Quarters Bed & Breakfast
109 Clay Street
(270) 831-2778
victorianquartersbb.com
Scenic mansion
overlooking the Ohio
River. Three rooms.

MAYFIELD

Super 8 Motel
1100 Links Lane
(270) 247-8899

MURRAY

Quality Inn
1210 North Twelfth Street
(270) 759-5910

Holiday Inn Express
U.S. Highway 641 North
(270) 759-4449

PADUCAH

1857's
127 Market House Square
(270) 444-3960 or
(800) 264-5607
A three-story brick lodging
on the National Register
of Historic Places. Some
pets and children allowed.
Pool table and hot tub.

Fox Briar Farm Inn
515 Schmidt Road
(270) 554-1774
foxbriarinn.com
Charms include a hundred
wooded acres, lake,
and 2,000-square-foot
covered porch.

More Fun Places to Eat in Western Kentucky

BENTON

Catfish Kitchen
136 Teal Run Circle
(270) 362-7306
Lakeside dining; great
seafood and homemade
desserts.

CADIZ

Ferrell's
2021 Main Street
(270) 522-3418
Hamburger-and-fries joint.

Lake Barkley State Resort Park
off US 68
(270) 924-1131
parks.ky.gov/parks/
resortparks/Lake-Barkley/
default.aspx
Spacious dining room
with fireplace; regional
specialties.

GRAND RIVERS

Dockers Grille Turtle Bay Resort
overlooking Lake Barkley
(800) 498-0248
greenturtlebay.com
Breakfast and lunch; try
the "turtle burger."

Knoth's Bar-B-Que
728 U.S. Highway 62
(270) 362-8580
Lunch and dinner with—
guess what—barbecue.
Notable sauce. If inclined,
you can buy a whole pork
shoulder to take home.

Miss Scarlett's Restaurant
708 Complex Drive
(270) 928-3126
exit31rvpark.com
Traditional Southern
and regional fare, with
homemade breads and
soups.

HOPKINSVILLE

Woodshed Pit Bar-B-Que
1821 West Seventh Street
(270) 885-8144
Barbecue and other
American fare.

KUTTAWA

Hu-B's at Kuttawa Harbor Marina
1709 Lake Barkley Drive
(270) 388-9563
kuttawaharbormarina.com
Indoor and outdoor dining.

MURRAY

Sammon's Bakery
874 Chestnut Street
(270) 753-5434
Cheeseburgers on
homemade buns,
doughnuts, and pastries.

OWENSBORO

Old Hickory Pit
338 Washington Avenue
(270) 926-9000
oldhickorybar-b-q.com
Smoked mutton and great
desserts.

Ole South Barbeque
3523 Highway 54
(270) 926-6464
More barbecue and
accoutrements.

PADUCAH

Cynthia's Ristorante
125 Market House Square
(270) 443-3319
cynthiasristorante.com
Menu changes weekly
for top-notch cuisine in
beautiful setting.

Flamingo Row West
2100 Broadway
(270) 442-0460
flamingorow.com
Famous for more than
20 varieties of "stuffed
bread." You can't
miss the super-bright
building facade made of
handmade tiles. Outdoor
dining.

Index

A

Abbey of
Gethsemani, 68
Abraham Lincoln
Birthplace National
Historic Site, 175
Actors Theatre, 59
Adsmore Museum, 218
AK Steel Mill, 117
a la lucie, 78
Alfalfa Restaurant, 11
Alfred Duncan House
of Willow, 198
Alice Lloyd College, 103
Alvin Mountjoy
House, 131
American Cave Museum
and Hidden River
Cave, 164
American Printing
House for the
Blind, 65
America's Best Value
Inn, 124
Amerson Farm
Orchard, 21
Anderson Ferry, 140
Antique Junction, 117
Appalachian
Celebration, 123
Appalachia—Science
in the Public
Interest, 184
Appalshop, 92
AQS National
Quilt Show and
Contest, 208

Architectural
Salvage, 63
Asbury Meadow Bed
and Breakfast, 154
Ascension Episcopal
Church, 49
Ashland, 115
Ashland Plaza
Hotel, 124
Ashland, the Henry
Clay Estate, 10
Atkinson-Griffin
House, 177
Atomic Cafe, 10
Augusta, 147
Augusta Ferry, 148
Augusta General
Store, 148

B

Bad Branch Nature
Preserve, 92
Bar-B-Q Capital of the
World, 231
Bardstown, 66
Bardstown Art
Gallery, 68
Bardstown Historical
Museum, 68
Barlow House
Museum, 206
Barthell Mining
Camp, 187
Bat Cave, 121
Battle of Tebbs
Bend, 177

Baxter Avenue
Filmworks, 64
Beargrass Creek State
Nature Preserve, 55
Beattyville, 113
Beaumont Inn, The,
23, 76
Beautiful Dreamer Bed
& Breakfast, 76
Behringer-Crawford
Museum, 144
Bell County Chamber of
Commerce, 84
Bellevue, 146
Ben E. Clement Mineral
Museum, 215
Benham, 90
Bennett House, The, 77
Bennett's Grist Mill, 115
Bentham School House
Inn, The, 91
Benton, 196
Berea, 44
Bernheim Forest
Arboretum and
Nature Center, 65
Berryman's
Tastytreat, 47
Berry, Wendell, 134
Bert & Bud's Vintage
Coffins, 198
Best Western, 154, 191
Best Western Gold
Vault Inn, 191
Bethany Spring, 72
Betty Thomas Teddy
Bears, 189

Biancke's Restaurant,
78, 155
Big Black Mountain, 91
Big Bone Gardens, 137
Big Bone Lick State
Park, 137
Big Singing Day, 196
Big South Fork National
River and Recreation
Area, 186
Big South Fork Scenic
Railway, 186
Big Spring Park, 220
Billy Ray's Playhouse-
Restaurant, 126
Bi-Water Farm, 21
Black Gold Festival, 105
Blaine, 119
Bluegrass Heritage
Museum, 47
Blue Grass Railroad
Museum Inc., 29
Blue Grass Tours, 4
Bluegrass Wood and
Leather Craft, 183
Blue Heron, 187
Blue Licks Battlefield
State Resort
Park, 151
Boat Store, The, 118
Bobby Davis
Museum, 105
Bobby Mackey's, 145
Boone Tavern Hotel
and Restaurant, 46
Boone Tavern
Restaurant, 78
Botts School, 111
Bowling Green, 156
Boyd Orchard, 29
Bread of Life Cafe, 193

Breaks Interstate
Park, 96
Breathitt County
Museum, 113
Brickyard Cafe, 192
Brown Hotel, The, 77
Brown-Pusey
House, 171
Brownwood Bed
& Breakfast &
Cabins at Cave Run
Lake, 125
Buckhorn Lake, 106
Buckhorn Lake
Presbyterian
Church, 106
Buckhorn Lake State
Resort Park, 106,
124, 125
Buckley Wildlife
Sanctuary, 31
Burke's Bakery, 35
Burkesville, 176
Burlington Antique
Show, 139
Burlington's Willis
Graves B&B Inn, 138
Burnside, 183, 184
Butcher Hollow, 99
Butler County Park
and Green River
Museum, 163
Butler Turpin
House, 135

C
Cabin Arts and Quilt
Shop, 139
Cabin Creek
Bridge, 150
Cabin Fever, 191
Cadiz, 217

Campbellsville, 177
Campbellsville Cherry
Reproductions,
Inc., 178
Campbellsville
Handmade Cherry
Furniture, 178
Camp Nelson Heritage
Park, 41
Camp Nelson National
Cemetery, 42
Camp Wildcat Civil War
Battle Site, 189
Cane Ridge Meeting
House Shrine, 16
Canoe Kentucky, 52
Capitol Arts Center, 160
Caproni's on the
River, 150
Carcassonne Dance, 94
Cardome Centre, 19
Carlisle, 153
Carmichael's
Bookstore, 64
Carnegie Visual and
Performing Arts
Center, 142
Carr Creek State
Park, 105
Carr Folk Lake, 105
Carriage Museum, 151
Carrollton, 134
Carry A. Nation's
birthplace, 40
Carter Caves State
Resort Park, 121
Cascade Caverns, 121
Casey County Apple
Festival, 180
Catfish Kitchen, 236
Cathedral Basilica of
the Assumption, 141

Cathedral Museum, 141
Cave-in-Rock Ferry, 216
Cave Run Lake, 122
Cave Run Muskie Guide
  Service, 122
C. B. Caudill Store and
  History Center, 94
Center for Rural
  Economic
  Development, 182
Center Furnace
  Trail, 212
Central City, 228
Central Kentucky
  Antique Mall, 18
Central Park, 116
Charles Heigold
  House, 56
Cherokee Park, 64
Chimney Corner
  Cafe, 125
Chirico's Ristorante, 97
Chrisman Mill Vineyards
  and Winery, 41
Christmas in the
  Country, 173
Christmas in the
  Park, 171
Christopher's Bed &
  Breakfast, 146
Churchill Weavers, 45
Claiborne Farm, 16
Clark, Billy C., 118
Clarkson, 170
Clifty Wilderness, 110
Clinton, 202
Clinton Furnace, 119
Coal House Museum,
  The, 85
Coal Miner's Park, 91
Columbia, 176
Columbus, 204

Columbus-Belmont
  Battlefield State
  Park, 204
Colville Covered
  Bridge, 48
Community Arts
  Center, 37
Completely
  Kentucky, 52
Constitution Square
  State Park, 35
Cooper's
  Restaurant, 155
Cora Wilson Stewart
  Moonlight
  School, 123
Corbin, 188
Country Charm Historic
  Farmhouse Bed and
  Breakfast, 77
covered bridge at
  Dover, 149
Covington, 141
Covington's Anchor
  Grill, 144
Cozy Corner Crafts, 93
Cranks Creek Lake, 88
Crazy Daisy Antique
  Mall, 63
Creelsboro Natural
  Bridge, 180
Crisp's Dairy Treat, 125
Crittenden County
  Historical
  Museum, 215
Cumberland, 90
Cumberland Crafts, 84
Cumberland Falls, 185
Cumberland Falls State
  Resort Park, 185,
  191, 192

Cumberland Gap
  National Historic
  Park, 83
Cumberland Inn, 192
Cumberland Manor, 85
Cumberland Mountain
  Fall Festival, 85
Cumberland Museum,
  Inn, and Center
  for Leadership
  Studies, 187
Curtis Gates Lloyd
  Wildlife Management
  Area, 136
Cynthiana, 127
Cynthiana/Harrison
  County Museum, 129
Cynthia's Ristorante, 237

D
Dale Hollow, 179
Dale Hollow Lake State
  Resort Park, 192
Danville, 34
David A. Zegeer Coal-
  Railroad Museum, 95
David School, 103
Days Inn, 125, 154
Dee Felice Cafe, 143
Depot Branch, 161
Diamond Caverns, 167
Diamond Lake
  Resort and
  Campground, 233
Dils Cemetery, 97
Dinsmore Homestead,
  The, 139
Dockers Grille Turtle
  Bay Resort, 237
Doctor's Inn, The, 76
Donathan Rock, 111

Don F. Pratt Memorial
    Museum, 222
Donna's Place, 154
Downtown After
    Dinner, 210
Draffenville, 197
Dr. Thomas Walker
    State Historic Site, 83
Duncan Hines Scenic
    Byway, 162
Duncan Tavern, 15
Dundee, 229
DuPont Mansion Bed
    and Breakfast, 77
Dutchman's Market, 183

E
East Kentucky Science
    Center, 103
1857's, 236
1817 Saddle Factory
    and Museum, 225
1869 Homestead Bed &
    Breakfast, 191
Elizabethtown Historic
    Walking Tours, 170
Elk & Bison Prairie, 212
Elk Creek Hunt
    Club, 132
Elk Creek Vineyard, 132
Elkhorn City Railroad
    Museum, 98
Elkton, 225
El Midway Cafe, 155
Emma Reno Connor
    Black History
    Gallery, 169
Ephraim McDowell
    House and
    Apothecary, 35
Equus Run
    Vineyards, 55

Evans Farm Orchard, 21
Explorium, 9

F
Fairview, 224
Falls of the Ohio, 56
Fancy Farm Picnic, 203
Farmington, 57
Farnsley-Moreman
    House, 57
Fava's Restaurant, 17
Ferrell's, 237
Ferrell's
    Hamburgers, 222
Filson Club Historical
    Society, 58
First Farm Inn, 154
Fishtrap Lake, 95
Flame Run Gallery and
    Studio, 61
Flamingo Row
    West, 237
Flocoe Restaurant, 86
Forkland Community
    Center, 38
Fort Boonesborough
    State Park, 46
Fort Duffield, 172
Fort McCook, 83
440 Main Restaurant
    and Bar, 192
Four Seasons Country
    Inn, 191
Fox Briar Farm Inn, 236
Frances' Diner, 126
Frankfort, 51
Frazier International
    History Museum, 62
Freddie's Restaurant, 34
French Quarter Inn, 154
Friendly Farms Bed &
    Breakfast, 232

Friendship School, 178
Frontier Nursing
    Service, 106
Fulton, 204
Furnace Mountain
    Inc., 112

G
Gaitskill Mound, 47
Gallatin County
    Historical
    Society, 136
Galt House, 77
Garrard County Jail
    Museum, 39
Gary Humphress &
    Sons, 178
Gate Capital of the
    World, 182
Gateway Bed and
    Breakfast, 154
General Burnside Island
    State Park, 184
General Butler State
    Resort Park, 135,
    154, 155
George Beard's House
    of Willow, 198
George Rogers Clark
    Park, 142
Georgetown, 17
Georgetown and Scott
    County Museum, 19
Georgetown Antique
    Mall, 18
Georgetown/Scott
    County Tourism, 20
Gibby's, 78
Ginkgo Tree, 11
Ginza Japanese
    Restaurant, 192

Giuseppe's Ristorante
Italiano, 12
Gladie Creek Cabin, 109
Gladie Creek Historic
Site/Environmental
Learning Center, 109
Glasgow, 168
Glassworks, 60
Glendale, 173
Glendale Crossing
Festival, 174
Glitz, The, 28
Godbey Appalachian
Cultural and Fine
Arts Center, 90
Goddard (White)
Covered Bridge, 153
Golden Lion Bed &
Breakfast, 76
Goose Nest Sink, 84
Grace Manor Bed and
Breakfast, 154
Grand Rivers Inn, 236
Gratz Park Inn, 76
Graves County Art
Guild, 203
Grayson Lake State
Park, 121
Great American Brass
Band Festival, 36
Great American
Dulcimer Festival, 86
Greenbo Lake State
Resort Park, 114, 126
Green River Lake State
Park, 177
Greensburg, 179
Greenup, 115
Greenup's walking
tour, 115
Greenville, 229
Greyhound Tavern, 155

Guerrant Mountain
Mission Bed and
Breakfast, 47, 77
Guthrie, 225

H
Hall Place Bed and
Breakfast, 168
Hall's on the River, 79
Hampton Inn
Bardstown, 76
Hampton Inn,
Hazard, 124
Haney's Appledale
Farm, 182
Harlan, 87
Harlan Boys' Choir, 87
Harland Sanders Cafe &
Museum, 188
Harlan Musettes,
The, 87
Harmon Station, 101
Harper's, 193
Harriet Beecher Stowe
Slavery to Freedom,
Museum, 151
Harrodsburg, 22
Harrodsburg Historical
Society Museum, 23
Harry C. Miller Lock
Collection, 41
Hart County Historic
Society and
Museum, 167
Hatfield and McCoy
Reunion, 97
Hawkins-Kirby
House, 136
Hazard, 105
Hazel, 200
Headley-Whitney
Museum, 8

Heaven Hill
Distilleries, 66
Heine Brothers'
Coffee, 64
Heirlooms and
Gretchen's, 18
Hemlock Garden
Trail, 86
Henderson
Settlement, 87
Henning's
Restaurant, 74
Hensley Settlement, 84
Henson Broom Shop
Museum, 211
Hickman County
Museum, 202
Hickman-Dorena
Ferry, 200
Higdon-Strecker
Studio, 9
High Bridge, 26
Highland Games and
Gathering of Scottish
Clans, 168
Hillsboro Bridge, 153
Hindman
Settlement, 104
Historic and Horse
Farm Tours Inc., 4
Hodgenville, 74, 175
Hofbräuhaus, 155
Holiday Inn Express,
125, 236
Holly Hill Inn, 32
Homeplace 1850,
The, 212
Hopewell Museum, 16
Hopkinsville, 220
Horse Cave, 164
House of Onyx, 229

House on Belmont
B&B, 77
Hu-B's at Kuttawa
Harbor Marina, 237
Hummel
Planetarium, 43
Hunt-Morgan House,
The, 7

I
Indian Rocks, 84
International Bar-B-Q
Festival, 230
International Bluegrass
Music Museum, 231
International Museum
of the Horse, 6
Interstate Greenhouse &
Nursery, 135
Irish Acres Antiques, 28
Iron Hill Furnace, 120
Iroquois Park, 64
Irvinton House
Museum, 43
Isaac Shelby Cemetery
State Historic Site, 37

J
Jack Jouett House, 31
Jackson, 113
Jackson Inn, 124
Jack Thomas
House, 175
Jacob Hiestand
House, 177
Jailer's Inn, 76
James D. Veatch
Camp Breckinridge
Museum and Arts
Center, 234
Janice Mason Art
Museum, 218

Jefferson Davis
Monument State
Historic Site, 224
Jenkins, 95
Jenkins Homecoming
Days Festival, 95
Jenny Wiley State
Resort Park, 101,
125, 126
Jenny Wiley Summer
Music Theatre, 101
Jenny Wiley Train
Heritage Byway, 101
Jesse Stuart State Nature
Preserve, 114
Jim Beam American
Stillhouse, 66
Jim's Seafood, 78
Joe Bologna's, 11
Joe Ley Antiques, 62
John A. Roebling
Suspension
Bridge, 143
John B. Begley
Chapel, 176
John C. C. Mayo
Museum, 98
John Fitch's grave, 67
John James Audubon
State Park, 234, 236
Johnson Creek Covered
Bridge, 152
Jones Visual Arts Center
at Centre College, 36
Jordan Farm, 76
Joseph Byrd
Brannen & Co.,
Antique Furniture
Reproductions, 149
Jot 'Em Down Store, 5
Judy's Castle, 192

K
Kathy's Country
Kitchen, 125
Keeneland Race
Course, 6
Kentucky Artisan
Center, 44
Kentucky Center for the
Arts, 59
Kentucky Coal Mining
Museum, 91
Kentucky Coal Museum
and Portal 31
Exhibition Mine
Tour, 91
Kentucky Dam
Village State Resort
Park, 236
Kentucky Derby, 54
Kentucky Derby
Museum, 55
Kentucky Folk Art
Center, The, 123
Kentucky Fudge
Company and
Cafe, 78
Kentucky Gateway
Museum Center, 149
Kentucky Guild
of Artists and
Craftsmen, 45
Kentucky Highlands
Museum and
Discovery
Center, 116
Kentucky Horse Park, 5
Kentucky Museum of
Art and Craft, 59
Kentucky Museum,
The, 156

Kentucky Music
Hall of Fame and
Museum, 190
Kentucky Opry, 197
Kentucky Railway
Museum, 70
Kentucky Reptile
Zoo, 108
Kentucky Ridge State
Forest, 85
Kentucky's Country
Music Highway, 102
Kentucky Theater, 10
Kincaid Regional
Theatre, 131
Kingdom Come State
Park, 90
Kirchhoff's Bakery and
Deli, 209
Kizito Cookies, 62
Knob Creek Farm, 176
Knobs Haven
Retreat, 71
Knoth's Bar-B-Que, 237
Kuttawa, 214

L
Labrot & Graham,
The Bourbon
Homeplace, 30
La Fonda Restaurant, 24
Lake Barkley State
Resort Park, 236, 237
Lake Cumberland, 179
Lake Cumberland State
Resort Park, 191
Lake Malone State
Park, 229
Lakes Creek Bed &
Breakfast, 124
Lamp Post Café, 125
Lancaster, 39

Lancaster Homes and
Holiday, 39
Land Between the
Lakes, 212
Landmark Inn, 125
Larkspur Press, 133
Laurel Cove Trail, 86
Lawrenceburg, 50
Lebanon, 72
Lebanon's National
Cemetery, 74
Leeds Center for the
Arts, 47
Leeds Theatre, 47
Leitchfield, 175
Leslie Morris Park on
Fort Hill, 52
Levi Jackson State
Park, 188
Lexington, 3
Lexington Children's
Theatre, 10
Lexington Convention
and Visitors
Bureau, 4
Lexington Walk and
Bluegrass Country
Driving Tour, 4
Lilley Cornett
Woods, 94
Lilly's, 79
Lincoln Days
Celebration, 176
Lincoln Heritage
House, 171
Lincoln Homestead
State Park, 74
Lincoln Marriage
Shrine, 23
Lincoln Museum, 176
Little Britain Farm, 139
Little Eagle Falls, 186

Little Shepherd Trail,
The, 88
L&N Bed and
Breakfast, 236
Lodge Restaurant,
The, 193
Log House Craft
Gallery, 46
London, 188
Loretto
Motherhouse, 71
Lost River Cave and
Valley, 161
Loudoun House, 8
Louisa, 118
Louisa Needle
Dam, 119
Louisville, 54
Louisville Nature
Center, 55
Louisville Science
Center, 61
Louisville Slugger
Museum, 61
Louisville Zoological
Garden, 58
Lower Town, 210
Lynch, 91

M
Maines Hardware, 136
Main Strasse, 143
Maker's Mark
Distillery, 71
Mammoth Cave
Hotel, 191
Mammoth Cave
National Park, 163
Mannsville, 178
Mansion Museum, 23
Mantle Rock, 216

Mantle Rock Native
Education and
Cultural Center, 217
Maple Hill Manor Bed
and Breakfast, 77
Marie Stewart Crafts
Shop, 104
Marion, 215
Market House
Museum, 207
Market House
Theatre, 208
Markland Locks and
Dam, 136
Marshall Key's
Tavern, 155
Marshalls'
Strawberries, 17
Martins Fork Lake, 88
Masterson House, 135
Mayfield, 202
Mayo Methodist
Church, 99
Mays Lick, 151
Maysville, 149
Maysville Flood Wall
Murals, 149
McConnell Springs, 13
McCreary County
Museum, 187
Meadowgreen Park, 113
Meeting House, The, 76
Melini Cucina Italian
Ristorante, 79, 126
Merchants' Row, 38
Merton Center, 69
Metropolis Lake, 206
Midway, 31
Miguel's Pizza, 108
Mill Springs
Battlefield, 182
Mill Springs Mill, 181

Minor E. Clark Fish
Hatchery, 123
Miss Scarlett's
Restaurant, 237
Monkey's Eyebrow, 205
Monte Casino
Chapel, 147
Montgomery Inn, 77
Moonlite Bar-B-Q
Inn, 231
Morehead, 122
Morgan County
Sorghum
Festival, 124
Morgan Row, 23
Morgan Station, 49
Morgantown, 163
Mother Goose
House, 105
Mountain Arts
Center, 102
Mountain Home
Place, 98
Mountain Laurel
Festival, 86
Mountain Mushroom
Festival, 108
Mountain Springs
Inn, 125
Mount Saint Joseph
Center and
Community of
Ursuline Sisters, 232
Mount Savage
Furnace, 120
Mount Sterling, 47
Mount Vernon, 189
Mount Zion Bridge, 74
Muhlenberg County
Music Museum, 228
Mullins Log Cabin, 130
Munfordville, 168

Murdock
Mausoleum, 200
Murray, 197
Museum of the
American Quilter's
Society, 208
Mutter Gottes
Kirch, 142
My Old Kentucky
Dinner Train, 67
My Old Kentucky
Home State Park, 66
Myrtledene Bed and
Breakfast, 72

N
Nada Tunnel, 109
Nannine Clay Wallis
Arboretum, 16
Natasha's Bistro &
Bar, 78
National Corvette
Museum, 160
National Historic
Landmark, 102
Natural Arch Scenic
Area, 184
Natural Bridge State
Resort Park, 107, 126
Needle Nest, The, 54
New Haven, 70
Newport, 145
Newport Aquarium, 144
Newsom's Old Mill
Store, 219
Nicholasville, 40
Nolin River Nut Tree
Nursery, 175
Nonesuch, 28
Norton Center for the
Arts, 34

Nostalgia Station Toy
Train Museum, 29

O
Oakroom, 63
Official Kentucky State
Championship
Old-time Fiddling
Contest, 174
Offutt-Cole Tavern, 32
Olde Towne Park, 24
Old Fort Harrod State
Park, 22
Old Guides
Cemetery, 164
Old Hickory Pit, 237
Old Jail, 40
Old Mud Meeting
House, 24
Old Mulkey Meeting
House, 169
Old Nicholas County
Jail, 153
Old Owl Tavern, 24, 78
"Old Reliable, The"
Germantown
Fair, 148
Old Scott County Jail
Complex, 18
Old Simpson
County Jailer's
Residence, 164
Old Stone Jail, 134
Old Talbott Tavern, 67
Oldtown Covered
Bridge, 115
Ole South
Barbeque, 237
Oscar Getz Museum of
Whiskey History, 68
Owensboro, 231

Owensboro Area
Museum of Science
and History, 231
Owensboro Museum of
Fine Art, 232
Owenton, 133

P
Pactolus, 120
Paducah, 207
Paducah Flood Wall
Murals, 210
Paintsville, 98
Palisades, The, 26
Paradise, 228
Paradise Cafe, 79
Paramount Arts
Center, 116
Parkette Drive-In, 79
Parkview Country Inn,
The, 148
Pathway of Peace: The
Danville Labyrinth
Project, 34
Patti's 1880s
Settlement, 213
Patton Museum
of Cavalry and
Armor, 172
Paxton Inn, 151
Peking Chinese
Restaurant, 126
Penchem Tack
Store, 225
Penn Country
Hams, 178
Penn's Store, 37
Pennyrile Forest State
Resort Park, 236
Pennyroyal Area
Museum, 220
Perryville, 38

Perryville Battlefield
State Historic Site, 38
Pete's Custom Saddle
Shop, 224
Phoenix Theatre, 161
Pikeville, 97
Pikeville College, 97
Pikeville Cut-Thru, 97
Pilot Knob State Nature
Preserve, 112
Pine Mountain/Letcher
County Crafts
Co-op, 93
Pine Mountain
Settlement
School, 88
Pine Mountain State
Resort Park, 85, 126
Pioneer Playhouse, 35
Pioneer Telephone
Museum, 47
Pioneer Village, 104
Pioneer Weapons
Hunting Area, 111
Planet Thai, 79
Pleasant Retreat, 40
Point Park, 155
Poke Sallet Festival, 87
Pompilios, 146
Poor Fork Arts and
Craft Guild, 90
Poor Richard's
Books, 52
Portland Museum, 57
Port Royal, 133
Prestonsburg, 102
Princess Furnace, 119
Princeton, 218
Princeton Art Guild, 219
Proof on Main, 60

Q
Quality Inn, 236
Queen of Sheba, 79
Quilt Box, The, 131
Quilter's Alley, 209

R
Rabbit Hash, 138
Rabbit Hash General
Store, 138
Railway Museum
of Greater
Cincinnati, 143
Ramsey's Diner, 79
Ramsi's Café on the
World, 64
Raven Run Nature
Sanctuary, 12
Rebecca-Ruth Candy
Inc., 51
Red Bird Mission
Crafts, 87
Red Carpet Inn, 154
Red Mile Harness
Track, 6
Red River Gorge, 107
Red River Historical
Museum, 113
Reed Valley, 17
Reelfoot Lake, 201
Reid's Orchard, 234
Renfro Valley, 190
Rhodes Hall Art
Gallery, 72
Richmond, 43
Ridge Trail, 83
Ringos Mills, 153
River Discovery
Center, 209
Riverview at Hobson
Grove, 159
Robert Penn Warren
Museum, 225

Rock Hotel Trail, 86
Roe Wells School, 111
Rooster Run General
Store, 66
Rough River Dam State
Resort Park, 191, 192
Royal Spring, 20
Rudy's Restaurant, 197
Russell, 117
Ruth Hunt Candies, 49

S
Sahara Steak
House, 192
Saint Catharine
Motherhouse, 75
Saint Joseph Proto-
Cathedral, 67
Saint Rose Proto-
Priory, 75
Sammon's Bakery, 237
Samuel May House, 103
Sarah Bush
Johnston Lincoln
Memorial, 171
sassafras tree, 231
Schlabach's Bakery, 225
Schneider's Sweet
Shop, 146
School House Inn, 124
Science Hill, 53
Science Hill Inn, 53
Seamen's Church
Institute/Center for
Maritime Education
Paducah, 209
Seelbach Hilton, 77
Seigel Pottery, 133
Serafini Broadway at
the Saint Clair, 78
Shaker Tavern Bed and
Breakfast, 227

Shaker Village of
Pleasant Hill, 25
Shelbyville, 53
Sheltowee Trace, 110
Sheltowee Trace
Outfitters, 96, 186
Sherwood Inn, 77, 79
Shooting Star
Nursery, 21
Simpson County
Archives and
Museum, 164
Smith's Grove, 163
Snug Hollow Farm Bed
& Breakfast, 124
Somerset, 182
Southern Deposit
Bank, 226
South Union Post
Office, 227
South Union Shaker
Village, 226
Spalding Hall, 67
Speed Art Museum, 58
Springfield, 75
Stab, 185
Stanford, 39
Static, 179
St. Clare Catholic
Church, 45
St. Joseph Catholic
Church, 161
Stone Hearth
Restaurant, 192
Stone Mountain, 88
strawberry kings, 225
Sun Valley Pizza, 154
Super 8 Motel, 124,
125, 236
Swann's Nest at Cygnet
Farm, 76
Switzer Covered
Bridge, 48

Swope's Cars of
Yesteryear
Museum, 169

T
Tater Day, 197
Tattoo Charlie's, 63
Tewes Poultry
Farm, 140
Thaxton's Licking River
Canoe Rental and
Paddlers' Inn, 130
Thomas B. Clark
Center for Kentucky
History, 51
Thoroughbred Center,
The, 14
Three Chimneys, 4
Tilghman Civil War
Museum, 210
Tippedore's, 155
Tompkinsville, 168
Tony York's on
Maine, 174
Tousey House
Tavern, 138
Townsend's Sorghum
Mill, 49
Toyota Motor
Manufacturing,
Kentucky, Inc., 22
Tracks Restaurant, 154
Trail of Tears
Commemorative
Park, 221
Trail of Tears Intertribal
Indian Pow
Wow, 222
Travelwise Motor
Inn, 124

Treehouse at Stoner
Creek Bed and
Breakfast, The, 77
Trigg County Country
Ham Festival, 217
21C Museum Hotel, 59

U
United States Treasury
Department Gold
Depository, 172

V
Valley of the Winds Art
Gallery, 92
Valley View Ferry, 42
Value Stay, 154
Van Lear Historical
Society Coal Miners'
Museum, 99
Van Lear Town
Celebration, 99
Vent Haven
Museum, 139
Vernon-Douglas State
Nature Preserve, 173
Versailles, 28
Victorian House Bed
and Breakfast, 192
Victorian Quarters Bed
& Breakfast, 236
Village Inn, The, 78
Village Players of Fort
Thomas, 147
Vincenzo's, 79

W
Wacinton, 207
Wakefield-Scearce
Galleries, 54
Walcott Covered
Bridge, 148

Walk Through Time, 17
Wallace Station, 33
Walter T. Kelley Co.
Inc., 170
Warren A. May's
Woodworking
Shop, 45
Warsaw, 136
Washington, 151
Washington County
Courthouse, 75
Water Mill
Restaurant, 192
Waveland State Historic
Site, 12
Wayne Bates Studio &
Gallery 121, 198
Weisenberger Mill, 32
Welch's Riverside
Restaurant, 155
Weller Haus Bed and
Breakfast, 146
Wertheim's, 155
Western Kentucky
Museum, 203
West Point, 172
Whistle Stop
Restaurant, 173
White Eagle
Antiques, 117
White Hall State
Historic Site, 43
Whitehaven Welcome
Center, 207
Whitesburg, 92
Wickliffe Mounds
Research Center, 205
Wigwam Village, 165
Wild Turkey
Distillery, 50
Williamsburg, 187
Williamstown, 130

William Whitley House
   State Historic Site, 39
Winchester, 46
Windy Hollow
   Raceway, Park,
   Restaurant and
   Museum, 233
Wolf Creek National
   Fish Hatchery, 180
Wolfe County Historical
   Museum, 110

Woodford County
   Historic Society
   Museum, 28
Woodshed Pit Bar-B-
   Que, 237
Wooldridge
   Monuments,
   The, 202
Woolly Worm
   Festival, 113
World Peace Bell, 145

Y
Yahoo Falls, 186
Yatesville Lake State
   Park, 119
Yeiser Art Center, 207
Youngers Creek, 171
Yuko-En on the
   Elkhorn, 19

Z
Zephyr Gallery, 59
Zimmerman Farms
   produce stand, 224

About the Author

Zoé Strecker is an artist and writer who lives with her husband and daughters on a farm near the Kentucky River.

About the Editor

An award-winning journalist and photographer, Jackie Sheckler Finch has covered a wide array of topics, from birth to death, with all the joy and sorrow in between. She has written 25 books and had articles published in numerous newspapers and magazines. She has been named the Mark Twain Travel Writer of the Year by Midwest Travel Writers Association a record five times—in 1998, 2001, 2003, 2007, and 2011—and is a member of The Society of American Travel Writers. Jackie shares her home with Pepper, resident guard dog and entertainer. One of her greatest joys is taking to the road to find the fascinating people and places that wait over the hill and around the next bend.